COMMODORE 16 GAMES BOOK

Edited by
Richard Woolcock
and
Cameron Duffy

MELBOURNE HOUSE
PUBLISHERS

First Published in the United Kingdom by Melbourne House

This Remastered Edition
Published by
Acorn Books
www.acornbooks.co.uk

This book is a page-by-page reproduction of the original 1984 edition as published by Beam Software and Melbourne House. The entirety of the book (apart from a final publisher feedback section) is presented with no changes, corrections nor updates to the original text, images and layout; therefore no guarantee is offered as to the accuracy of the information within.

Contents

Contents (cont.)

Appendices

Preface

The Commodore 16 represents tremendous value and, while intended for the novice, has many surprises in store for the experienced programmer. The improved version of Commodore BASIC has many powerful graphics statements, making it ideal for developing games.

With this book, Melbourne House continues its tradition of producing high quality literature and software in support of personal computers.

Arrangement of Programs

The games programs are graded within the book from easy to difficult. However, because different people have preferences for particular kinds of games, they are listed in the Contents page grouped by type. If you enjoy strategy games, you will find them all by consulting the Contents.

Ease of Use

Like us, you have probably gone crosseyed while trying to type in programs from computer magazines. Counting spaces and trying to distinguish Commodore graphics characters are the two most frustrating experiences of program typing.

Be of good cheer! In this book programs have been formatted for greater clarity. Graphics characters have been redefined to resemble keyboard pictographs, and spaces within strings are indicated by small black pyramids.

To speed program debugging, the ChexSum utility program enables you to identify incorrectly-typed lines immediately. (This aid is unique to Melbourne House games books.)

But — and this is an important but — read the chapter 'Program Accuracy' first if you want to get the maximum benefit from all the aids to accurate transcription.

Programming Projects

We hope that as you read and use our book, you will absorb the principles of programming the Commodore 16 by osmosis. Lists of variables have been provided and subroutine names inserted in listings to help you discover how programs work.

We have also suggested improvements you may make to the games as a challenge to your programming skills.

Suggestions

Melbourne House is always interested in feedback from readers, whether it be suggestions, praise or complaints — see Appendix E, 'Reader Feedback'.

Happy computer gaming!

Richard Woolcock
Cameron Duffy
September 1984

Program Accuracy

Programs take a long time to type in and debug. To help make programs easier to read and debug, printouts have been specially formatted, and utilities have been provided to help you get programs running. Read the rest of this chapter, and enter the Merge and ChexSum programs before you enter any games programs.

FORMATTED LISTINGS

The program listings in this book have been processed through a formatting program to improve their appearance and readability. The formatter:

- Aligns statements at the left, avoiding the margin stepping that occurs as line numbers increase,
- Inserts spaces between keywords,
- Transforms SPACE characters occurring in strings, i.e. between quote marks ("), into a small black pyramid (▲),
- Makes the colon easier to see by redefining it as two small opposed triangles (⬍), and
- Redefines graphics characters to resemble the keyboard pictographs and inserts spaces between them so that they are readily distinguished.

Because the redefined alphanumeric and graphics characters do not exactly resemble the screen display, you may make typing errors until you become familiar with them. To assist you in determining which symbol corresponds to a particular key, tables of colour and control characters, and keyboard pictographs are illustrated overleaf.

These tables are also reproduced in Appendix D, 'Printout Symbols'. We suggest you photocopy or cut out Appendix D and keep it with you for ready reference.

KEYBOARD CHARACTERS*

Symbol in book	Key	Symbol in book	Key
┴	C= E		C= ↑
┤	C= W	┬	C= R
	C= D	├	C= Q
	C= C		C= F
	C= B		C= V
	C= T		C= +
	C= U		C= Y
	C= O		C= I
	C= @		C= P
	C= G		C= -
	C= J		C= H
	C= L		C= K
	C= M		C= N
	C= S		C= £
	C= A		C= X
	C= *		C= Z
└	SHIFT L	┘	SHIFT @
┌	SHIFT O	┐	SHIFT P
	SHIFT I		SHIFT U
	SHIFT K		SHIFT J
○	SHIFT W	●	SHIFT Q
┼	SHIFT +	╳	SHIFT V
╲	SHIFT M	╱	SHIFT N
◆	SHIFT Z	♥	SHIFT S
♣	SHIFT X	♠	SHIFT A
	SHIFT E		SHIFT D
	SHIFT *		SHIFT C
	SHIFT F		SHIFT R
	SHIFT T		SHIFT G
	SHIFT B		SHIFT -
	SHIFT H		SHIFT Y
◤	SHIFT £	←	SHIFT =
↑	SHIFT ZERO		

* These characters are designed to emulate the pictographs which appear on the front of the keys. The C= symbol is the special shift key located to the left of the left hand shift key.

Unfortunately different keyboard characters can produce identical symbols on the screen and printout. If a program doesn't work, these symbols may have been interchanged in a string:

	CTRL ,	CURSOR LEFT
	SHIFT *	SHIFT C
	SHIFT B	SHIFT -

COLOUR AND CONTROL CHARACTERS*

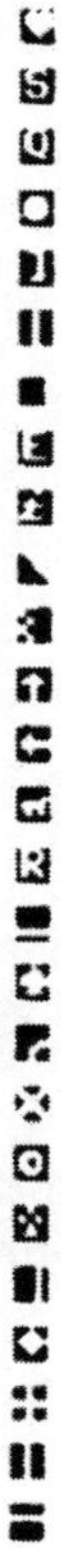

Symbol in book	Key
	CLR
	HOME
	CURSOR DOWN
	CURSOR UP
	CURSOR RIGHT
	CURSOR LEFT
	CTRL 1
	CTRL 2
	CTRL 3
	CTRL 4
	CTRL 5
	CTRL 6
	CTRL 7
	CTRL 8
	CTRL 9
	CTRL 0
	C= 1
	C= 2
	C= 3
	C= 4
	C= 5
	C= 6
	C= 7
	C= 8
	CTRL ,
	CTRL .

* These characters are designed to emulate the characters which appear on the screen.

TYPING RULES

In the program listings spaces have only been used as an aid to readability. For example, the line

```
100   POKE 54273, I : PRINT "▲ S T R I N G ▲ "
```

would be entered into your computer as

```
100POKE54273,I:PRINT"▲STRING▲"
```

Spaces are often used in strings but only enter a space when you see a (▲) symbol. This character does not appear on the keyboard but is used to tell you when to press the SPACE bar.

Character Confusion

In the printouts certain similar characters may be confused and entered incorrectly, and cause your program to crash: they are the letter I and the figure 1, and the letter O and the figure 0. In the text, figure zero (0) is shown cancelled (Ø). In listings these confusing characters are soon recognised:

CHARACTER	PRINTOUT
Letter I	I
Figure 1	1
Letter O	O
Figure Ø	Ø

If you are modifying programs and entering code from your own notes, a number of handwritten characters are easily confused unless clearly distinguished. We offer you this guide:

CONFUSED CHARACTERS	RECOMMENDED FORM
Letter Z, figure 2	Z, 2
Letter O, figure Ø	O, Ø
Letter S, figure 5	S, 5
Letter I, figures 1 and 7	I, 1, 7

Punctuation may also be a trap:

- Commas (,) and full stops or periods (.) are not interchangeable.
- Colons (:) and semi-colons (;) are not interchangeable.
- Apostrophes (') and double quotes (") are not interchangeable.
- Use parentheses () and not brackets []. Always ensure that parentheses are correctly paired: a quick check is to make sure that you have as many righthand as lefthand parentheses in a mathematical expression.
- The SHIFT key must be pressed when some characters (such as ! " # $ %, etc.) are entered.

SAVE Before RUNning

Do you remember the old proverb?

Programs typed and SAVEd today, live to RUN another day.

Be sure to progressively SAVE the programs onto cassette or disk as you enter the listings. From time to time the keyboard may lock up, especially if you try to RUN a program that contains an error. We strongly recommend that you keep SAVEing copies of the program as you enter it into the computer and debug any typing errors.

Note Some programs contain loaders to place machine language routines in high memory and which may alter certain system pointers. If such a program is RUN and crashes, the machine language program and the pointers will remain as they were even when the NEW command has been entered. When debugging programs, SAVE your work before RUNning and always reset the computer after a crash to avoid crashing a program subsequently entered or loaded.

CHEXSUM PROGRAM VERIFICATION

When games programs such as these are keyed in, invariably reading and typing mistakes creep in. You then spend ages trying to sort out where and what is causing the error. Even experienced programmers often cannot easily identify an error and need to do the tedious job of double-checking with the book, especially with DATA statements.

To avoid this major cause of frustration when entering the programs, there are two short routines in this book which you should enter and save before you enter other programs:

- Merge and
- ChexSum.

The program ChexSum calculates a unique check-sum number for each line of a games program, then prints out a table of program line-numbers and their corresponding line check-sums, plus a grand total for the whole program.

When you have entered a game program, run ChexSum and compare the check-sum table with that in the book. Any discrepancies immediately identify a mistyped line.

Other versions of BASIC have a MERGE command which enables you to construct new programs by combining pre-written subroutines or sections of existing programs. To use ChexSum it must be appended to the end of the games program it is to check. The Merge utility program performs this job and overcomes the lack of a MERGE command in Commodore BASIC. (Merge may also be used to join other programs — see Appendix C, 'Merging Programs'.)

Saving Merge and ChexSum

Follow these instructions to enter Merge and ChexSum, and save them to tape or disc. If saving to tape, do not put games programs on the same tape or you will spend considerable time winding and rewinding the tape to, first, load your program and, second, to load and use ChexSum.

1 Type in the Merge and ChexSum listings below and SAVE them before you do anything else.
Note Hand check Merge character by character after you have saved it. Merge is the only program in the book which cannot be verified by ChexSum. Why? Because you need Merge to load ChexSum to verify Merge and, if Merge is incorrect, this won't happen.

2 Load ChexSum and RUN it. It will first of all process itself, generating a table of line sums and a grand total for the whole program.

3 At this point you may or may not have had a crash. If a table was successfully generated, compare your table with that given below. If the grand totals differ, check the line sums to find the incorrect line.

4 Repeat steps 2 and 3 until ChexSum is debugged.

5 In line 62Ø2Ø, alter the value of E = 62194 to E = 61999. Save a copy to tape or disk.

Note This is your working copy used to check all the other programs in the book. Make sure you don't confuse it with your initial version, which is used only to verify ChexSum itself.

MERGE PROGRAM

```
5      POKE 55,202:POKE 56,63:CLR
10     FOR I=16331 TO 16331+34:READA:POKE I,A:C=C+A:NEXT
20     IF C<>4094THEN PRINT "C H E C K S U M ▲ E R R O R "
       :STOP
100    DATA165,43,141,238,63,165,44,141,239,63,56,165,45,2
       33,2,133,43,165
110    DATA46,233,0,133,44,96,173,238,63,133,43,173,239,63
       ,133,44,96
120    NEW
```

CHEXSUM PROGRAM

```
62000 T=PEEK(62)*256+PEEK(61)+1
62005 INPUT  "F R O M ▲ L I N E ▲ ";FROM
62010 INPUT "T O ▲ P R I N T E R ▲ ( Y / N ) ";Q$
62011 IF  Q$<>"Y "THEN 62020
62015 CLOSE4:OPEN4,4:CMD4:PRINT CHR$(1);CHR$(129)
62020 LINK=PEEK(44)*256+PEEK(43):E=62194
62120 T=LINK
62130 LINK=PEEK(T+1)*256+PEEK(T)
62135 LN=PEEK(T+3)*256+PEEK(T+2):IF LN<FROMTHEN 62120
62136 IF LN>ETHEN PRINT :PRINT "T O T A L = ";CH:CLOSE4:
      END
62137 S$=STR$(LN):L=LEN(S$)-1:S$=MID$(S$,2,L)+MID$("▲ ▲ ▲
       ▲ ▲ ▲ ",1,6-L)
```

```
62138 PRINT S$;
62140 CS=0:N=0:C=0
62150 FOR P=T+4 TO LINK-2:PK=PEEK(P)
62160 IF PK=143THEN P=LINK-2:GOTO 62190
62165 IF PK=34THEN C=(C=0)
62170 IF C=0ANDPK=32THEN 62190
62180 IF PK=137THEN N=N+1:CS=CS+(203ORN):PK=164
62185 N=N+1:CS=CS+(PKORN)
62190 NEXT:CH=CH+CS
62192 H$=STR$(CS):Y=LEN(H$):H$=MID$(H$,2,Y):H$=MID$("▲ ▲
      ▲ ▲ ▲ ",1,5-(Y-1))+H$
62194 PRINT "= ▲ ";H$:GOTO 62120
62196 REM
```

ChexSum Tables

62000 = 1848	62130 = 2067	62160 = 2373
62005 = 1332	62135 = 3540	62165 = 1431
62010 = 1618	62136 = 2407	62170 = 1554
62011 = 1281	62137 = 4234	62180 = 3320
62015 = 2020	62138 = 338	62185 = 1862
62020 = 2502	62140 = 1142	62190 = 1001
62120 = 577	62150 = 2251	62192 = 4892
		62194 = 1247
		TOTAL = 44837

Using ChexSum

The greatest problem encountered when typing in programs from a book is errors made by the user. Most of these are picked up when the computer responds to the RUN command with the 'Syntax Error' message. The user then has only to LIST the line and compare it with the line in the book. Unfortunately, some errors are more subtle and not fatal to program operation. These types of errors will cause the program to run, but incorrectly, and the computer will not be able to detect them as such.

Checksum is a special program which generates a unique sum for each line in a program and a grand total of all line sums. After each program listing is a table of check sums. You need only compare the numbers in the ChexSum table for each program with those generated by ChexSum. If two numbers differ, check that particular line.

1 Load and run the Merge program by typing LOAD "MERGE" (for tape) or LOAD "MERGE",8 (for disk), and then entering RUN.

2 From your games tape or disk, load the program you want to verify.

Note Always SAVE your program to tape before running ChexSum.

For the first program, enter LOAD "BLOCKADE" for tape or LOAD "BLOCKADE", 8 for disk. Do not RUN the program at this point.

3 Enter SYS16331 to protect the first game program, i.e. BLOCKADE.

4 Load ChexSum by entering LOAD "CHEXSUM" for tape or LOAD "CHEXSUM", 8 for disk.

5 Enter SYS16355 to merge the game program BLOCKADE with ChexSum.

6 Enter RUN 62ØØØ to activate ChexSum.

7 The program will respond with the prompt:

LINE NUMBER: ?

Pressing the RETURN key at this point will cause ChexSum to start with the first line of your program. Entering a line number will start ChexSum at that line.

8 ChexSum next prompts with:

PRINTER (Y/N) ?

A 'Y' will send the ChexSum table to the printer or an 'N' will send it to the screen.

9 Check your grand total with that in the book. If they differ, a line has been typed incorrectly. Compare line numbers until you locate the bad lines and then edit them.

10 Repeat steps 6 to 8 until the games program is debugged. In step 6, enter the number of the first bad line to avoid ChexSum verifying the games program from the first line.

DEBUGGING HINTS

Limitations of ChexSum

ChexSum is not entirely foolproof and cannot detect two errors which give a (seemingly) correct output:

1 If your grand total is correct but the program crashes, two lines have been typed in incorrectly and, although their individual line sums are incorrect, they cancel. Please check that all line sums are correct.

2 At certain column positions in a statement line, a full point (.) and a comma (,) may be interchanged and yet still give a correct line sum. When occurring in a DATA statement a (.) for (,) substitution will cause two adjacent integer numbers to be read as a single real number and will usually generate an 'Out of Data' message. When either possible substitution occurs in a program statement, a 'Syntax Error' message will be generated.

It is impossible for ChexSum to completely eliminate typing errors — it merely reduces the probability of them occurring to a very low level.

Pointer Corruption

Sometimes a program will run incorrectly even when thoroughly debugged by ChexSum and by hand. In this case there are two possibilities:

- The program is wrong — please write and tell us (see Appendix E, 'Reader Feedback').
- A previous run has left system pointers corrupted and they continue to crash the program despite the use of the NEW command. Always reset the computer after a crash to avoid this problem.

Blockade

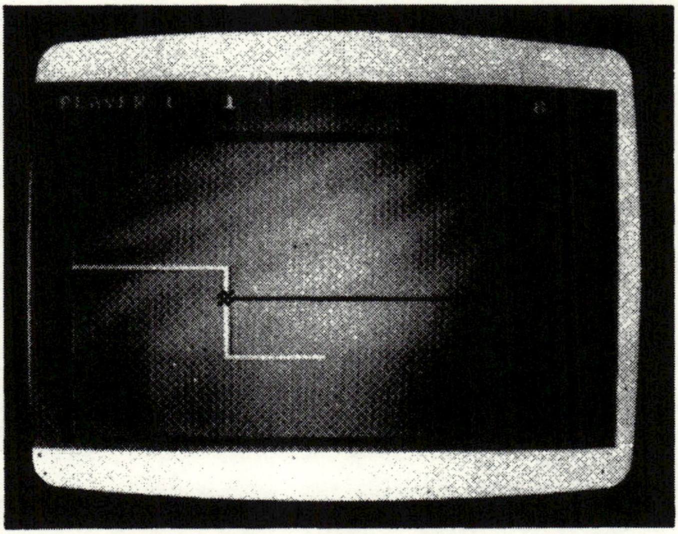

CLASSIFICATION: Evasion

In this fast-paced game, your goal is to build a wall in front of your opponent so that he crashes into it. Only by quick maneouvres, either left or right, can you avoid the walls. May you outlast your opponent.

The controls are:

Player 1, Q move left, Z move right; player 2, I move left, P move right.

PROGRAMMING SUGGESTIONS

Add a computer opponent. Give the computer limited (or perhaps random!) intelligence when making a decision to turn left or right at each step.

Add obstacles to the board. Set up a routine in the board so that non-blank characters on the field will act as obstacles.

PROGRAM
Variables

CH	Wall characters
CX, CY	Corner characters
X1, Y1	Player 1 co-ordinates
X2, Y2	Player 2 co-ordinates
P1, P2	Scores, player 1 and player 2
D1, D2	Direction of players 1 and 2
A1, B1	Player 1 step value
A2, B2	Player 2 step value
W	Winner

Listing

Initialisation

```
10    COLOR0,2,5:COLOR4,15:VOL 8:P1=0:P2=0
20    X$="█ █ █ █ █ █ █ █ █ █ █ █ ":DIMCH(1,1):CH(1,0)=64:C
      H(0,1)=93:DIMCX(3):DIMCY(3)
30    CX(0)=109:CX(1)=125:CX(2)=110:CX(3)=112
40    CY(0)=112:CY(1)=109:CY(2)=125:CY(3)=110
50    B$="▀ ▀ ▀ ▀ ▀ ▀ ▀ ▀ ▀ ▀ ▀ ▀ ▀ ▀ ▀ ▀ ▀ ▀ ▀ ▀ ▀ ▀ ▀ ▀ ▀ ▀
       ▀ ▀ ▀ ▀ ▀ ▀ ▀ ▀ ▀ ▀ ▀ ▀ ▀ "
60    L$="▴ ▴ ▣ ▐ ▀ ▴ ▴ ▴ ▴ ▴ ▴ ▴ ▴ ▴ ▴ ▴ ▴ ▴ ▴ ▴ ▴ ▴ ▴ ▴ ▴
       ▴ ▴ ▴ ▴ ▴ ▴ ▴ ▴ ▴ ▴ ▴ ▴ ▴ ▴ ▴ ▴ ▴ ▴ ▐ ▴ ▴ "
70    COLOR1,16,4:PRINT "▚ ▣ ▣ ▣ ▣ ▴ ▴ ▴ ┬ ═ ╗ ▴ ┬ ▴ ▴ ▴
      ╔ ═ ╗ ▴ ╔ ═ ╗ ▴ ┬ ▴ ┬ ▴ ▴ ╔ ═ ╗ ▴ ┬ ═ ╗ ▴ ┌ ═ ╗ ▴ ▴
       ║ "
80    PRINT "▴ ▴ ▴ ├ ═ ┤ ▴ ║ ▴ ▴ ▴ ║ ▴ ║ ▴ ║ ▴ ▴ ▴ ├ ═ ╝
      ▴ ▴ ├ ═ ┤ ▴ ║ ▴ ║ ▴ ├ ═ ▴ ▴ ▴ ║ "
90    PRINT "▴ ▴ ▴ ┴ ═ ╝ ▴ ╚ ═ ╝ ▴ ╚ ═ ╝ ▴ ╚ ═ ╝ ▴ ┴ ▴ ╚
      ▴ ▴ ┴ ▴ ┴ ▴ ┴ ═ ╝ ▴ ╚ ═ ╝ ▴ ▴ ● "
100   COLOR1,9,4:PRINT :PRINT :PRINT "▴ ▴ ▴ ▴ ▴ ▴ ▴ ▴ ▴ ▴ ▴
       ▴ ▴ ▴ ▴ C O N T R O L S "
110   PRINT :PRINT "▴ ▴ ▴ ▴ ▴ ▴ ▴ ▴ ▴ ▴ ▴ P L A Y E R 1 ▴ ▴ ▴
       ▴ ▴ P L A Y E R ▴ 2 "
120   PRINT :PRINT "▴ L E F T ▴ ▴ : ▴ ▴ ▴ < Q > ▴ ▴ ▴ ▴ ▴
       ▴ ▴ ▴ ▴ < + > "
130   PRINT :PRINT "▴ R I G H T ▴ : ▴ ▴ ▴ < Z > ▴ ▴ ▴ ▴ ▴
       ▴ ▴ ▴ ▴ < / > "
140   COLOR1,7,4:PRINT :PRINT :PRINT :PRINT "▴ ▴ ▴ ▴ ▴ H
      I T ▴ < R E T U R N > ▴ T O ▴ C O N T I N U E . . .
       "
150   PRINT :PRINT "▴ ▴ ▴ ▴ ▴ ▴ ▴ ▴ ▴ ▴ ▴ < E > ▴ T O ▴ E X I
       T . "
160   GETA$:IF A$=""THEN 160
170   IF A$="E "THEN PRINT "▚ ▣ ▣ █ █ T H E ▴ E N D . . .
       ":END
180   IF ASC(A$)<>13THEN 160
190   COLOR1,3,3:PRINT "▚ ▴ ▴ ▴ ▴ ▴ ▴ ▴ ▴ ▴ ▴ ▴ ▴ ▴ ▴ ▴ ▴ ▴ ▴ ▴ B
       L O C K A D E ":PRINT :PRINT :PRINT "▴ ▴ ▙ ";B$;"▜
       "
200   COLOR1,3,3:FOR I=1 TO 20:PRINT L$:NEXT:PRINT "▴ ▴ ▛
       ▣ ";B$;"▀ ▐ ";
210   COLOR1,8:PRINT "▩ ▣ ▴ ▴ P L A Y E R ▴ 1 "
220   COLOR1,15,2:PRINT "▩ ▣ █ █ █ █ █ █ █ █ █ █ █ █ █ █ █ █
      █ █ █ █ █ █ █ █ █ █ █ █ █ P L A Y E R ▴ 2 "
230   X1=2:X2=37:Y1=12:Y2=14:A1=1:A2=-1:B1=0:B2=0:D1=0:D2
      =2:S=0
```

```
240   COLOR1,2:PRINT "■ ■ ■ ";X$;"▲ ▲ ▲ ▲ ▲ ▌▌ ▌▌ ▌▌ ▌▌ ▌▌ ";P
      1;X$;"■ ■ ■ ■ ■ ■ ▲ ▲ ▲ ▲ ▲ ▌▌ ▌▌ ▌▌ ▌▌ ";P2
```

Get Player Input

```
250   GETA$:C1=CH(ABS(A1),ABS(B1)):C2=CH(ABS(A2),ABS(B2))
      :S=S+1:IF S=2THEN S=0
260   X1=X1+A1:X2=X2+A2:Y1=Y1+B1:Y2=Y2+B2
270   IF A$="Q "THEN C=B1:B1=-A1:A1=C:D1=INT(((D1+1)/4-
      INT((D1+1)/4))*4):C1=CX(D1)
280   IF A$="+ "THEN C=B2:B2=-A2:A2=C:D2=INT(((D2+1)/4-
      INT((D2+1)/4))*4):C2=CX(D2)
290   IF A$="Z "THEN C=-B1:B1=A1:A1=C:D1=INT((ABS((D1+3)
      /4)-INT(ABS((D1+3)/4)))*4):C1=CY(D1)
300   IF A$="/ "THEN C=-B2:B2=A2:A2=C:D2=INT((ABS((D2+3)
      /4)-INT(ABS((D2+3)/4)))*4):C2=CY(D2)
```

Collision Detection

```
310   IF PEEK(3072+40*Y1+X1)<>32THEN A1=0:B1=0:P2=P2+1:W
      =2:X=X1:Y=Y1:GOSUB 400:GOTO 160
320   IF PEEK(3072+40*Y2+X2)<>32THEN A2=0:B2=0:P1=P1+1:W
      =1:X=X2:Y=Y2:GOSUB 400:GOTO 160
330   GOSUB 350
340   GOTO 250
```

Draw New Bricks In Each Player's Wall

```
350   POKE 3072+40*Y1+X1,C1:POKE 2048+40*Y1+X1,119
360   POKE 3072+40*Y2+X2,C2:POKE 2048+40*Y2+X2,46
370   IF S=0THEN SOUND 1,400+20*D1,5
380   IF S=1THEN SOUND 1,320+20*D2,5
390   RETURN
400   SOUND 3,850,20:SOUND 3,800,100
410   FOR I=1 TO 10:POKE 3072+40*Y+X,102:POKE 2048+40*Y
      +X,96:FOR J=1 TO 20:NEXTJ
420   POKE 3072+40*Y+X,230:POKE 2048+40*Y+X,44:FOR J=1
       TO 20:NEXTJ
430   NEXTI
```

Determine Winner

```
440   IF W=1THEN COLOR1,8:PRINT "■ ■ ■ ▲ ▲ P L A Y E R ▲
      1 ■ "
```

```
450  IF W=2THEN COLOR1,15,2:PRINT "▌▐█▐▐▐▐▐▐▐▐▐
     ▐▐▐▐▐▐▐▐▐▐▐▐▐▐▐▐▐PLAYER 2▀
     "
460  COLOR1,2:PRINT "█▐▐ ";X$;"      ▌▌▌▌▌ ";P
     1;X$;"▐▐▐▐▐▐     ▌▌▌▌ ";P2
470  RETURN
```

ChexSum Tables

10	= 2228	170	= 2259	330	= 299
20	= 4384	180	= 1378	340	= 526
30	= 2904	190	= 4121	350	= 3105
40	= 2916	200	= 3324	360	= 3055
50	= 6342	210	= 1453	370	= 1843
60	= 2670	220	= 2559	380	= 1844
70	= 6651	230	= 5263	390	= 143
80	= 4821	240	= 4358	400	= 1419
90	= 5645	250	= 5280	410	= 4997
100	= 2784	260	= 3367	420	= 4047
110	= 2292	270	= 6413	430	= 206
120	= 1992	280	= 6374	440	= 2432
130	= 2051	290	= 7025	450	= 3738
140	= 4049	300	= 6980	460	= 4358
150	= 1745	310	= 6585	470	= 143
160	= 1214	320	= 6593	TOTAL	= 160175

Zapp

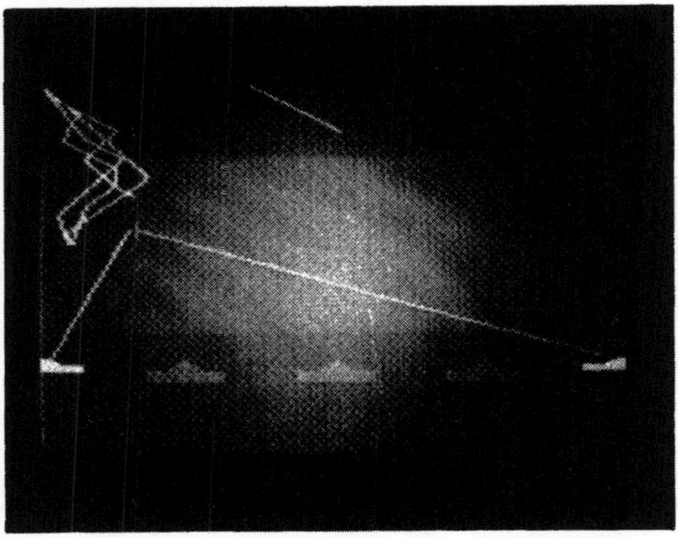

CLASSIFICATION: Shoot Up

Control your gunsights to target the attacking pods: fire either 1 or 2 zaps to destroy them and to protect your cities and weapon emplacements. You have only limited energy reserves, so zap sparingly. You receive bonus points for remaining energy. Be prepared to zap heavily when later waves of high-tech pods swarm in. The game is over when all cities are destroyed.

Controls are:

Q up, Z down, I left, P right, SPACE fire.

PROGRAMMING SUGGESTIONS

Create a new type of pod — one that must take more zaps to be destroyed, or perhaps one that can split open to drop more pods. Increase the speed of the game with each level. Give some special pods more intelligence — have them either home in on the gun emplacements or on the cities. Give bonus cities for surviving each wave.

PROGRAM
Variables

NM	Pod co-ordinates
E	Energy
LX, LY	Co-ordinates of sights
G%	Gun damage
C%	City damage
LV	Level
SC	Score
T	Speed of pods
MV	Gunsight step distance

Listing

Select Graphics Mode and Initialise

```
10      DIMNM%(3,2):C%=7:T=0:G%=3:SC%=0:LV=1:LX=79:LY=79:
        GRAPHIC4,1
20      COLOR0,2,2:COLOR4,1:COLOR1,8:COLOR2,3,4:COLOR3,15,5
        :VOL 8
30      GOSUB 400
```

Get Player's Input, Fire Remaining Zappers Draw Gunsight

```
40      GETA$:T=T+1:GOSUB 190:IF T=6-LVTHEN GOSUB 220
50      IF A$="I "THEN GOSUB 200:LX=LX-7:IF LX<4THEN LX=4
60      IF A$="P "THEN GOSUB 200:LX=LX+7:IF LX>155THEN LX
        =155
70      IF A$="Q "THEN GOSUB 200:LY=LY-9:IF LY<5THEN LY=5
80      IF A$="Z "THEN GOSUB 200:LY=LY+9:IF LY>147THEN LY
        =147
90      IF A$<>"▲ "ORG%=0THEN GOTO 40
100     IF (G%AND2)=2THEN DRAW1,3,148 TO LX-2,LY
110     IF (G%AND1)=1THEN DRAW1,156,148 TO LX+2,LY
120     DRAW0,3,148 TO LX-2,LY:DRAW0,156,148 TO LX+2,LY:
        SOUND 3,1000,15
130     FOR I=0 TO 3:IF NM%(I,0)<=0THEN 160
140     IF NM%(I,0)<LX-3ORNM%(I,0)>LX+3ORNM%(I,1)<LY-5ORNM%
        (I,1)>LY+5THEN 160
150     SOUND 3,900,25:SC%=SC%+LV*5:NM%(I,0)=-1:CIRCLE2,LX,
        LY,2,4:K%=K%+1
160     NEXTI
170     IF K%=LV*4THEN LV=LV+1:SCNCLR:K%=0:PRINT "◣ ▣ ▣ ▣ ▣
         ▣ ▣ ▣ ▣ ▣ ▣ ▣ ▣ ▣ ▣ ▣ ▣ ▣ ▣ ▣ ▣ ▣ S C O R E ";SC%:
        GOSUB 400
```

Move Pods, Check If Pods Hit Cities or Zappers. End Game

```
180     GOTO 40
190     B%=2:GOTO 210
200     B%=0
210     DRAWB%,LX,LY-5 TO LX,LY+5:DRAWB%,LX-3,LY TO LX+3,LY
        :RETURN
220     FOR I=0 TO 3
230     IF NM%(I,0)>0THEN 260
240     IF RND(1)>.08*LVTHEN 390
250     NM%(I,0)=INT(RND(1)*140+5):NM%(I,1)=0
```

```
260   IF RND(1)<.3THEN NM%(I,2)=INT(RND(1)*11-5)
270   IF NM%(I,0)+NM%(I,2)<5THEN NM%(I,2)=INT(RND(1)*6)
280   IF NM%(I,0)+NM%(I,2)>154THEN NM%(I,2)=-INT(RND(1)
      *6)
290   NM%(I,0)=NM%(I,0)+NM%(I,2):NM%(I,1)=NM%(I,1)+5
300   DRAW3,NM%(I,0),NM%(I,1) TO NM%(I,0)-NM%(I,2),NM%(I,
      1)-5
310   IF NM%(I,1)<154THEN 380
320   IF (C%AND1)>0ANDNM%(I,0)>24ANDNM%(I,0)<56THEN C%=C%
      -1:D%=0:GOSUB 510
330   IF (C%AND2)>0ANDNM%(I,0)>64ANDNM%(I,0)<96THEN C%=C%
      -2:D%=1:GOSUB 510
340   IF (C%AND4)>0ANDNM%(I,0)>104ANDNM%(I,0)<136THEN C%
      =C%-4:D%=2:GOSUB 510
350   IF NM%(I,0)<13THEN G%=(G%AND1):CHAR1,1,19,"* "
360   IF NM%(I,0)>147THEN G%=(G%AND2):CHAR1,38,19,"* "
370   IF C%=0THEN CHAR1,12,12,"G A M E _ O V E R ":END
380   IF NM%(I,1)>159THEN NM%(I,0)=-1
390   NEXTI:T=0:RETURN
400   IF (G%AND2)=0THEN 430
```

Draw Screen

```
410   DRAW3,0,148 TO 3,148 TO 6,151 TO 12,151 TO 12,154
       TO 0,154 TO 0,148:PAINT3,3,151
420   DRAW3,159,148 TO 156,148 TO 153,151 TO 147,151
       TO 147,154 TO 159,154 TO 159,148:PAINT3,156,150
430   IF (G%AND1)=0THEN 450
440   DRAW3,159,148 TO 156,148 TO 153,151 TO 147,151
       TO 147,154 TO 159,154 TO 159,148:PAINT3,156,150
450   FOR I=0 TO 2:IF (C%AND(2↑I))=0THEN 500
460   DRAW2,25+I*40,154 TO 25+I*40,159 TO 55+I*40,159
       TO 55+I*40,154 TO 53+I*40,154
470   FOR J=0 TO 3:DRAW2 TO 53+I*40-J*7,146 TO 48+I*40-J
      *7,146 TO 48+I*40-J*7,154
480   DRAW2 TO 46+I*40-J*7,154:NEXT
490   PAINT2,38+I*40,157
500   NEXTI:RETURN
510   CHAR1,7+D%*10,19,"# # # # # # ":SOUND 3,600,20:
      RETURN
```

ChexSum Tables

10	= 4555	180	= 476	350	= 2742
20	= 3054	190	= 349	360	= 2857
30	= 298	200	= 337	370	= 2404
40	= 2717	210	= 4134	380	= 2122
50	= 3199	220	= 655	390	= 791
60	= 3413	230	= 1210	400	= 1170
70	= 3216	240	= 1506	410	= 4163
80	= 3430	250	= 2754	420	= 5367
90	= 1955	260	= 2819	430	= 1169
100	= 2458	270	= 3286	440	= 5367
110	= 2601	280	= 3568	450	= 2261
120	= 3916	290	= 3479	460	= 5613
130	= 2102	300	= 3705	470	= 5875
140	= 5785	310	= 1313	480	= 1994
150	= 4962	320	= 4561	490	= 1212
160	= 206	330	= 4567	500	= 407
170	= 5460	340	= 4672	510	= 2571
				TOTAL	= 145403

Unscramble

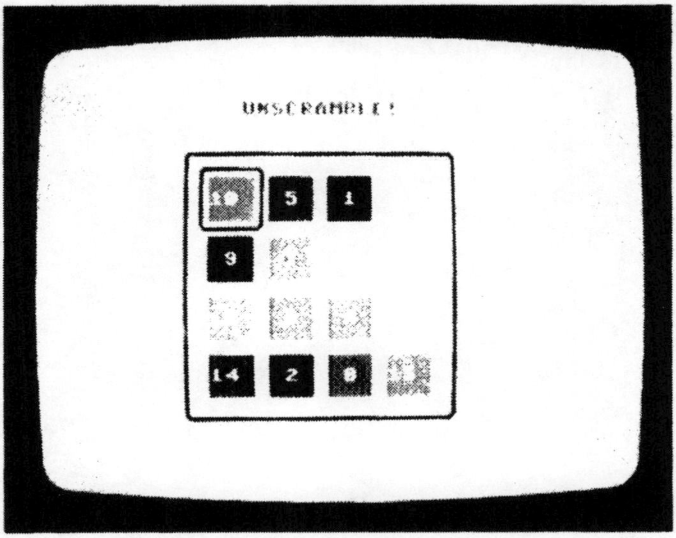

CLASSIFICATION: Logic COLOUR ILLUSTRATION OBC

A four-by-four matrix of numbers ranging from 1 to 15; 1 is blank and 15 are scrambled. You have to re-organise them into sequence from 1 in the top left to 15 in the bottom right. Use I and P to move the blinking cursor, then hit the SPACE bar to shift the pieces.

PROGRAMMING SUGGESTIONS

Increase the size of the matrix for a more challenging game.

PROGRAM
Variables

N	Board array
NZ$	Tile patterns
X, Y	Cursor co-ordinates
X1, Y1	Empty square co-ordinates

Listing

Initialise Game; Display Title and Define Tiles

```
10    COLOR0,2:COLOR4,2:VOL 8
20    DIMN(3,3):DIMNZ$(15)
30    X=0:Y=0:C2$="":C3$=""
40    TP$="▔ ▔ ▔ ▔ ▔ ▔ ▔ ▔ ▔ ▔ ▔ ▔ ▔ ▔ ▔ ▔ ▔ ▔ ▔ ":S$="▒ ◙ ▐▐
      ▒ ◙ ▐▐ ▒ ◙ ▐▐ ▒ ◙ ▐▐ ▒ ◙ ▐▐ ▒ ◙ ▐▐ ▒ ◙ ▐▐ ▒ ◙ ▐▐ ▒ ◙
      ▐▐ ▒ ◙ ▐▐ ▒ ◙ ▐▐ ▒ ◙ ▐▐ ▒ ◙ ▐▐ ▒ ◙ ▐▐ ▒ ◙ ▐▐ ▒ ◙ ▐▐ "
50    CX$="▲ ▲ ▲ ▲ ▲ ◙ ▐▐ ▲ ◙ ▐▐ ▲ ◙ ▐▐ ▲ ◙ ▐▐ ▲ ▐▐ ▐▐ ▲ ▐▐ ▐▐ ▲
      ▐▐ ▐▐ ▲ ▐▐ ▐▐ ▲ □ ▐▐ ▲ □ ▐▐ ▲ □ ▐▐ ▲ "
60    CD$="◙ ◙ ◙ ◙ ◙ ":CR$="◙ ◙ ◙ ◙ ◙ ◙ ◙ ◙ ◙ ◙ ◙ ◙ ◙ ":CS$="▒
      ▔ ▔ ▔ ▒ ◙ ▐▐ ▒ ◙ ▐▐ ▒ ◙ ▐▐ ▒ ◙ ▐▐ ▒ ▐▐ ▐▐ ▔ ▐▐ ▐▐ ▔ ▐▐ ▐▐ ▔ ▐▐
      ▐▐ ▒ □ ▐▐ ▒ □ ▐▐ ▒ □ ▐▐ ▒ "
70    BD$="◙ ◙ ◙ ◙ ◙ ◙ ◙ ◙ ":BR$="◙ ◙ ◙ ◙ ◙ ◙ ◙ ◙ ◙ ◙ ◙ ◙ ◙ ◙ ◙ ◙ "
80    COLOR1,3,3:PRINT "◙ ◙ ◙ ◙ ◙ ◙ ┬ ▲ ┬ ┬   ┬ ▒ ▔ ▒ ▒ ▔
      ▒ ┌ ▔ ▒ ▒ ▔ ▒ ▒ ▒ ▒ ▒ ┌ ▔ ▒ ┬ ▲ ┌ ▔ "
90    PRINT "◙ ◙ ◙ ◙ ▒ ▲ ▒ ▒ ╲ ▒ ▒ ▔ ▒ ▒ ▲ ▲ ├ ┬ ▒ ├ ▔ ┤
      ▒ ▒ ▒ ▒ ├ ▔ ┤ ▒ ▲ ├ ▔ "
100   PRINT "◙ ◙ ◙ ◙ ▒ ▔ ▒ ┴   ┴ ▒ ▔ ▒ ▒ ▔ ▒ ┴ ▒ ▲ ┴   ┴
      ┴   ┴ ▒ ▔ ▒ ▒ ▔ ▒ ▔ ▲ ● "
110   COLOR1,9,4:PRINT "◙ ◙ ◙ ◙ ◙ ◙ ◙ ◙ ◙ ◙ ◙ ◙ ◙ ◙ ◙ ◙ ◙ ◙ I N
      S T R U C T I O N S "
120   PRINT "◙ ◙ ◙ ◙ ◙ ◙ ◙ ◙ ◙ ◙ ◙ ◙ ◙ ' I ' ▲ ▲ ▲ ▲ C U R S
      O R ▲ L E F T "
130   PRINT "◙ ◙ ◙ ◙ ◙ ◙ ◙ ◙ ◙ ◙ ◙ ◙ ◙ ' P ' ▲ ▲ ▲ ▲ C U R S O
      R ▲ R I G H T "
140   PRINT "◙ ◙ ◙ ◙ ◙ ◙ ◙ ◙ ◙ ◙ ◙ ◙ ◙ ' Q ' ▲ ▲ ▲ ▲ C U R S O
      R ▲ U P "
150   PRINT "◙ ◙ ◙ ◙ ◙ ◙ ◙ ◙ ◙ ◙ ◙ ◙ ◙ ' Z ' ▲ ▲ ▲ ▲ C U R S O
      R ▲ D O W N "
160   PRINT "◙ ◙ ◙ ◙ ◙ ◙ ◙ ◙ ◙ ◙ ◙ ◙ ◙ S P A C E ▲ ▲ ▲ S H I F
      T ▲ P I E C E S "
170   PRINT "◙ ◙ ◙ ◙ ◙ ◙ ◙ ◙ ◙ ◙ ◙ ◙ ◙ ◙ ( H I T ▲ R E T U R N
      ▲ T O ▲ S T A R T ) "
180   GETA$:IF ASC(A$)<>13THEN 180
190   NZ$(0)="◙ ◙ ▲ ▲ ▲ ◙ ▐▐ ▐▐ ▐▐ ▲ ▲ ▲ ◙ ▐▐ ▐▐ ▐▐ ▲ ▲ ▲ "
200   NZ$(1)="■ ◙ ▲ ▲ ▲ ◙ ▐▐ ▐▐ ▐▐ ▲ 1 ▲ ◙ ▐▐ ▐▐ ▐▐ ▲ ▲ ▲ "
210   NZ$(2)="◙ ◙ ▲ ▲ ▲ ◙ ▐▐ ▐▐ ▐▐ ▲ 2 ▲ ◙ ▐▐ ▐▐ ▐▐ ▲ ▲ ▲ "
220   NZ$(3)="◣ ◙ ▲ ▲ ▲ ◙ ▐▐ ▐▐ ▐▐ ▲ 3 ▲ ◙ ▐▐ ▐▐ ▐▐ ▲ ▲ ▲ "
230   NZ$(4)="◙ ◙ ▲ ▲ ▲ ◙ ▐▐ ▐▐ ▐▐ ▲ 4 ▲ ◙ ▐▐ ▐▐ ▐▐ ▲ ▲ ▲ "
240   NZ$(5)="◙ ◙ ▲ ▲ ▲ ◙ ▐▐ ▐▐ ▐▐ ▲ 5 ▲ ◙ ▐▐ ▐▐ ▐▐ ▲ ▲ ▲ "
250   NZ$(6)="◙ ◙ ▲ ▲ ▲ ◙ ▐▐ ▐▐ ▐▐ ▲ 6 ▲ ◙ ▐▐ ▐▐ ▐▐ ▲ ▲ ▲ "
260   NZ$(7)="◙ ◙ ▲ ▲ ▲ ◙ ▐▐ ▐▐ ▐▐ ▲ 7 ▲ ◙ ▐▐ ▐▐ ▐▐ ▲ ▲ ▲ "
270   NZ$(8)="◙ ◙ ▲ ▲ ▲ ◙ ▐▐ ▐▐ ▐▐ ▲ 8 ▲ ◙ ▐▐ ▐▐ ▐▐ ▲ ▲ ▲ "
280   NZ$(9)="◙ ◙ ▲ ▲ ▲ ◙ ▐▐ ▐▐ ▐▐ ▲ 9 ▲ ◙ ▐▐ ▐▐ ▐▐ ▲ ▲ ▲ "
```

```
290   NZ$(10)="⌘ ◙ ▲ ▲ ▲ ◙ ▐▐ ▐▐ ▐▐ 1 0 ▲ ◙ ▐▐ ▐▐ ▐▐ ▲ ▲ ▲ "
300   NZ$(11)="▣ ◙ ▲ ▲ ▲ ◙ ▐▐ ▐▐ ▐▐ 1 1 ▲ ◙ ▐▐ ▐▐ ▐▐ ▲ ▲ ▲ "
310   NZ$(12)="▩ ◙ ▲ ▲ ▲ ◙ ▐▐ ▐▐ ▐▐ 1 2 ▲ ◙ ▐▐ ▐▐ ▐▐ ▲ ▲ ▲ "
320   NZ$(13)="▮ ◙ ▲ ▲ ▲ ◙ ▐▐ ▐▐ ▐▐ 1 3 ▲ ◙ ▐▐ ▐▐ ▐▐ ▲ ▲ ▲ "
330   NZ$(14)="◘ ◙ ▲ ▲ ▲ ◙ ▐▐ ▐▐ ▐▐ 1 4 ▲ ◙ ▐▐ ▐▐ ▐▐ ▲ ▲ ▲ "
340   NZ$(15)="▦ ◙ ▲ ▲ ▲ ◙ ▐▐ ▐▐ ▐▐ 1 5 ▲ ◙ ▐▐ ▐▐ ▐▐ ▲ ▲ ▲ "
350   FOR I=0 TO 3:FOR J=0 TO 3:N(I,J)=I*4+J:NEXTJ,I
360   PRINT "◘ ◙ ▐ ▐ ▐ ▐ ▐ ▐ ▐ ▐ ▐ ▐ ▐ ▐ ▐ ▐ ▐ U N S C R A
      M B L E ! ":GOSUB 550
```

Shuffle Tiles Randomly; Draw Cursor

```
370   X1=0:Y1=0:X=0:Y=0:Z=20+INT(RND(0)*25)
380   FOR J=1 TO Z:X=INT(RND(0)*4):GOSUB 620:Y=INT(RND(0)
      *4):GOSUB 620:NEXT
390   COLOR1,3,3:PRINT CD$;CR$;"▐ ◙ ";C2$;C3$;CS$;"▩ ":X
      =0:Y=0
```

Get Input; Move and Draw Cursor

```
400   GETA$:IF A$<>"▲ "ANDA$<>"P "ANDA$<>"I "ANDA$<>"Q "
      ANDA$<>"Z "THEN 400
410   IF A$="▲ "AND(X1=XORY1=Y)THEN GOSUB 620:GOTO 400
420   PRINT CD$;CR$;"◙ ▐ ";C2$;C3$;CX$
430   IF A$<>"▲ "THEN SOUND 1,400,7
440   IF A$="P "THEN X=X+1:C2$=C2$+"▐ ▐ ▐ ▐ ":IF X>3
      THEN X=0:C2$=""
450   IF A$<>"I "THEN 480
460   X=X-1:IF X>=0THEN C2$=LEFT$(C2$,X*4):GOTO 520
470   X=3:C2$="▐ ▐ ▐ ▐ ▐ ▐ ▐ ▐ ▐ ▐ ▐ ▐ ":GOTO 520
480   IF A$<>"Q "THEN 510
490   Y=Y-1:IF Y>=0THEN C3$=LEFT$(C3$,Y*4):GOTO 520
500   Y=3:C3$="◙ ◙ ◙ ◙ ◙ ◙ ◙ ◙ ◙ ◙ ◙ ◙ "
510   IF A$="Z "THEN Y=Y+1:C3$=C3$+"◙ ◙ ◙ ◙ ":IF Y>3
      THEN Y=0:C3$=""
520   COLOR1,3,3:PRINT CD$;CR$;"◙ ▐ ";C2$;C3$;CS$
530   GOTO 400
540   END
```

Draw Board and Tiles On Screen

```
550   COLOR1,1:PRINT CD$;CR$;"▧ ";TP$;"▨ ◙ ▐▐ ";S$;
560   PRINT CD$;CR$;"◙ ";S$;"▨ ";TP$;"▧ ";
570   PRINT CD$;"◙ ◙ ◙ ◙ ";
580   FOR I=0 TO 3:PRINT CR$;"▐ ▐ ";:FOR J=0 TO 3
590   PRINT "□ □ ";NZ$(I*4+J);"▀ ▲ ";:N(I,J)=I*4+J
600   NEXTJ:PRINT :PRINT :PRINT :PRINT :NEXTI
610   RETURN
```

Shuffle Tiles

```
620   IF X1=XANDY1=YTHEN RETURN
630   IF Y<Y1THEN FOR I=Y1-1 TO Y STEP -1:N(I+1,X)=N(I,X)
      :GOSUB 680:Y1=Y:NEXT
640   IF Y>Y1THEN FOR I=Y1+1 TO Y:N(I-1,X)=N(I,X):
      GOSUB 690:NEXT:Y1=Y:RETURN
650   IF X<X1THEN FOR I=X1-1 TO X STEP -1:N(Y,I+1)=N(Y,I)
      :GOSUB 710:NEXT:X1=X:RETURN
660   IF X>X1THEN FOR I=X1+1 TO X:N(Y,I-1)=N(Y,I):
      GOSUB 720:NEXT:X1=X:RETURN
670   PRINT BD$;BR$;NZ$(0):COLOR1,1:RETURN
```

Shuffle Down

```
680   Z$=BD$:BD$=LEFT$(BD$,I*4+7):GOTO 700
```

Shuffle Up

```
690   Z$=BD$:BD$=BD$+"■ ■ ■ ■ "
700   SOUND 1,1000-5*I,2:GOSUB 670:PRINT Z$;BR$;NZ$(N(I,X
      )):RETURN
```

Shuffle Right

```
710   Z$=BR$:BR$=LEFT$(BR$,I*4+12):GOTO 730
```

Shuffle Left

```
720   Z$=BR$:BR$=BR$+"■ ■ ■ ■ "
730   SOUND 1,970+5*I,2:GOSUB 670:PRINT BD$;Z$;NZ$(N(Y,I)
      ):RETURN
```

ChexSum Tables

10	=	1171
20	=	1100
30	=	1770
40	=	12924
50	=	4369
60	=	9603
70	=	1522
80	=	6927
90	=	5657
100	=	6244
110	=	2443
120	=	1883
130	=	1952
140	=	1701
150	=	1892
160	=	2194
170	=	2257
180	=	1709
190	=	2137
200	=	2277
210	=	2155
220	=	2285
230	=	2285
240	=	2159
250	=	2161
260	=	2285
270	=	2277
280	=	2297
290	=	2351
300	=	2354
310	=	2349
320	=	2352
330	=	2347
340	=	2350
350	=	3185
360	=	2195
370	=	3202
380	=	4131
390	=	3259
400	=	4985
410	=	3011
420	=	1590
430	=	1525
440	=	4019
450	=	1124
460	=	3425
470	=	1840
480	=	1133
490	=	3428
500	=	1116
510	=	4014
520	=	2220
530	=	529
540	=	129
550	=	2587
560	=	2098
570	=	634
580	=	2142
590	=	3195
600	=	1351
610	=	143
620	=	1477
630	=	4803
640	=	4594
650	=	5030
660	=	4582
670	=	1709
680	=	2745
690	=	1489
700	=	3286
710	=	2848
720	=	1583
730	=	3212
TOTAL	=	203307

SAM

CLASSIFICATION: Shoot Up

You are the commander of a ground-based guided-missile launcher. You launch surface-to-air missiles at attacking enemy craft flying overhead, and try to intercept and destroy them. The smaller and faster the target, the more points you earn.

Use Q to move the missile up, Z down, I left and P right. The SPACE bar will launch a new missile and abort one currently zooming about.

PROGRAMMING SUGGESTIONS

Have the enemy shoot their own anti-missile missiles — you must evade them. Have the enemy drop paratroopers who will try to overrun your emplacement.

PROGRAM
Variables

DR%	Direction table
D	Current direction
SC	Screen memory
CL	Colour memory
MX, MY	Missile's (X, Y) co-ordinates
X, Y	Step values for missile
TG	Missile collision
EX, EY	Enemy (X, Y) co-ordinates
SX, SY	Enemy missile (X, Y) co-ordinates
S	Score

Listing

Draw Title Page and Initialise Game
Draw Screen and Start Game

```
10   VOL 8:COLOR0,14,6:COLOR4,6:SC=3072:CL=2048
20   DIMDR%(7,1):DIMMC%(7):EX=-1:LV=1
30   FOR I=0 TO 7:READDR%(I,0):READDR%(I,1):NEXT:FOR I
     =0 TO 7:READMC%(I):NEXT
40   DATA1,0,1,-1,0,-1,-1,-1,-1,0,-1,1,0,1,1,1,62,78,30,
     77,60,78,33,77
50   PRINT "▚▚▚▚▚"
60   PRINT "▲▲▲▲▲▲▲▲▲▲╭══╮▲▲▲╭══╮▲▲▲
     ╭═╮╭═╮"
70   PRINT "▲▲▲▲▲▲▲▲▲▲║▲▲┴▲▲▲║▲▲║▲▲▲
     ║▲║║▲║"
80   PRINT "▲▲▲▲▲▲▲▲▲▲╰══╮▲▲▲├══┤▲▲▲
     ║▲╰╯▲║"
90   PRINT "▲▲▲▲▲▲▲▲▲▲┬▲▲║▲▲▲║▲▲║▲▲▲
     ║▲▲▲▲║"
100  PRINT "▲▲▲▲▲▲▲▲▲▲╰══╯▲●▲┴▲▲┴▲●▲
     ┴▲▲▲▲┴▲●"
110  PRINT "■▚▚▲▲▲▲▲▲▲▲▲▲▲▲▲▲▲▲CONTRO
     LS"
120  PRINT "▚▚▚▲▲▲▲▲▲▲▲'I'▲▲TURN▲MIS
     SILE▲LEFT"
130  PRINT "▚▲▲▲▲▲▲▲'P'▲▲TURN▲MISSI
     LE▲RIGHT"
140  PRINT "▚▲▲▲▲▲▲▲▲SPACEBAR▲FIRES
     ▲MISSILE"
150  PRINT "▚▚▲▲▲▲▲▲▲▲▲▲▲▲RETURN▲TO▲
     START"
160  GETA$:IF A$=""THEN 160
170  IF ASC(A$)<>13THEN 160
180  PRINT "▚▚▲▲▲▲▲▲▲▲▲▲▲▲▲▲▲S.A.M."
190  GOSUB 670:K=0:N=LV*5:PC=0
200  FOR I=0 TO 39:POKE 4032+I,104:POKE 3008+I,57:NEXT
210  POKE 4050,85:POKE 4051,66:POKE 4052,73
220  MX=2:MY=22:D=2:F$=""
```

Get Player's Command, Move and Fire Missile
Generate and Move Enemy

```
230  GETA$:TN=TN+1
240  IF A$<>"▲"THEN 280
250  SOUND 3,750,5:SOUND 3,765,5:SOUND 3,780,5:SOUND 3,7
     95,10
260  PT=PT-1:PC=PC-1:GOSUB 670
```

```
270    POKE SC+40*MY+MX,32:MY=22:MX=19:D=2:POKE SC+40*MY
       +MX,MC%(D):F$="F "
280    IF F$=""THEN 380
290    POKE SC+40*MY+MX,32:POKE CL+40*MY+MX,0
300    MX=MX+DR%(D,0):MY=MY+DR%(D,1)
310    IF MX<0ORMX>39ORMY<2ORMY>23THEN 220
320    TG=PEEK(SC+40*MY+MX)
330    IF TG<>32THEN GOSUB 560:GOTO 230
340    POKE SC+40*MY+MX,MC%(D):POKE CL+40*MY+MX,0
350    IF A$="I "THEN D=D+1:IF D>7THEN D=0
360    IF A$="P "THEN D=D-1:IF D<0THEN D=7
370    SOUND 1,1000-ABS(EX-MX)-ABS(EY-MY),3
380    IF TN<6-LVTHEN 230
390    TN=0:IF EX>=0ANDEX<=39THEN 430
400    FOR I=1 TO 10:SOUND 2,900-5*I,4:FOR J=1 TO 4:NEXTJ:
       NEXTI
410    EX=0:ED=1:IF RND(0)>.5THEN EX=39:ED=5
420    EY=INT(RND(0)*8+RND(0)*8+2)
430    POKE SC+40*EY+EX,32
440    IF EY+DR%(ED,1)<3THEN EY=3:ED=INT(RND(0)*5+4):
       GOTO 510
450    IF EY+DR%(ED,1)>23THEN EY=23:ED=INT(RND(0)*5):
       GOTO 530
460    EX=EX+DR%(ED,0):EY=EY+DR%(ED,1)
470    ED=ED+INT(RND(0)*3)-1
480    IF EX<0THEN EX=1:ED=INT(RND(0)*4+6)
490    IF EX>39THEN EX=38:ED=INT(RND(0)*5+2)
500    IF ED<0THEN ED=ED+7
510    IF ED>7THEN ED=ED-7
520    EG=PEEK(SC+40*EY+EX)
530    POKE SC+40*EY+EX,65:POKE CL+40*EY+EX,49
540    IF EG<>32THEN GOSUB 560
550    GOTO 230
```

Collision Detection and Scoring

```
560    POKE SC+40*MY+MX,42:PT=PT+5*LV+1:PC=PC+5*LV+1
570    FOR I=1 TO 25:SOUND 3,1000-5*I,5:NEXT
580    FOR I=60 TO 127:POKE CL+40*MY+MX,I:NEXT
590    F$="":POKE SC+40*MY+MX,32:X=19:MY=22:EX=-1:K=K+1
600    IF K<>NTHEN 670
610    FOR I=1 TO 20+2*LV:SOUND 1,600+I*5,5:SOUND 2,900-4
       *I,5:FOR J=1 TO 5:NEXTJ:NEXTI
620    PRINT "■ ▣ ▣ ▣ ▣ ▣ ▤ ▤ ▤ ▤ L E V E L ▲ ";LV;"▲ C O
       M P L E T E D . "
630    PRINT "▣ ▲ ▲ ▲ ▲ K I L L ▲ R A T I O ▲ = ▲ ";100*PC
       /(N*5*LV);"% "
640    PRINT "▣ ▣ ▥ ▲ ▲ ▲ ▲ R E T U R N ▲ T O ▲ C O N T I
       N U E "
```

```
650   LV=LV+1:IF LV>5THEN LV=5
660   PRINT "▣ ▣ ▲ ▲ ▣ S C O R E ▲ ▣ ";PT:GOTO 160
670   PRINT "▣ ▣ ▲ ▲ ▣ S C O R E ▲ ▣ ▲ ▲ ▲ ▲ ▲ ▲ ▲ ▮▮ ▮▮ ▮▮ ▮▮
      ▮▮ ▮▮ ";PT:RETURN
```

ChexSum Tables

10	= 2655	240	= 1080	470	= 1705
20	= 2292	250	= 2687	480	= 2669
30	= 4029	260	= 1939	490	= 2795
40	= 3521	270	= 5684	500	= 1413
50	= 471	280	= 848	510	= 1414
60	= 3899	290	= 2988	520	= 1752
70	= 2879	300	= 2541	530	= 3050
80	= 3489	310	= 2810	540	= 1257
90	= 2556	320	= 1768	550	= 528
100	= 3365	330	= 1868	560	= 4370
110	= 1732	340	= 3299	570	= 2187
120	= 2443	350	= 2361	580	= 2607
130	= 2345	360	= 2367	590	= 4326
140	= 2395	370	= 2672	600	= 995
150	= 1986	380	= 1242	610	= 5218
160	= 1214	390	= 2358	620	= 2482
170	= 1378	400	= 3350	630	= 3194
180	= 1434	410	= 2830	640	= 2149
190	= 1868	420	= 2213	650	= 1928
200	= 2771	430	= 1435	660	= 1851
210	= 1759	440	= 4053	670	= 2740
220	= 1813	450	= 3927	TOTAL	= 163007
230	= 1075	460	= 2682		

Tank Ambush

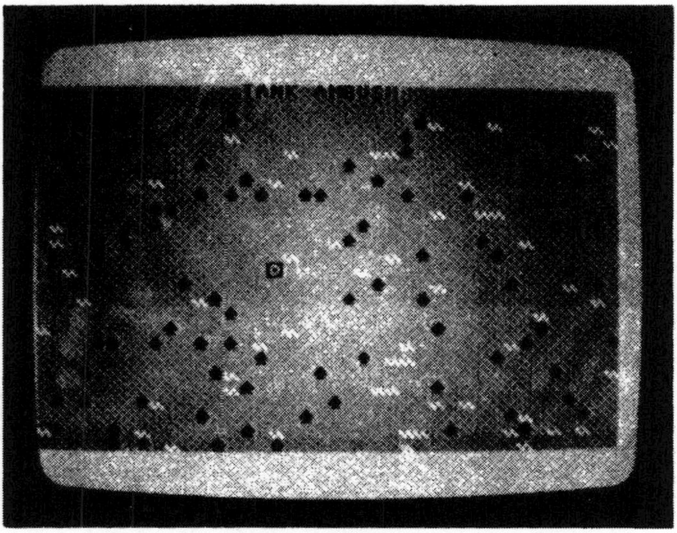

CLASSIFICATION: Shoot Up

The hunter against the hunted: hiding within the woods or lying behind hedges are devious infantrymen with dangerous heat-seeking missiles.

These missiles will always home in on your tank. You can shoot them with keys 1 to 8, or manoeuvre by pressing Q for up, Z for down, I for left and Z for right.

PROGRAMMING SUGGESTIONS

Have an enemy helicopter that fires heat-seeking missiles at your tank — shoot them or avoid them by manoeuvring. Introduce limited ammunition in the tank and ammunition dumps (where the tank must wait until it is reloaded). Give the killer tank hit points so it can suffer up to five hits before being destroyed. Also, create a repair station to fix up damages, and create the fuel for the killer tank and fuel dumps where it can refuel.

PROGRAM
Variables

SC	Screen memory
CC	Colour memory
BR	Background brightness level
LV	Level of difficulty
TB, TC	Character and colour beneath tank
F$	Fired flag
X, Y	Co-ordinates of tank
E	Delay for moving misSile
EX, EY	Co-ordinates of enemy missile
EB, EC	Character and colour behind missile
SX, SY	Howitzer shell co-ordinates
GB, GC	Character and colour behind shell
D	Firing direction
PT	Score

Listing

Title Screen and Instructions; Initialise game

```
10    VOL 8:SC=3072:CL=2048:BR=7:COLOR0,2,BR:Y=12:X=0
20    PRINT "[graphics]"
30    PRINT "[graphics]"
40    PRINT "[graphics]"
50    PRINT "[graphics]INSTRUCTIONS"
60    PRINT "[graphics]YOUR TANK":PRINT "[graphics]ENEMY MISSILE ([graphics]SHOOT[graphics])"
70    PRINT "[graphics]LAND MINE      ([graphics]AVOID[graphics])":PRINT "[graphics]TREE/HEDGE"
80    PRINT "[graphics]FIRING                 MOVEMENT"
90    PRINT "[graphics]8 1 2      [graphics]         Q"
100   PRINT "[graphics]\[graphics]/       [graphics]RETURN[graphics]         [graphics]"
110   PRINT "[graphics]7[graphics]3      [graphics] TO   [graphics]      I[graphics]P"
120   PRINT "[graphics]/[graphics]\       [graphics]BEGIN.[graphics]         [graphics]"
130   PRINT "[graphics]6 5 4      [graphics]         Z"
140   GETA$:IF ASC(A$)<>13THEN 140
150   GOSUB 710:GOSUB 660
160   TB=PEEK(SC+40*Y+X):TC=PEEK(CL+40*Y+X)
170   POKE SC+40*Y+X,215:POKE CL+40*Y+X,0
```

Get Input; Move Missile In; Move and Fire Tank

```
180   GETA$
190   IF F$="F "THEN GOSUB 450
200   E=E+1:IF E<8-LVTHEN 340
210   E=0
```

```
220   POKE SC+40*EY+EX,EB:POKE CL+40*EY+EX,EC:SOUND 1,100
      0-ABS(EX-X)-ABS(EY-Y),2
230   IF EY=YANDABS(EX-X)>1THEN EY=EY+INT(RND(0)*3-1):
      GOTO 260
240   IF EY<YTHEN EY=EY+1
250   IF EY>YTHEN EY=EY-1
260   IF EX=XANDABS(EY-Y)>1THEN EX=EX+INT(RND(0)*3-1):
      GOTO 290
270   IF EX<XTHEN EX=EX+1
280   IF EX>XTHEN EX=EX-1
290   IF EY<2THEN EY=3:
300   IF EY>24THEN EY=24
310   IF EX<0THEN EX=1
320   IF EX>39THEN EX=38
330   GOSUB 670
340   IF A$=""THEN 180
350   POKE SC+40*Y+X,TB:POKE CL+40*Y+X,TC
360   IF A$="Q "THEN Y=Y-1:SOUND 3,400,10:IF Y<2THEN Y=2
370   IF A$="Z "THEN Y=Y+1:SOUND 3,380,10:IF Y>24THEN Y
      =24
380   IF A$="I "THEN X=X-1:SOUND 3,420,10:IF X<0THEN X=0
390   IF A$="P "THEN X=X+1:SOUND 3,440,10:IF X>39THEN X
      =39
400   IF VAL(A$)>0ANDF$=""THEN F$="F ":SX=X:SY=Y:D=VAL(A$
      ):TS=0:GB=215:GC=0:SOUND 3,800,20
410   TB=PEEK(SC+40*Y+X):TC=PEEK(CL+40*Y+X):IF TB=42
      THEN 780
420   IF TB=43THEN TB=GB:TC=GC
430   POKE SC+40*Y+X,215:POKE CL+40*Y+X,0
440   GOTO 180
450   POKE SC+40*SY+SX,GB:POKE CL+40*SY+SX,GC
460   IF D=8ORD=1ORD=2THEN SY=SY-1:IF SY<2THEN SY=2:
      GOTO 640
470   IF D=2ORD=3ORD=4THEN SX=SX+1:IF SX>39THEN SX=39:
      GOTO 640
480   IF D=4ORD=5ORD=6THEN SY=SY+1:IF SY>24THEN SY=24:
      GOTO 640
490   IF D=6ORD=7ORD=8THEN SX=SX-1:IF SX<0THEN SX=0:
      GOTO 640
500   GB=PEEK(SC+40*SY+SX):GC=PEEK(CL+40*SY+SX)
```

Shell Collision With Missile; Increase Level

```
510   IF GB=215THEN GB=TB:GC=TC
520   IF GB<>81ANDEB<>43THEN 610
530   PRINT "■ ":IF BR=7THEN PRINT "■ "
540   SOUND 3,1000,15:PT=PT+1:PRINT "■ ■ ■ ■ S C O R E ";
      PT:GB=42:GC=0:GOSUB 660
```

```
550   PU=PU+1:IF PU=LV+1THEN BR=BR-1:PU=0
560   IF BR>=0THEN 600
570   IF BR=-1THEN COLOR0,1:GOTO 640
580   BR=7:COLOR0,2,BR:LV=LV+1:IF LV>8THEN LV=8
590   FOR I=1 TO 500:NEXT:PRINT "▚ ▆ ▆ ▆ ▆ ▆ ▆ ▆ ■ L E V E
      L ";LV;"▲ C O M P L E T E D ":FOR I=1 TO 1000:
      NEXT:GOTO 150
600   COLOR0,2,BR:GOTO 640
610   POKE SC+40*SY+SX,43:POKE CL+40*SY+SX,0
620   TS=TS+1:IF TS>10THEN 640
630   RETURN
640   POKE SC+40*SY+SX,GB:POKE CL+40*SY+SX,GC
650   F$="":RETURN
```

Initialise Enemy Missile Location

```
660   EX=INT(RND(0)*40):EY=INT(RND(0)*22+2)
670   EB=PEEK(SC+40*EY+EX):EC=PEEK(CL+40*EY+EX)
680   IF EX=XANDEY=YTHEN 780
690   POKE SC+40*EY+EX,81:POKE CL+40*EY+EX,0
700   RETURN
```

Display Score and Generate Background; End Game

```
710   PRINT "▚ ■ ▲ ▲ ▲ ▲ ▲ ▲ ▲ ▲ ▲ ▲ ▲ ▲ ▲ ▲ ▲ ▲ ▲ ▲ T A N K ▲ A
      M B U S H "
720   PRINT "▆ ▆ ▲ ▲ S C O R E ";PT;"/ ";LV+1
730   A=INT(RND(0)*50+50-6*LV)
740   FOR I=1 TO A:B=INT(RND(0)*920+80):POKE SC+B,65:
      POKE CL+B,53:NEXT
750   A=INT(RND(0)*30+30-3*LV)
760   FOR I=1 TO A:B=INT(RND(0)*920+80):POKE SC+B,104:
      POKE CL+B,88:NEXT
770   RETURN
780   POKE SC+40*Y+X,102:FOR I=1 TO 15:COLOR0,I:SOUND 3,8
      00+10*I,9:FOR J=1 TO 50:NEXTJ:NEXTI
790   COLOR0,2,7:PRINT "▚ ▆ ▆ ▆ ▆ ▆ ▆ ▆ ▆ ▆ ▆ ▆ ▆ ▆ ▆ ▆ ▆
      ▆ G ▲ A ▲ M ▲ E ▲ ▲ ▲ O ▲ V ▲ E ▲ R ▀ "
800   PRINT "▆ ▆ ▆ ▆ ▆ ▆ ▆ ▆ ▆ ▆ ▆ ▆ ▆ ▆ ▆ ▆ ▆ ▆ ■ S C O R
      E ";PT;"/ ";LV+1:END
```

ChexSum Tables

10	= 3640	280	= 1494	550	= 3158
20	= 6091	290	= 1171	560	= 1050
30	= 4916	300	= 1229	570	= 1875
40	= 4620	310	= 1109	580	= 3168
50	= 1932	320	= 1238	590	= 5518
60	= 6531	330	= 302	600	= 1203
70	= 5860	340	= 843	610	= 3007
80	= 2724	350	= 2824	620	= 1773
90	= 3249	360	= 3174	630	= 143
100	= 3413	370	= 3288	640	= 3168
110	= 3391	380	= 3160	650	= 570
120	= 2854	390	= 3284	660	= 2876
130	= 3121	400	= 6547	670	= 3747
140	= 1705	410	= 4483	680	= 1550
150	= 679	420	= 1843	690	= 2987
160	= 3403	430	= 2704	700	= 143
170	= 2704	440	= 533	710	= 2125
180	= 267	450	= 3168	720	= 1724
190	= 1079	460	= 4302	730	= 2055
200	= 1753	470	= 4401	740	= 4273
210	= 298	480	= 4404	750	= 2050
220	= 5929	490	= 4298	760	= 4321
230	= 4367	500	= 3797	770	= 143
240	= 1496	510	= 1882	780	= 5514
250	= 1495	520	= 1912	790	= 3027
260	= 4377	530	= 1585	800	= 2529
270	= 1495	540	= 4226	TOTAL	= 220287

Alien Overrun

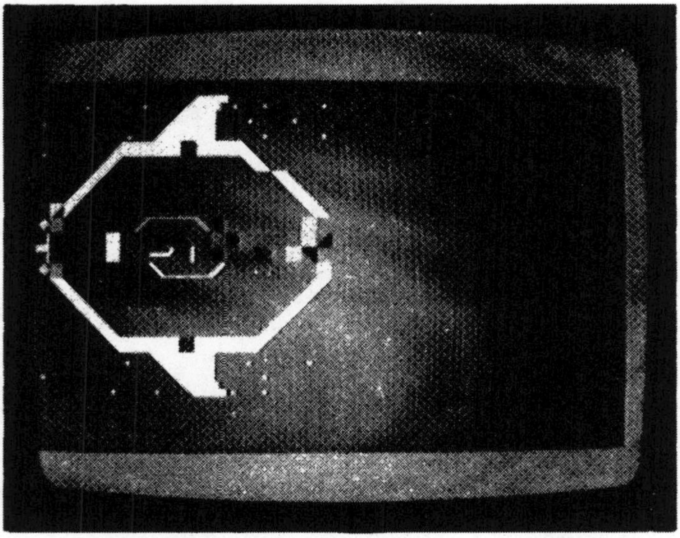

CLASSIFICATION: Defender

Your spaceship has been invaded by hordes of menacing aliens and they are multiplying prodigiously. You must move around your spaceship for as long as possible without being destroyed. Wipe the aliens out by moving onto the green chequered squares. Don't stand still as you don't score when you're still.

PROGRAMMING SUGGESTIONS

Make your ship a multi-level vehicle and arm your man with more than one weapon.

PROGRAM
Variables

X1, Y1	Next position of player
X, Y	Current position of player
Z	Level of difficulty
SC	Score
X( ), Y( )	Array of locations of each alien
A, B	Location of a particular alien
A1, B1	Next location of a particular alien
N	Number of aliens

Listing

```
10      REM ALIEN OVERUN
20      COLOR4,5,5:COLOR0,7,4
```

Input Difficulty Level, Define Variables and Draw the Spaceship

```
30      INPUT "▣ D I F F I C U L T Y ▲ 1 - 5 ";Z:Z=Z*10
40      IF Z>50ORZ<10THEN 30
50      C=2048:S=3072:SC=0:DIMX(Z),Y(Z):X=6:Y=10:N=1
60      PRINT "▣ ▣ ▣ ▲ ▲ ▲ · ▲ ▲ ▲ · ▲ ▲ ▣ ◤ ▲ ▣ ▬ · ▲ · ▲
        ▲ ▲ · "
70      PRINT ". ▲ ▲ ▲ ▲ ▲ ▲ ▲ ▲ ▣ ◤ ▲ ▲ ▬ ▣ ▲ · ▲ ▲ · "
80      PRINT "▲ ▲ ▲ ▲ ▲ ▲ · ▲ ▣ ◤ ▲ ▲ ▲ ▬ ▣ ▲ ▲ · ▲ ▲ ▲ ·
        "
90      PRINT ". ▲ ▲ ▲ ▲ ▣ ◤ ▲ ▲ ▲ ▲ ▣ ▬ ✱ ▣ ▣ ▲ ▲ ▣ ▲ ◥ "
100     PRINT "▲ ▲ ▲ ▲ ▣ ◤ ▬ ◤ ▲ ▲ ▣ ▲ ▲ ▲ ▲ ▲ ▲ ▲ ◥ ▣ ◥ "
110     PRINT "▲ ▲ ▲ ▣ ◤ ▬ ◤ ▲ ▲ ▲ ▲ ▲ ▲ ▲ ▲ ▲ ▲ ▲ ▲ ◥ ▣ ◥ "
120     PRINT "▲ ▲ ▣ ◤ ▬ ◤ ▲ ▲ ▲ ▲ ▲ ▲ ▲ ▲ ▲ ▲ ▲ ▲ ▲ ▲ ◥ ▣ ◥
        "
130     PRINT "▲ ▣ ◤ ▬ ◤ ▲ ▲ ▲ ▲ ▲ ▲ ▲ ▲ ▲ ▲ ▲ ▲ ▲ ▲ ▲ ▲ ◥ ▣
        ◥ "
140     PRINT "▣ ◆ ◣ ▣ ▲ ▬ ▲ ▲ ▲ ▲ ▣ ▲ ▣ ╱ ▢ ▢ ▢ ╲ ▲ ▲ ▲ ▲
        ▲ ▲ ◣ ▣ ▲ "
150     PRINT "▣ ┘ ▣ ✱ ▲ ▲ ▲ ▣ ▣ ▲ ▬ ▲ ▲ ▣ ✱ ▣ ▣ ▤ ▣ ▢ ▲ ▲
        ▣ ◆ ▣ ▲ ▲ ▬ ▲ ◣ ▣ ▲ ▣ ◤ "
160     PRINT "▣ ┐ ▣ ✱ ▲ ▲ ▲ ▣ ▣ ▲ ▬ ▲ ▣ ▣ ▣ ▤ ▣ ▢ ▲ ▲ ▣ ◆
        ▣ ▲ ▬ ▣ ✱ ▲ ◣ ◣ ▣ ▲ ▬ ▣ ◥ "
170     PRINT "▣ ◆ ◣ ▣ ▲ ▬ ▲ ▲ ▲ ▲ ▲ ▲ ▲ ▣ ╲ ▢ ▢ ▢ ╱ ▲ ▲ ▲ ▲
        ▲ ▲ ◣ ▣ ▲ "
180     PRINT "▣ ▲ ◥ ▬ ▣ ◥ ▬ ▲ ▲ ▲ ▲ ▲ ▲ ▲ ▲ ▲ ▲ ▲ ▲ ▲ ▲ ▲
        ▣ ◤ ▬ ◤ "
190     PRINT "▣ ▲ ▲ ◥ ▬ ▣ ◥ ▬ ▲ ▲ ▲ ▲ ▲ ▲ ▲ ▲ ▲ ▲ ▲ ▲ ▲ ▲ ▣
        ◤ ▬ ◤ "
200     PRINT "▣ ▲ ▲ ▲ ◥ ▬ ▣ ◥ ▬ ▲ ▲ ▲ ▲ ▲ ▲ ▲ ▲ ▲ ▲ ▲ ▲ ▣ ◤
        ▬ ◤ "
210     PRINT "▣ ▲ ▲ ▲ ▲ ◥ ▬ ▣ ◥ ▬ ▲ ▲ ▲ ▲ ▲ ▲ ▲ ▲ ▲ ▲ ▲ ▣ ◤ ▬
        ◤ "
220     PRINT "▲ ▲ ▲ ▲ ▲ ◥ ▣ ▲ ▲ ▲ ▲ ▲ ▣ ✱ ▣ ▲ ▲ ▲ ▲ ▲ ▬ ◤ "
230     PRINT "▲ ▲ ▲ ▲ ▲ ▲ · ▲ ◥ ▣ ▲ ▲ ▲ ▬ ▣ ▲ · ▲ ▲ ▲ · "
240     PRINT ". ▲ ▲ ▲ ▲ ▲ ▲ ▲ ▲ ◥ ▣ ▲ ▲ ▬ ▣ ▲ ▲ · "
250     PRINT "▲ ▲ ▲ ▲ ▲ · ▲ ▲ · ▲ ◥ ▣ ▲ ▣ ▬ · ▲ · "
260     A=14:B=10:FOR I=0 TO N
270     X(I)=A:Y(I)=B:POKE C+B*40+A,2:POKE S+B*40+A,81
280     A1=A+INT(RND(1)*3-1):B1=B+INT(RND(1)*3-1)
290     IF PEEK(S+B1*40+A1)<>32THEN 280
300     B=B1:A=A1:NEXT
```

```
310   FOR I=0 TO N:PRINT "▚ ■ ▲ S C O R E : ";SC;:IF SC
      <10THEN PRINT "▌▌ ▲ "
320   C1=1:A=X(I):B=Y(I)
330   IF RND(1)>.7THEN 350
340   A1=A+(A>X)-(A<X):B1=B+(B>Y)-(B<Y):GOTO 360
350   B1=B+INT(RND(1)*3-1):A1=A+INT(RND(1)*3-1)
360   IF PEEK(S+B1*40+A1)=32ORPEEK(S+B1*40+A1)=81ORPEEK(S
      +B1*40+A1)=88THEN 400
370   C1=C1+1:IF C1<10THEN 350
380   IF I<NTHEN A=X(I+1):B=Y(I+1)
390   GOTO 410
400   POKE S+B*40+A,32
410   A=A1:B=B1:IF A=XANDB=YTHEN 580
420   X(I)=A:Y(I)=B:POKE C+B*40+A,2:POKE S+B*40+A,81
```

Scan Keyboard; Move Player in Response; Multiply and Move Aliens

```
430   GETA$:IF A$<>"A "ANDA$<>"D "ANDA$<>"W "ANDA$<>"X "
      THEN 530
440   X1=X+(A$="A ")-(A$="D "):Y1=Y+(A$="W ")-(A$="X ")
450   P=PEEK(S+Y1*40+X1)
460   IF P=81THEN 580
470   IF P<>32ANDP<>102ANDP<>230THEN 530
480   SC=SC+1
490   POKE C+Y1*40+X1,7:POKE S+Y1*40+X1,88:POKE S+Y*40+X,
      32:Y=Y1:X=X1
500   IF P<>102ANDP<>230THEN 530
510   FOR J=0 TO N:POKE S+Y(J)*40+X(J),32:NEXT:SC=SC-30:
      IF SC<0THEN SC=0
520   N=1:GOTO 260
530   IF N<ZANDRND(1)>.8THEN N=N+1:X(N)=X(N-1):Y(N)=Y(N
      -1)
540   IF N=ZTHEN FOR J=1 TO Z:POKE S+Y(J)*40+X(J),32:
      NEXT:N=1
550   NEXTI:GOTO 310
560   POKE S+Y(0)*40+X(0),32:IF C1=10THEN 430
570   GOTO 310
580   REM
590   FOR I=1 TO 500:NEXT
```

Print the Score and Ask Player If He Wants Another Game

```
600   FOR I=1 TO 1000:NEXT:PRINT "▙ ■ T H E ▲ ▩ ▩ A L I E
       N S ▀ ■ ▲ G O T ▲ Y O U ! ! ":PRINT :PRINT "■ ▌▌ ▌▌
      ▌▌ ▌▌ S C O R E "SC
610   PRINT :PRINT "■ A N O T H E R ▲ G A M E ? "
620   GETA$:IF A$<>"Y "ANDA$<>"N "THEN 620
```

```
630   IF A$="N "THEN PRINT :PRINT "■ B Y E ▲ B Y E ▲ T H
      E N . ":END
640   PRINT :PRINT :PRINT "■ * * * S T A N D ▲ B Y * * *
      "
650   FOR I=1 TO 1500:NEXT
660   RUN
```

ChexSum Tables

10	= 0	230	= 1612	450	= 1582
20	= 1058	240	= 1442	460	= 848
30	= 2270	250	= 1457	470	= 2637
40	= 1392	260	= 1572	480	= 716
50	= 3678	270	= 3668	490	= 5141
60	= 1863	280	= 3417	500	= 1897
70	= 1508	290	= 2231	510	= 4892
80	= 1612	300	= 1009	520	= 917
90	= 1624	310	= 3376	530	= 4296
100	= 1768	320	= 1544	540	= 3756
110	= 1858	330	= 1117	550	= 803
120	= 1915	340	= 4067	560	= 2548
130	= 1961	350	= 3419	570	= 526
140	= 2813	360	= 5833	580	= 0
150	= 3311	370	= 1624	590	= 964
160	= 3668	380	= 2236	600	= 5627
170	= 2852	390	= 530	610	= 1617
180	= 2360	400	= 1167	620	= 2337
190	= 2295	410	= 2247	630	= 2654
200	= 2235	420	= 3668	640	= 1778
210	= 2180	430	= 4118	650	= 1021
220	= 1621	440	= 4047	660	= 139
				TOTAL	= 147939

Micro Minotaur

CLASSIFICATION: Educational

This is a smaller version of the number guessing game Minotaur. The objective is to guess a number in the range of 0 to 99. You do it by moving a piece around a board of numbers. As you pass over a number, it is removed from the board and added to your score. If you pass over an X, a clue appears at the top of the board for a short time. If you pass over a question mark, a random number is added to your Score.

If you pass over a number greater than five as you move around the board, you are pursued by a minotaur. If he captures you, you're dead. Remember, once you pass over a number it is removed from the board and you cannot pass over spaces. If you become encircled by spaces, press T to escape. Move your piece around using I for left, P for right, Q for up and Z for down. When you have guessed the number, move your piece to the white cursor.

PROGRAMMING SUGGESTIONS

Add different pieces to the board, such as bombs and mines. Place temporary barriers in the path of both the player and the minotaur.

PROGRAM

Variables

SC	Screen memory
CO	Colour memory
H$	Characters to place on screen
R	Row co-ordinate of player's piece
C	Column co-ordinate of player's piece
PO	Player's pieces position
PE	Player's pieces previous position
BE	Start of matrix on screen
C1	Column position of minotaur
R1	Row position of minotaur
MA	Minotaur's screen position

Listing

```
10     REM MICRO MINOTAUR
20     CLR
```

Draw Border, Rows of Numbers; Generate Number to Guess

```
30     SCNCLR:VOL 8:COLOR1,1,3
40     SC=3072:CO=2048:COLOR0,7,4:COLOR4,6,4:C=0:R=0:PO=SC
       +(R*40)+C:BE=SC+130
50     PRINT "■ ";
60     FOR I=1 TO 24:RR$=RR$+"■ ":NEXT
70     FOR I=1 TO 40:CC$=CC$+"■ ":NEXT
80     FOR I=1 TO 34:CL$=CL$+"▲ ":NEXT
90     H$="1 2 3 4 5 6 7 8 9 ? "+CHR$(24):DIMCL$(10)
100    FOR I=SC TO SC+39:POKE I,160:NEXT
110    FOR I=SC+(24*40) TO SC+(24*40)+39:POKE I,160:NEXT
120    FOR I=SC TO SC+(24*40) STEP 40:POKE I,160:NEXT
130    FOR I=SC+39 TO SC+(24*40)+39 STEP 40:POKE I,160:
       NEXT
140    PRINT "■ ■ ▲ ▲ ▲ ▲ ▲ ▲ ▲ ▲ ▲ ▲ M I C R O ▲ M I N O T
       A U R ";"■ ▲ ▲ ▲ ▲ ▲ P L A Y E R "
150    FOR I=SC+130 TO SC+850 STEP 80
160    FOR J=I TO I+18 STEP 2
170    Q=INT(RND(1)*12):IF Q=0THEN 170
180    A=ASC(MID$(H$,Q,1))
190    POKE J,A:NEXT:NEXT
200    NU=INT(RND(1)*100):IF NU=0THEN 200
210    NU$=STR$(NU):RA=INT(RND(1)*3):IF RA=0THEN GOTO 210
220    IF NU<10THEN NU$="0 "+NU$
```

Make up Clues About Random Number

```
230    IF RA=1THEN CL$(1)="F I R S T ▲ D I G I T ▲ E Q U A
        L S ▲ "+MID$(NU$,2,1)
240    IF RA=2THEN CL$(1)="S E C O N D ▲ D I G I T ▲ E Q U
        A L S ▲ "+MID$(NU$,3,1)
250    CN=2:FOR I=2 TO NU-1
260    A=NU/I:B=INT(A):IF A<>BTHEN 290
270    IF CN=7THEN 300
280    CL$(CN)="A ▲ F A C T O R ▲ O F ▲ T H E ▲ N U M B E
       R ▲ I S ▲ "+STR$(A):CN=CN+1
290    NEXT
300    IF NU/2=INT(NU/2)THEN CL$(CN)="T H E ▲ N U M B E R
       ▲ I S ▲ E V E N "
```

```
310   IF NU/2<>INT(NU/2)THEN CL$(CN)="T H E ▲ N U M B E R
       ▲ I S ▲ O D D "
320   GB=VAL(MID$(NU$,3,1)):FOR I=2 TO 9:A=GB/I:IF A=
      INT(GB/I)THEN GOSUB 1060:GOTO 340
330   NEXT
340   GB=VAL(MID$(NU$,2,1)):FOR I=2 TO 9:A=GB/I:IF A=
      INT(GB/I)THEN GOSUB 1070:GOTO 360
350   NEXT
360   SD=VAL(MID$(NU$,2,1)):IF SD/2=INT(SD/2)THEN CL$(7)
      ="F I R S T ▲ D I G I T ▲ I S ▲ E V E N "
370   IF SD/2<>INT(SD/2)THEN CL$(7)="F I R S T ▲ D I G I
      T ▲ I S ▲ O D D "
380   SD=VAL(MID$(NU$,3,1)):IF SD/2=INT(SD/2)THEN CL$(8)
      ="S E C O N D ▲ D I G I T ▲ I S ▲ E V E N "
390   IF SD/2<>INT(SD/2)THEN CL$(8)="S E C O N D ▲ D I G
      I T ▲ I S ▲ O D D "
400   FOR I=1 TO 9:IF I*I=NUTHEN CL$(9)="N U M B E R ▲ I
      S ▲ T H E ▲ P R O D U C T ▲ O F ▲ A ▲ S Q U A R E "
```

Place Minotaur and Player On Board; Move Them Around

```
410   NEXT
420   HO=BE+10:POKE HO,160
430   C1=6:R1=6:MA=BE+(R1*40)+C1:VE=PEEK(MA):POKE MA,13
440   C=10:R=18:PO=BE+(R*40)+C:VA=PEEK(PO):POKE PO,209
450   A=PEEK(198):POKE MA,13:IF A=64THEN 550
460   IF A=62THEN GOSUB 560
470   IF A=12THEN GOSUB 620
480   IF A=33THEN GOSUB 680
490   IF A=41THEN GOSUB 740
500   IF A=22THEN GOTO 1040
510   GOSUB 850:SOUND 2,15,12:SOUND 1,23,23
520   PRINT "■ ";LEFT$(RR$,2);LEFT$(CC$,2);CL$;
530   TT=TT+CU
540   PRINT "■ ";LEFT$(RR$,23);LEFT$(CC$,7);"■ L A S T ▲
      S C O R E : ■ ";CU;"▲ ▲ ■ T O T A L ▲ S C O R E : ■
       ";TT;
550   CU=0:POKE MA,141:GOTO 450
560   IF R=0THEN RETURN
570   R=R-2:PE=PO:PO=BE+(R*40)+C:DA=PEEK(PO):IF DA=32
      THEN R=R+2:PO=BE+(R*40)+C:RETURN
580   IF DA=13THEN GOTO 920
590   GOSUB 800
600   POKE PE,VA:FL=PEEK(PE):CU=VAL(CHR$(FL)):POKE PE,32:
      VA=PEEK(PO)
610   POKE PO,209:RETURN
620   IF R=18THEN RETURN
630   R=R+2:PE=PO:PO=BE+(R*40)+C:DA=PEEK(PO):IF DA=32
      THEN R=R-2:PO=BE+(R*40)+C:RETURN
```

```
640   IF DA=13THEN GOTO 920
650   GOSUB 800
660   POKE PE,VA:FL=PEEK(PE):CU=VAL(CHR$(FL)):POKE PE,32
670   VA=PEEK(PO):POKE PO,209:RETURN
680   IF C=0THEN RETURN
690   C=C-2:PE=PO:PO=BE+(R*40)+C:DA=PEEK(PO):IF DA=32
      THEN C=C+2:PO=BE+(R*40)+C:RETURN
700   IF DA=13THEN GOTO 920
710   GOSUB 800
720   POKE PE,VA:FL=PEEK(PE):CU=VAL(CHR$(FL)):POKE PE,32
730   VA=PEEK(PO):POKE PO,209:RETURN
740   IF C=18THEN RETURN
750   C=C+2:PE=PO:PO=BE+(R*40)+C:DA=PEEK(PO):IF DA=32
      THEN C=C-2:PO=BE+(R*40)+C:RETURN
760   IF DA=13THEN GOTO 920
770   GOSUB 800
780   POKE PE,VA:FL=PEEK(PE):CU=VAL(CHR$(FL)):POKE PE,32
790   VA=PEEK(PO):POKE PO,209:RETURN
800   IF DA=63THEN CU=INT(RND(1)*10)
810   FU=INT(RND(1)*10):DI=(40-LEN(CL$(FU)))/2
820   IF DA=24THEN PRINT "◙ ";LEFT$(CC$,DI);LEFT$(RR$,2);
      CL$(FU);:GOSUB 1050
830   IF DA=160THEN GOSUB 1000
840   RETURN
```

Work Out Minotaur's Position and Move Him Closer To You

```
850   IF CU<5THEN RETURN
860   IF C1>CTHEN C1=C1-2
870   IF C1<CTHEN C1=C1+2
880   IF R1>RTHEN R1=R1-2
890   IF R1<RTHEN R1=R1+2
900   POKE MA,VE:MA=BE+(R1*40)+C1:IF PEEK(MA)=209THEN
      GOSUB 920:STOP
910   VE=PEEK(MA):POKE MA,13:RETURN
920   PRINT "▙ ";LEFT$(RR$,10);"T H E ▲ M I N O T A U R ▲
       H A S ▲ E A T E N ▲ Y O U "
930   PRINT "◙ ";LEFT$(RR$,13);"T H E ▲ N U M B E R ▲ W A
       S ";NU;
940   PRINT :PRINT :PRINT
950   PRINT "D O ▲ Y O U ▲ W A N T ▲ A N O T H E R ▲ G A
      M E ( Y / N ) : ";
960   GETA$:IF A$=""THEN 960
970   IF A$="Y "THEN GOTO 20
980   IF A$="N "THEN END
990   GOTO 960
1000  PRINT "▙ ";LEFT$(RR$,2);LEFT$(RR$,3);"W H A T ▲ I S
       ▲ T H E ▲ N U M B E R ";:INPUT VT
```

```
1010  IF VT<>NUTHEN PRINT "W R O N G , ▲T H E ▲N U M B
      E R ▲ W A S ▲ ";NU:GOTO 940
1020  PRINT "C O N G R A T U L A T I O N S ▲Y O U ▲H A
      V E ▲B E A T E N ▲M I N O T A U R"
1030  GOTO 940
1040  PRINT "[illegible] ";:GOTO 930
1050  FOR I=1 TO 1200:NEXT:RETURN
1060  CL$(6)="A ▲ F A C T O R ▲ O F ▲ S E C O N D ▲D I G
       I T ▲ I S "+STR$(I):RETURN
1070  CL$(5)="A ▲ F A C T O R ▲ O F ▲F I R S T ▲D I G I
       T ▲ I S "+STR$(I):RETURN
```

ChexSum Tables

10	=	0	370	=	4090	730	=	1614
20	=	157	380	=	5953	740	=	809
30	=	1125	390	=	4216	750	=	7311
40	=	5999	400	=	5668	760	=	1287
50	=	295	410	=	131	770	=	302
60	=	1942	420	=	1346	780	=	3195
70	=	1892	430	=	4005	790	=	1614
80	=	1914	440	=	3984	800	=	2033
90	=	2293	450	=	2185	810	=	3162
100	=	1868	460	=	986	820	=	3756
110	=	3341	470	=	982	830	=	1175
120	=	2612	480	=	982	840	=	143
130	=	3242	490	=	982	850	=	839
140	=	2922	500	=	1278	860	=	1363
150	=	1872	510	=	1647	870	=	1364
160	=	1222	520	=	2034	880	=	1425
170	=	2025	530	=	857	890	=	1426
180	=	1198	540	=	5677	900	=	3944
190	=	739	550	=	1579	910	=	1533
200	=	2287	560	=	761	920	=	3677
210	=	3559	570	=	7374	930	=	2735
220	=	1726	580	=	1287	940	=	585
230	=	3881	590	=	302	950	=	2628
240	=	4040	600	=	4201	960	=	1214
250	=	1484	610	=	729	970	=	1271
260	=	2422	620	=	824	980	=	895
270	=	857	630	=	7373	990	=	535
280	=	4306	640	=	1287	1000	=	4192
290	=	131	650	=	302	1010	=	3955
300	=	4034	660	=	3195	1020	=	3802
310	=	4141	670	=	1614	1030	=	533
320	=	5441	680	=	746	1040	=	1051
330	=	131	690	=	7312	1050	=	1226
340	=	5443	700	=	1287	1060	=	3662
350	=	131	710	=	302	1070	=	3546
360	=	5832	720	=	3195	TOTAL	=	250979

Dumper

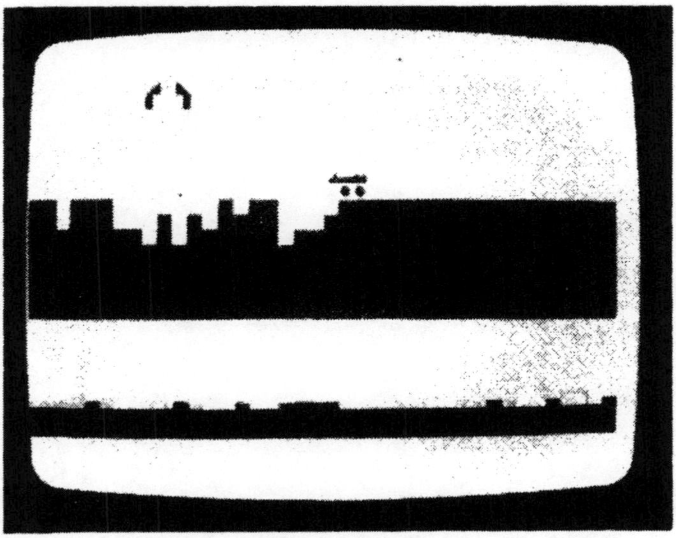

CLASSIFICATION: Defender COLOUR ILLUSTRATION OBC

An alien spacecraft is dropping bombs on your city's shield and gradually eating it away. You have three dumper trucks with which to drop bricks onto the shield and rebuild it. (Be careful, the trucks can be destroyed by the UFO's bombs.) Use the I key to move left, the P key to move right, and the SPACE bar to drop bricks on the shield.

PROGRAMMING SUGGESTIONS

Change or vary the effect of the alien's bombs so that one bomb may take one piece of the shield and another several pieces. Also give bonus points each time the UFO's bombs break the shield if you reseal it before the city is destroyed.

PROGRAM
Variables

HS	Highest score
S	Score
B	Position of bomb
G$	INKEY$
AL	Alien
P	Position of dumper
DI	Holes
DU	Number of dumpers

Listing

```
10     REM DUMPER
20     HS=0:VOL 8
30     COLOR0,4,5:COLOR4,2,5
40     PRINT "◣ ⓤ ⓤ ⓤ ⓤ ⓤ ⓤ ⓤ ⓤ ⓤ ⓤ ⓤ ▣ ⓚ ";
```

Set the Colors; Draw the Sky, Shield and City; Define the Alien

```
50     FOR I=1 TO 8:PRINT "▲ ▲ ▲ ▲ ▲ ▲ ▲ ▲ ▲ ▲ ▲ ▲ ▲ ▲ ▲ ▲
        ▲ ▲ ▲ ▲ ▲ ▲ ▲ ▲ ▲ ▲ ▲ ▲ ▲ ▲ ▲ ▲ ▲ ▲ ▲ ▲ ▲ ▲ ▲ ▲ ";
       :NEXT
60     PRINT "▀ ⓤ ⓤ "TAB(8)"ⓖ ▒ ⓤ ▌ + ⓤ ▌ ▒ ⓤ ▌ ⓚ ▲ "
70     PRINT "□ ⓡ ▄ ▄ ▄ ⓚ ▲ ▔ ▔ ▀ ▲ ▐ ◩ ◪ ■ ▄ ⓡ ▄ ⓖ ╱ ╲ ▣
       ▄ ⓡ ┌ ┐ ▲ ■ ▄ ▄ ▄ ";
80     PRINT "ⓡ ▄ ▄ ▄ ⓚ ▲ ▔ ▔ ▀ ▲ ▐ ◩ ◪ ■ ▄ ⓡ ▄ ⓖ ╱ ╲ ▣ ▄
       ⓡ ┌ ┐ ▲ ■ ▄ ";
90     PRINT "ⓚ ▲ ▲ ▲ ▲ ▲ ▲ ▲ ▲ ▲ ▲ ▲ ▲ ▲ ▲ ▲ ▲ ▲ ▲ ▲ ▲ ▲
       ▲ ▲ ▲ ▲ ▲ ▲ ▲ ▲ ▲ ▲ ▲ ▲ ▲ ▲ ▲ ▲ ▲ ▲ ▲ ";
100    PRINT "ⓚ ▲ ▲ ▲ ▲ ▲ ▲ ▲ ▲ ▲ ▲ ▲ ▲ ▲ ▲ ▲ ▲ ▲ ▲ ▲ ▲ ▲
       ▲ ▲ ▲ ▲ ▲ ▲ ▲ ▲ ▲ ▲ ▲ ▲ ▲ ▲ ▲ ▲ ▲ ▲ ▲ ";
110    PRINT "□ □ □ ▐ ▐ ▐ ▐ ▀ ▣ ▄ ▐ ▐ ▐ ▐ ▐ ▐ ▐ ▐ ▐ ▐ ▐ ▐
       ▄ "
120    DU=3:S=0
130    AL=1:A$="▲ ▣ ⓚ ◤ ⓒ ▀ ● ▣ ⓚ ◥ ▀ ▲ ⓤ ▌ ▌ ▌ ▌ ▌ ▲ ▐ ⓖ
       ▔ ▣ ⓚ ▌ ▀ ▲ "
140    P=3387
150    B=0
160    K=64:GOTO 220
170    GETG$
180    IF G$=""THEN K=64
190    IF G$="I "THEN K=12
200    IF G$="P "THEN K=20
210    IF G$="▲ "THEN 450
220    D=(K=12)-(K=20)*2+P:IF D<3351THEN 310
230    IF PEEK(D)=160THEN D=D-40
240    IF D>PTHEN D=D-1
250    POKE P,32:POKE P-41,32:POKE P-39,32:POKE P+1,32:
       POKE P-40,32
260    POKE P-81,32:POKE P-80,32:POKE P-79,32:POKE P-121,3
       2:POKE P-119,32:P=D
270    POKE P,81:POKE P+1,81:POKE P-41,233:POKE P-40,98:
       POKE P-39,248
280    IF PEEK(P+40)<>32ANDPEEK(P+40)<>160THEN 520
290    IF PEEK(P+40)=160THEN 310
300    D=P+40:GOTO 250
310    AL=AL+INT(RND(1)*3-1):IF AL<0THEN AL=0
320    IF AL>18THEN AL=18
```

Move the Alien Invader Along the Top of the Screen and the Dumper

```
330   PRINT "▣ "TAB(AL)A$
340   IF B>0THEN 370
350   IF RND(1)<.8THEN 440
360   B=3154+AL
370   POKE B,32:B=B+40:IF PEEK(B)=32THEN 430
380   IF PEEK(B)<>160THEN 410
390   POKE B,32
400   B=0:GOTO 440
410   IF B>3711THEN 520
420   GOTO 540
430   POKE B,46
440   GOTO 170
450   DI=P-1:IF PEEK(DI+40)<>160THEN S=S+5
460   POKE P-41,95
470   POKE P-41,233:GOTO 500
480   S=S+1:POKE DI,160
490   FOR I=1 TO 10:NEXT
500   IF PEEK(DI+40)=160ORDI>3671THEN 310
510   POKE DI,32:DI=DI+40:GOTO 480
520   GOTO 530
530   GOTO 610
```

Generate Sound, Print the Score and Prompt for Another Game

```
540   REM SOUND
550   SOUND 2,55,5:POKE B-1,77:POKE B,121:POKE B+1,78
560   IF DU=1THEN 610
570   POKE B,32:POKE B-1,32:POKE B+1,32
580   POKE P,32:POKE P+1,32:POKE P-41,32:POKE P-40,32:
      POKE P-39,32
590   PRINT "▣ "TAB(AL+1)"▴ ▴ ▴ ▴ ▣ ▮▮ ▮▮ ▮▮ ▴ ▴ ▴ "
600   DU=DU-1:GOTO 140
610   FOR I=1 TO 1000:NEXT:PRINT "▣ ▣ ▣ ■ S C O R E "S
620   IF S>HSTHEN HS=S
630   PRINT "▣ H I ▴ ▴ ▴ "HS
640   PRINT "▣ A N O T H E R ▴ G A M E ? ":POKE 198,0
650   GETA$:IF A$="Y "THEN 40
660   IF A$<>"N "THEN 650
670   PRINT :PRINT "▣ ▣ ▣ ▣ T O O ▴ T O U G H ▴ F O R ▴ Y
       O U , ▴ E H ▴ ? "
680   END
```

ChexSum Tables

10	= 0		240	= 1198		470	= 1347
20	= 736		250	= 3449		480	= 1161
30	= 1053		260	= 4378		490	= 908
40	= 720		270	= 3580		500	= 2316
50	= 3160		280	= 3058		510	= 1930
60	= 2018		290	= 1503		520	= 532
70	= 5020		300	= 1231		530	= 530
80	= 4551		310	= 2965		540	= 0
90	= 2151		320	= 1203		550	= 2477
100	= 2151		330	= 721		560	= 867
110	= 1716		340	= 769		570	= 1778
120	= 779		350	= 1113		580	= 3465
130	= 3865		360	= 781		590	= 1762
140	= 481		370	= 2315		600	= 1333
150	= 296		380	= 1393		610	= 2084
160	= 972		390	= 374		620	= 1179
170	= 271		400	= 903		630	= 696
180	= 1062		410	= 957		640	= 1746
190	= 1145		420	= 529		650	= 1243
200	= 1150		430	= 371		660	= 1128
210	= 905		440	= 528		670	= 2640
220	= 2971		450	= 2909		680	= 129
230	= 1652		460	= 679		TOTAL	= 106983

Scrambler

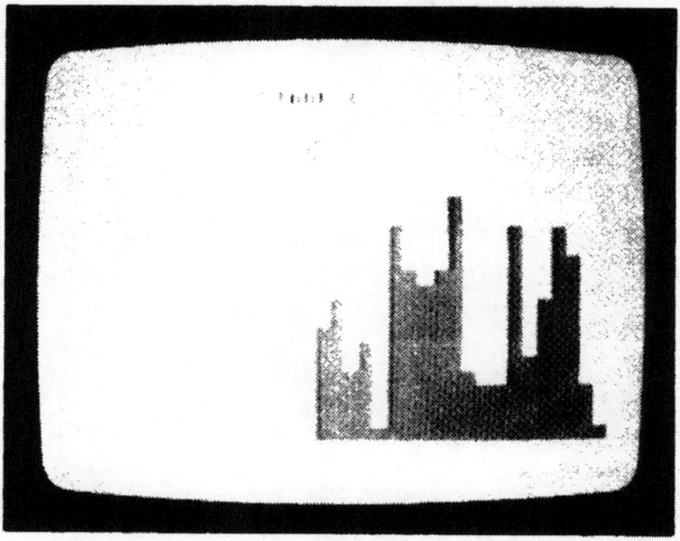

CLASSIFICATION. Evasion

You are the commander of a spaceship which must fly through an obstacle course of mountains, corridors and meteors. To move your space vehicle, use the Q key for up, the Z key for down. The program uses a small machine-language routine to scroll the screen, so the program should be saved before running in case you make a 'typo' and crash the program.

PROGRAMMING SUGGESTIONS

Give the player more landscapes to travel through. Cause a missile or a rocket to drift up from the ground occasionally. Give the player a fuel limit or a time limit to complete a given piece of scenery, otherwise he is destroyed.

PROGRAM
Variables

SA	Start of screen memory
PO	Position of spaceship
SL	Start of colour memory
R	Row position of spaceship
C	Column position of spaceship
P	Keyscan location
I$	Vertical bar
CC$	Column positioning variable
RR$	Row positioning variable
S1	Score

Listing

```
10    REM SCRAMBLER
20    POKE 55,16:POKE 56,39:CLR
30    GOSUB 450
40    T$="▣ ▲ ▀ ‖ □ ‖ □ ‖ □ ‖ □ ‖ □ ‖ □ ‖ ▣ ▲ ▀ "
50    COLOR0,7,5:COLOR4,7,5
60    K$="▣ ▲ ▀ □ ‖ ":FOR I=1 TO 19:I$=I$+K$:NEXT
70    SA$="▲ ▲ ▲ ▲ ▲ ◙ ‖ ‖ ‖ ‖ ‖ ▲ / □ \ ▲ ◙ ‖ ‖ ‖ ‖ ‖ ▲
      \ □ / ▲ ◙ ‖ ‖ ‖ ‖ ‖ ▲ ▲ ▲ "
80    RR$="◙ ":FOR I=1 TO 24:RR$=RR$+"◙ ":NEXT:FOR I=1
       TO 39:CC$=CC$+"◙ ":NEXT
90    W$="◙ "+LEFT$(RR$,22)+LEFT$(CC$,38)
```

Define Variables; Read Machine Program Into Memory

```
100   FOR I=11000 TO 11071:READA:POKE I,A:NEXT
110   PRINT "◙ ";:K1=11000
120   P=198:R=12:C=20:SA=3072:SL=2048:LM=300
130   PO=SA+(R*40)+C
140   PRINT "◙ ";TAB(16);"S T A G E ▲ O N E ▲ ▲ ";
```

Stage One: Fly Ship Over Mountains With Lowest Possible Altitude

```
150   FOR SC=1 TO 300:SYS K1:PRINT W$;LEFT$(I$,RND(1)*70)
      ;
160   IF PEEK(PO+83)=160ORPEEK(PO+82)=160THEN GOSUB 560:
      GOTO 140
170   A=PEEK(P):IF A=62THEN GOSUB 320
180   IF A=12THEN GOSUB 340
190   S1=S1+R-6:PRINT "◙ ▣ ";:PRINT USING"# # # ";S1;:
      PRINT "▀ ▲ ▲ ";
200   PRINT LEFT$(RR$,R);LEFT$(CC$,C);SA$;:NEXT
210   PRINT "◙ ";TAB(16);"S T A G E ▲ T W O ▲ ▲ ▲ ";
```

Stage Two: Fly Ship Through Meteor Storm and Keep Dodging Them

```
220   FOR SC=1 TO 300:SYS K1
230   IF SW=0THEN SW=1:GOTO 270
240   SW=0
250   HK=INT(RND(1)*22):IF HK<5THEN 250
260   FK=3072+(HK*40)+39:POKE FK,81
270   IF PEEK(PO+83)=81ORPEEK(PO+3)=160ORPEEK(PO+43)=81
      ORPEEK(PO+4)=81THEN GOSUB 560
280   A=PEEK(P):IF A=62THEN GOSUB 320
290   IF A=12THEN GOSUB 340
```

```
300   S1=S1+1:PRINT "▣ ▣ ";:PRINT USING"# # # ";S1;:
      PRINT "▀ ▲ ";
310   PRINT LEFT$(RR$,R);LEFT$(CC$,C);SA$;:NEXT:PRINT "▣
      Y O U R ▲ S C O R E ▲ W A S : ▲ ";SC:STOP
320   IF R=5THEN RETURN
330   R=R-1:PO=SA+(R*40)+C:RETURN
340   IF R=22THEN RETURN
350   R=R+1:PO=SA+(R*40)+C:RETURN
360   REM DATA FOR BLOCK MOVE
370   REM ===================
380   DATA173,11,255,201,204,208,249,160,0,162,199,185,20
      1,12,153,200,12,185
390   DATA145,13,153,144,13,185,89,14,153,88,14,185
400   DATA33,15,153,32,15,200,202,208,228,160,0,162
410   DATA5,142,238,46,169,32,153,239,12
420   DATA153,183,13,153,127,14,153,71,15,152,24,105,40,1
      68,174,238,46,202
430   DATA208,228,96
440   NEXT
450   PRINT "▣ ";TAB(14);"▣ S C R A M B L E R ▀ ";
460   PRINT :PRINT :PRINT "G U I D E ▲ T H E ▲ S H I P ▲
      A C R O S S ▲ T H E ▲ M O U N T A I N S . T H E ":
      PRINT
470   PRINT "L O W E R ▲ Y O U ▲ S T A Y ▲ T H E ▲ M O R
      E ▲ P O I N T S ▲ Y O U ▲ G A I N . ":PRINT
480   PRINT "I F ▲ Y O U ▲ L I F T ▲ Y O U R ▲ S H I P ▲
      T O ▲ I T S ▲ M A X I M U M ":PRINT
490   PRINT "H E I G H T ▲ Y O U ▲ W I L L ▲ B E G I N ▲
      L O S I N G ▲ P O I N T S . ":PRINT
500   PRINT "B E ▲ C A R E F U L ▲ N O T ▲ T O ▲ C R A S
      H ▲ I N T O ▲ M O U N T A I N S . ":PRINT
510   PRINT "O N C E ▲ Y O U ▲ H A V E ▲ P A S S E D ▲ T
      H E ▲ M O U N T A I N S ▲ Y O U ":PRINT
520   PRINT "W I L L ▲ H A V E ▲ T O ▲ S U R V I V E ▲ A
      ▲ M E T E O R ▲ S T O R M ":PRINT
530   PRINT TAB(10);"P R E S S ▲ A N Y ▲ K E Y ▲ T O ▲ S
      T A R T ";
540   GETA$:IF A$=""THEN 540
550   RETURN
560   FOR I=1 TO 15:FOR J=1 TO 99:NEXT:COLOR4,I,3:NEXT:
      RETURN
```

ChexSum Tables

10	=	0	200	=	2061	390	=	2422
20	=	1149	210	=	1761	400	=	2393
30	=	302	220	=	1205	410	=	1828
40	=	2859	230	=	1751	420	=	3852
50	=	1060	240	=	401	430	=	669
60	=	2816	250	=	2195	440	=	131
70	=	4857	260	=	2109	450	=	1946
80	=	4718	270	=	5547	460	=	4372
90	=	2201	280	=	1680	470	=	3855
100	=	2093	290	=	981	480	=	3518
110	=	1121	300	=	2697	490	=	3538
120	=	3254	310	=	4581	500	=	3769
130	=	1399	320	=	762	510	=	3716
140	=	1838	330	=	2296	520	=	3385
150	=	2911	340	=	819	530	=	2500
160	=	3748	350	=	2295	540	=	1212
170	=	1680	360	=	0	550	=	143
180	=	981	370	=	0	560	=	2797
190	=	3016	380	=	4072	TOTAL	=	125262

Siege

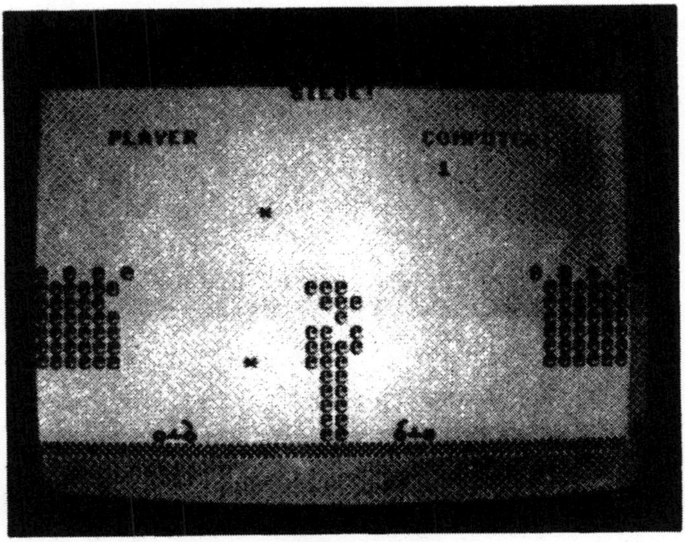

CLASSIFICATION: Shoot Up

It's you versus the Commodore 16. Use your ballista to lob huge rocks at the castle, trying to demolish it before it destroys your castle. You can raise and lower your ballista with Q and Z, and trundle it closer to or further away with P or I. Hitting the SPACE bar will fling your boulder.

PROGRAMMING SUGGESTIONS

Put flags on towers for extra points if hit. Have limited ammunition or reloading times. Have a different type of ammunition which starts fires which you must put out. You cannot shoot while extinguishing fires. Adapt the game for two players..

PROGRAM
Variables

CX	Computer position
PX	Player position
EV	Elevation of player's ballista
BY	Height of player's rock
VY	Velocity of player's rock
B%	Horizontal position of player's rock
CY	Height of computer's rock
FY	Velocity of computer's rock
C%	Horizontal position of computer's rock
PB	Bricks remaining in player's castle
CB	Bricks remaining in computer's castle
CH	Character beneath player's rock
C2	Character beneath computer's rock
F$	Player fired flag
F2$	Computer fired flag
M	Computer move distance

Listing

Title Screen

```
10   COLOR0,14:COLOR4,11:VOL 8:PRINT "▚ ":COLOR1,6,6
20   PRINT "▲▲▲▲▲▲▲▲▲▲▲▲▲▲▲▚═▚▲▛═▜▲┳▲▚═▚▲▛═▜"
30   PRINT "▲▲▲▲▲▲▲▲▲▲▲▲▲▲▲▐▲▲▲▐▲▲▲▐▲▐▲▲▲▐▲▲▲●"
40   PRINT "▲▲▲▲▲▲▲▲▲▲▲▲▲▲▲▚═▚▲┣═▲▲▐▲▐▲▲▲┣═"
50   PRINT "▲▲▲▲▲▲▲▲▲▲▲▲▲▲▲▐▲▐▲▲▲▐▲▐▲┳▲▐▲▲▲●"
60   PRINT "▲▲▲▲▲▲▲▲▲▲▲▲▲▲▲▚═▞▲▚═▞▲┻▲▚═▞▲▚═▞"
70   PRINT :PRINT :PRINT "▲▲▲▲▲▲▲▲▲▲▲▲▲▲▲▲▲▲█CONTROLS:"
80   PRINT :PRINT "▲▲▲▲▲▲▲▲█'█Q█'▲▲▲▲INCREASE▲RANGE"
90   PRINT :PRINT "▲▲▲▲▲▲▲▲'█Z█'▲▲▲▲DECREASE▲RANGE"
100  PRINT :PRINT "▲▲▲▲▲▲▲▲'█P█'▲▲▲▲MOVE▲BALLISTA▲RIGHT"
110  PRINT :PRINT "▲▲▲▲▲▲▲▲'█I█'▲▲▲▲MOVE▲BALLISTA▲LEFT"
120  PRINT :PRINT "▲▲▲▲▲▲▲█SPACE▲▲▲█FIRES▲BALLISTA"
130  PRINT :PRINT :PRINT :PRINT "▲▲▲▲▲▲▲▲▲▲▲▲▲(HIT▲RETURN▲TO▲BEGIN)"
```

Initialise Game and Draw Game Screen

```
140  GETA$:IF A$=""THEN 140
150  IF ASC(A$)<>13THEN 140
160  PRINT "▚ ":CD$="▜▣▣▣▣▣▣▣▣▣▣▣▣▣▣▣▣▣▣▣▣▣▣"
170  CR$="":CC$="▙▙▙▙▙▙▙▙▙▙▙▙▙▙▙▙▙▙▙▙▙▙▙▙▙▙▙▙▙▙▙▙"
180  CX=4:PX=1:EV=1.9:B%=0:BY=0:VY=0:CH=32:C%=0:CY=0:FY=0:C2=32:PB=40:CB=40
190  B$="▲●┻●▲"
200  B1$="▲▲*▚▲▣▐▐▐▐▐":C1$="▲▚*▲▣▐▐▐▐"
210  B2$="▲▲▲▐▣▐▐▐▐":C2$="▲▐▲▣▐▐▐"
220  B3$="▙▲▲▚▲▣▐▐▐▐▐":C3$="▲▚▲▲▣▐▐▐▐"
```

```
230   CT$="e ▲ e ▲ e ▲ e "‡CW$="e e e e e "‡SP$="▲ ▲ ▲
      ▲ ▲ ▲ ▲ ▲ ▲ ▲ ▲ ▲ ▲ "
240   COLOR1,9,5‡PRINT "▣ ▲ ▲ ▲ ▲ ▲ ▲ ▲ ▲ ▲ ▲ ▲ ▲ ▲ ▲ ▲ ▲ ▲ ▲
      ▲ S I E G E ! "‡PRINT "▣ ▣ ▣ ▣ ▮ ▮ ▮ ▮ ▮ P L A Y E
      R ";
250   COLOR1,15,5‡PRINT "▲ ▲ ▲ ▲ ▲ ▲ ▲ ▲ ▲ ▲ ▲ ▲ ▲ ▲ ▲ ▲ ▲ ▲ C
      O M P U T E R "‡COLOR1,2,3
260   PRINT "▣ ▣ ▣ ▣ ▣ ▣ ▣ ▣ ▣ ▣ ▣ ▣ ▣ ▣ ▣ ";CT$;SP$;"▲ ▲ ";S
      P$;CT$;
270   FOR I=1 TO 6‡PRINT CW$;SP$;"e e e e ";SP$;CW$;‡
      PRINT ‡NEXT
280   PRINT ,"▲ ▲ ▲ ▲ ▲ ▲ ▲ ▲ ▲ ▲ ▲ e e ▣ ■■ ■■ e e ▣ ■■ ■■ e e ▣
      ■■ ■■ e e ▣ ■■ ■■ e e "‡COLOR1,10,2
290   PRINT "※ ※ ※ ※ ※ ※ ※ ※ ※ ※ ※ ※ ※ ※ ※ ※ ※ ※ ※ ※ ※ ※ ※ ※
      ※ ※ ※ ※ ※ ※ ※ ※ ※ ※ ※ ※ ※ ※ ※ ※ ";‡POKE 4071,102‡
      POKE 3047,31
300   F$=""‡F2$=""‡BX$=B1$‡CX$=C1$
```

Get Input

```
310   GETA$
320   COLOR1,10,4‡PRINT CD$;CR$;BX$;B$;CD$;CC$;CX$;B$
330   IF A$="I "THEN PX=PX-1‡SOUND 2,100,2‡CR$=LEFT$(CR$,
      PX)‡IF PX<1THEN PX=1
340   IF A$="P "THEN PX=PX+1‡SOUND 2,100,2‡CR$=CR$+"▮ "‡
      IF PX>14THEN PX=14‡CR$=LEFT$(CR$,14)
350   IF A$="Q "THEN EV=EV+.01‡SOUND 2,1000,1‡IF EV>2.4
      THEN EV=2.4
360   IF A$="Z "THEN EV=EV-.01‡SOUND 2,1000,1‡IF EV<1.5
      THEN EV=1.5
370   IF RND(0)<.5THEN 430
380   M=INT(RND(0)*3)-1
390   CX=CX+M‡IF CX>15THEN CX=15‡M=0
400   IF CX<4THEN CX=4‡M=0
410   IF M=1THEN CC$=LEFT$(CC$,36-CX)
420   IF M=-1THEN CC$=CC$+"▮ "
430   IF F$="F I R E D "THEN GOSUB 510
440   IF F2$="F I R E D "THEN GOSUB 610‡GOTO 470
```

Fire Computer's Ballista

```
450   F2$="F I R E D "‡PRINT CD$;CC$;C2$;B$;CD$;CD$;CC$;C
      3$;B$;‡FY=1.5+RND(0)*.24‡Y=1
460   SOUND 2,850,1‡CX$=C3$‡F2=37-CX‡GOSUB 620
```

Fire Player's Ballista

```
470  IF A$<>"▲ "ORF$="F I R E D "THEN 310
480  PRINT CD$;CR$;B2$;B$;CD$;CD$;CD$;CR$;B3$;B$;
490  VY=EV*.7071:BY=1:SOUND 3,200,10
500  BX$=B3$:FS=PX+2:F$="F I R E D ":GOSUB 520:GOTO 310
```

Move Player's Rock and Check For Collision

```
510  POKE 3992+FS-INT(BY)*40+B%,CH
520  B%=B%+1:BY=BY+VY:VY=VY-.1
530  CH=PEEK(3992+FS-INT(BY)*40+B%):IF CH=32THEN 590
540  SOUND 1,0,0:SOUND 3,800,10
550  IF CH=42THEN POKE 3992+FS-INT(BY)*40+B%,32:F$="":B%
     =0:BY=0:VV=0:BX$=B1$:GOTO 700
560  IF B%>16ANDCH<>32ANDCH<>102THEN P1=P1+1:COLOR1,3,4:
     PRINT "▣ ◘ ◘ ◘ ◘ ◘ ▮ ▮ ▮ ▮ ▮ ▮ ";P1
570  POKE 3992+FS-INT(BY)*40+B%,32:IF B%>16ANDCH=0
     THEN CB=CB-1
580  IF CB=0THEN SOUND 1,1000,9:PRINT "▣ ◘ ▲ ▲ ▲ ▲ ▲ ▲ ▲ ▲
     ▲ ▲ ▲ ▲ ▲ ▲ ▲ ▲ ▲ ▲ Y O U ▲ W O N ! ! ! ":GOTO 710
590  IF CH=32ANDB%+FS<40ANDINT(BY)>0THEN POKE 3992+FS-
     INT(BY)*40+B%,42:RETURN
600  F$="":B%=0:BY=0:VY=0:BX$=B1$:RETURN
```

Move Computer's Rock and Check For Collision

```
610  POKE 3992+F2-INT(CY)*40-C%,C2
620  C%=C%+1:CY=CY+FY:FY=FY-.1
630  C2=PEEK(3992+F2-INT(CY)*40-C%):IF C2=32THEN 690
640  SOUND 1,0,0:SOUND 3,900,20
650  IF C2=42THEN POKE 3992+FS-INT(BY)*40+B%,32:F$="":B%
     =0:BY=0:VY=0:BX$=B1$:GOTO 700
660  IF C%>17ANDC2<>32ANDC2<>102THEN P2=P2+1:PRINT "▣ ▣
     ◘ ◘ ◘ ◘ ◘ ▮ ▮ ▮ ▮ ▮ ▮ ▮ ▮ ▮ ▮ ▮ ▮ ▮ ▮ ▮ ▮ ▮ ▮ ▮ ▮ ▮ ▮
     ▮ ▮ ▮ ▮ ▮ ";P2
670  POKE 3992+F2-INT(CY)*40-C%,32:IF C%>17ANDC2=0
     THEN PB=PB-1
680  IF PB=0THEN PRINT "▣ ◘ ▲ ▲ ▲ ▲ ▲ ▲ ▲ ▲ ▲ ▲ ▲ ▲ ▲ T H E
     ▲ ▮ C O M P U T E R ▬ ▲ W O N . . . ":GOTO 710
690  IF C2=32ANDC%-F2<0ANDINT(CY)>0THEN POKE 3992+F2-
     INT(CY)*40-C%,42:RETURN
700  F2$="":C%=0:CY=0:FY=0:CX$=C1$:RETURN
```

End Game

```
710   PRINT "█ █ █ █ █ █ █ ▲ ▲ ▲ ▲ ▲ A N O T H E R ▲ G A
      M E ▲ ? "
720   GETA$:IF A$=""THEN 720
730   IF A$="Y "THEN RUN160
740   PRINT "█ ":END
```

ChexSum Tables

10	= 2374	260	= 2126	510	= 2177
20	= 3574	270	= 3028	520	= 2471
30	= 2694	280	= 3522	530	= 3512
40	= 2946	290	= 8556	540	= 1191
50	= 2824	300	= 2230	550	= 6534
60	= 3571	310	= 267	560	= 5001
70	= 2244	320	= 2868	570	= 4406
80	= 2784	330	= 4963	580	= 4037
90	= 2590	340	= 6143	590	= 5127
100	= 3098	350	= 3827	600	= 2659
110	= 2957	360	= 3835	610	= 2106
120	= 2752	370	= 1113	620	= 2457
130	= 3162	380	= 1326	630	= 3426
140	= 1212	390	= 2455	640	= 1191
150	= 1376	400	= 1497	650	= 6510
160	= 1513	410	= 2015	660	= 5810
170	= 2362	420	= 1669	670	= 4350
180	= 6916	430	= 1396	680	= 4119
190	= 1063	440	= 2055	690	= 4913
200	= 3213	450	= 5624	700	= 2711
210	= 2774	460	= 2504	710	= 1784
220	= 3206	470	= 2084	720	= 1216
230	= 3005	480	= 2727	730	= 1096
240	= 3853	490	= 2179	740	= 569
250	= 2898	500	= 3343	TOTAL	= 223686

Hunter

CLASSIFICATION: Evasion COLOUR ILLUSTRATION OBC

You are a wild animal in a maze being pursued by a hunter. You can move yourself around the maze by pressing the keys I, P, Q and Z. No matter where you go in the maze, the hunter will know where you are and seek you out. As you move through the maze you eat munchies. When you have eaten all the munchies, you win. There are four levels.

PROGRAMMING SUGGESTIONS

Add a facility at the hardest level of the game so that the player can 'teleport' to another part of the board. He can't, however, control his destination, so he might land on top of the hunter.

PROGRAM
Variables

F$	Barriers of maze
D$	Munchies
SC	Screen start in memory
CC$	Horizontal position string
RR$	Vertical position string
R	Row position of animal
C	Column position of animal
PO	Current position of animal
T1	Previous position of animal
C1	Column position of hunter
R1	Row position of hunter
PC	Hunter's previous position
P1	Hunter's current position

Listing

```
10      REM HUNTER
20      CLR:COLOR0,8,3:COLOR4,7,3:COLOR1,2,7
30      GOSUB 710
40      GOSUB 850
```

Draw the Border, Maze, Power Pills and Define Variables

```
50      SCNCLR
60      SC=3072:CO=2048:BE=3072+207
70      A$="▣ ▲ ▲ ▬ ":B$="▲ ":C$=A$+B$
80      E$="▲ ▲ ● "
90      FOR I=1 TO 40:CC$=CC$+"▣ ":NEXT
100     FOR I=1 TO 25:RR$=RR$+"▣ ":NEXT
110     FOR I=SC TO SC+39:POKE I,160:POKE I+960,160:NEXT
120     FOR I=SC TO SC+999 STEP 40:POKE I,160:POKE I+39,160
        :NEXT
130     PRINT "▣ ";TAB(18);"▣ H U N T E R ";
140     FOR I=1 TO 8:F$=F$+E$:NEXT
150     FOR I=1 TO 10:D$=D$+C$:NEXT:PRINT :PRINT :PRINT :
        PRINT :PRINT
160     FOR I=1 TO 5:PRINT TAB(7);D$:PRINT TAB(7);D$:
        PRINT TAB(7);F$:NEXT
170     PRINT TAB(7);D$:PRINT TAB(7);D$
180     R=2:C=0
190     PO=BE+(R*40)+C:POKE PO,102
200     C1=26:R1=16:P1=BE+(R1*40)+C1:VE=PEEK(P1):POKE P1,86
```

Move Your Piece Up, Down, Left and Right; Move the Hunter

```
210     A=PEEK(198):IF A=62THEN GOSUB 370
220     IF A=12THEN GOSUB 420
230     IF A=33THEN GOSUB 470
240     IF A=41THEN GOSUB 520
250     GOSUB 290
260     IF CN=40THEN GOSUB 640:GOTO 10
270     PRINT "▣ ";LEFT$(RR$,3);LEFT$(CC$,16);"▣ S C O R E
        ▲ ";S1;"▬ ";
280     GOTO 210
290     IF SW<>AWTHEN SW=SW+1:RETURN
300     SW=0
310     PC=P1:IF C1<CTHEN C2=C1:C1=C1+1:P1=BE+(R1*40)+C1:
        IF PEEK(P1)=160THEN C1=C2:P1=PC
320     IF C1>CTHEN C2=C1:C1=C1-1:P1=BE+(R1*40)+C1:IF
        PEEK(P1)=160THEN C1=C2:P1=PC
```

```
330   IF R1<RTHEN R2=R1:R1=R1+1:P1=BE+(R1*40)+C1:IF
      PEEK(P1)=160THEN R1=R2:P1=PC
340   IF R1>RTHEN R2=R1:R1=R1-1:P1=BE+(R1*40)+C1:IF
      PEEK(P1)=160THEN R1=R2:P1=PC
350   POKE PC,VE:VE=PEEK(P1):IF VE=102THEN GOSUB 600:
      GOTO 10
360   POKE P1,86:RETURN
370   IF R=0THEN RETURN
380   T1=PO:R=R-1:PO=BE+(R*40)+C:IF PEEK(PO)=160THEN PO
      =T1:R=R+1:RETURN
390   IF PEEK(PO)=13THEN GOSUB 570
400   IF PEEK(PO)=81THEN S1=S1+1:CN=CN+1
410   POKE T1,32:POKE PO,102:RETURN
420   IF R=16THEN RETURN
430   T1=PO:R=R+1:PO=BE+(R*40)+C:IF PEEK(PO)=160THEN PO
      =T1:R=R-1:RETURN
440   IF PEEK(PO)=81THEN S1=S1+1:CN=CN+1
450   IF PEEK(PO)=86THEN GOSUB 570
460   POKE T1,32:POKE PO,102:RETURN
470   IF C=0THEN RETURN
480   T1=PO:C=C-1:PO=BE+(R*40)+C:IF PEEK(PO)=160THEN C=C
      +1:PO=T1:RETURN
490   IF PEEK(PO)=81THEN CN=CN+1:S1=S1+1
500   IF PEEK(PO)=86THEN GOSUB 570
510   POKE T1,32:POKE PO,102:RETURN
520   IF C=28THEN RETURN
530   T1=PO:C=C+1:PO=BE+(R*40)+C:IF PEEK(PO)=160THEN C=C
      -1:PO=T1:RETURN
540   IF PEEK(PO)=81THEN CN=CN+1:S1=S1+1
550   IF PEEK(PO)=86THEN GOSUB 570
560   POKE T1,32:POKE PO,102:RETURN
```

You Ran Into the Hunter; You Won the Game; Print Instructions

```
570   SCNCLR:PRINT "Y O U ▲ R A N ▲ S T R A I G H T ▲ I N
       T O ▲ T H E ▲ H U N T E R ! ! ! ! "
580   PRINT :PRINT :PRINT TAB(13);"Y O U   ▲ A T E ▲ ";CN
      ;"P O W E R ▲ P I L L S "
590   PRINT :PRINT :GOSUB 680:GOTO 10
600   SCNCLR:PRINT "▲ ▲ ▲ Y O U ▲ W E R E ▲ C A P T U R E
       D ▲ B Y ▲ T H E ▲ H U N T E R ! ! ! ! ! ! ":
      PRINT :PRINT
610   PRINT TAB(10);"Y O U ▲ A T E ▲ ";CN;"▲ P O W E R ▲
      P I L L S ":PRINT :PRINT
620   GOSUB 680
630   RETURN
640   SCNCLR
650   PRINT "◣ ";TAB(13)"C O N G R A T U L A T I O N S "
```

```
660   PRINT :PRINT :PRINT :PRINT TAB(5);"Y O U ▲ H A V E
      ▲ C O M P L E T E D ▲ L E V E L : ";TY
670   PRINT :PRINT :GOSUB 680:RETURN
680   PRINT TAB(8);"P R E S S ▲ A N Y ▲ K E Y ▲ T O ▲ C O
       N T I N U E ";:FOR I=1 TO 20:GETA$:NEXT
690   GETA$:IF A$=""THEN 690
700   RETURN
710   SCNCLR:PRINT TAB(16);"▣ H U N T E R "
720   PRINT :PRINT :PRINT "M O V E ▲ A R U N D ▲ T H E ▲
      S C R E E N ▲ F O R ▲ A S ▲ L O N G ▲ A S ":
      PRINT
730   PRINT "P O S S I B L E ▲ W I T H O U T ▲ B E I N G
      ▲ D E S T R O Y E D ▲ B Y ▲ T H E ":PRINT
740   PRINT "H U N T E R . ▲ Y O U ▲ G E T ▲ P O I N T S
      ▲ F O R ▲ E A T I N G ▲ T H E ":PRINT
750   PRINT "P O W E R ▲ P I L L S . W H E N ▲ A L L ▲ A
      R E ▲ G O N E ▲ Y O U ▲ G E T ":PRINT
760   PRINT "A N O T H E R ▲ G A M E , M O V E ▲ Y O U R
      ▲ M A N ▲ W I T H ▲ T H E S E ":PRINT
770   PRINT "K E Y ▲ C O M B I N A T I O N S - ":PRINT
780   PRINT :PRINT
790   PRINT TAB(15);"I ▲ - ▲ L E F T "
800   PRINT TAB(15);"P ▲ - ▲ R I G H T "
810   PRINT TAB(15);"Q ▲ - ▲ U P "
820   PRINT TAB(15);"Z ▲ - ▲ D O W N ":PRINT :PRINT
830   GOSUB 680:COLOR1,2,7
840   RETURN
850   SCNCLR:PRINT "D I F F I C U L T Y ▲ L E V E L ▲ ( 1
       - 4 ) ";
860   GETA$:IF A$<"1 "THEN 860ORA$>"4 "THEN 860
870   TY=VAL(A$):AW=4-TY:RETURN
880   FOR I=1  TO 255:GETKEYA$:POKE 3072,I:NEXT
```

ChexSum Tables

10	= 0
20	= 1877
30	= 299
40	= 306
50	= 233
60	= 2185
70	= 1988
80	= 656
90	= 1892
100	= 1942
110	= 2799
120	= 3115
130	= 1374
140	= 1664
150	= 2794
160	= 3016
170	= 1266
180	= 682
190	= 1935
200	= 4078
210	= 1779
220	= 980
230	= 986
240	= 978
250	= 302
260	= 1620
270	= 3012
280	= 526
290	= 2023
300	= 401
310	= 6496
320	= 6003
330	= 6080
340	= 6079
350	= 3206
360	= 648
370	= 761
380	= 5535
390	= 1389
400	= 2636
410	= 1283
420	= 818
430	= 5535
440	= 2636
450	= 1392
460	= 1283
470	= 746
480	= 5439
490	= 2556
500	= 1392
510	= 1283
520	= 810
530	= 5439
540	= 2556
550	= 1392
560	= 1283
570	= 3479
580	= 3170
590	= 1301
600	= 4057
610	= 3192
620	= 306
630	= 143
640	= 233
650	= 2157
660	= 3740
670	= 943
680	= 4171
690	= 1213
700	= 143
710	= 1437
720	= 3957
730	= 3862
740	= 3592
750	= 3579
760	= 3604
770	= 1778
780	= 366
790	= 1147
800	= 1250
810	= 1019
820	= 1597
830	= 867
840	= 143
850	= 2250
860	= 2286
870	= 1804
880	= 2167
TOTAL	= 231234

Chess

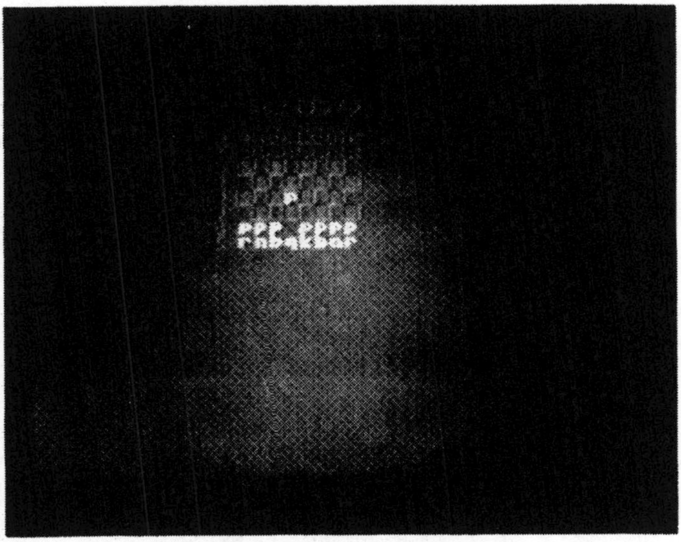

CLASSIFICATION: Logic

This game plays a subset of the standard chess game against you. You move around the screen by entering the starting position and then the destination position in the format (X, Y). The pieces are represented on the screen by the following symbols:

King	K	or	k
Queen	Q	or	q
Rook	R	or	r
Knight	N	or	n
Pawn	P	or	p

You play red from the bottom. When your pawn reaches the top, you must enter the initial of the piece you want to exchange it with, using the same system as above. The computer will tell you when you are in checkmate. If this happens, type 999999 when it is your move. You always go first and the game does not permit castling nor *en passant* moves.

PROGRAMMING SUGGESTIONS

Increase the game's central logic so that it can handle castling and *en passant* moves. Add to the number of pieces that can be fielded by both sides and replace symbols with user-defined characters.

PROGRAM

Variables

B% ( )	Numerical representation of the chess board
D% ( )	Chess board
A$ ( )	Chess in character format
XB, YB	Position of player's next move
X, Y	Position variable
KX, KY	Starting position for Commodore 16
F$	Flag for checkmate

Listing

```
10   REM CHESS
20   COLOR4,10,5:COLOR0,10,5
30   PRINT "♥■ ▲ ▲P L E A S E ▲W A I T "
40   KX=5:KY=8:DIMB%(8,8),D%(6,8,2),P%(6),A$(6):FOR Y=1
      TO 8:FOR X=1 TO 8
```

Read in Data for Pieces Representation on Board

```
50   B%(X,Y)=0:IF  Y=1 THEN  READ B%(X,Y)
60   IF Y=8THEN B%(X,Y)=-B%(X,1)
70   IF Y=2THEN B%(X,Y)=-1
80   IF Y=7THEN B%(X,Y)=1
90   NEXTX,Y
100  DATA-4,-2,-3,-5,-6,-3,-2,-4
110  FOR X=1 TO 6:P%(X)=2:FOR Y=1 TO 8:IF Y<3ORY=8
     THEN D%(X,Y,2)=1
120  IF Y>1ANDY<5THEN D%(X,Y,1)=1
130  IF Y>5THEN D%(X,Y,1)=-1
140  IF Y>3ANDY<7THEN D%(X,Y,2)=-1
150  NEXTY:IF X<>2THEN 190
160  FOR Y=1 TO 4:READD%(X,Y,1),D%(X,Y,2):D%(X,Y+4,1)=
     -D%(X,Y,1):D%(X,Y+4,2)=D%(X,Y,2)
170  NEXT
180  DATA -2,1,-1,2,1,2,2,1
190  IF X=1THEN P%(X)=8
200  IF X>4THEN P%(X)=1
210  NEXT:FOR  X=1 TO 6:READA$(X):NEXT
220  DATAP,N,B,R,Q,K
230  PRINT "♥ ":GOTO 620
```

Clear All the Variables to Zero and Work Out Next Move

```
240  XB=0:YB=XB:DB=XB:CL=1:BP=XB:X=9:AX=KX:AY=KY:F1$="":
     GOSUB 750:F1$=F$
250  FOR Y=1 TO 8:FOR X=1 TO 8:TB=0:C=1:TY=0:TX=0:D=0
260  IF  B%(X,Y)<1 THEN 600
270  P=B%(X,Y):FOR I=1 TO 8:DY=D%(P,I,2):DX=D%(P,I,1):AX
     =KX:AY=KY:C1=1:PO=0
280  IF X+DX<1ORX+DX>8ORY+DY<1ORY+DY>8THEN 530
290  IF P>2ANDP<6THEN 440
300  IF DY>-1ANDP=1THEN 530
310  IF Y>1ORP>1THEN 360
320  FOR I1=5 TO 1 STEP -1
330  IF P%(I1)<2THEN P%(I1)=P%(I1)+1:B%(X,Y)=I1:I1=1
340  NEXTI1
```

```
350  GOTO 530
360  IF DX<>0ANDB%(X+DX,Y+DY)>-1THEN 530
370  IF P=6THEN KX=X:KY=Y:AX=X+DX:AY=Y+DY:GOSUB 740:
     IF F$="1 "THEN 530
380  IF DX=0ANDB%(X,Y+DY)<>0THEN 530
390  PO=8-P-B%(X+DX,Y+DY)*3
400  IF Y<>7ORDX<>0ORB%(X,5)<>0ORP>1THEN 530
410  IF  F1$="1 " THEN  GOSUB  740:IF F$="" THEN  530
420  IF  F1$="1 " OR RND(1)>.3 THEN  C1=2
430  GOTO 530
440  X1=X:Y1=Y
450  IF P=3ANDINT(I/2)*2<ITHEN 530
460  IF P=4ANDINT(I/2)*2=ITHEN 530
470  IF X1+DX<1ORX1+DX>8ORY1+DY<1ORY1+DY>8THEN C1=C1-1:
     GOTO 530
480  IF B%(X1+DX,Y1+DY)>0THEN C1=C1-1:GOTO 530
490  PO=8-P+INT(RND(1)*3)-B%(X1+DX,Y1+DY)*3
500  IF F1$="1 "THEN GOSUB 740:IF F$=""THEN PO=PO+50:
     GOTO 570
510  IF B%(X1+DX,Y1+DY)<>0THEN 530
520  C1=C1+1:X1=X1+DX:Y1=Y1+DY:GOTO 470
530  IF PO=0THEN 570
540  IF F1$="1 "THEN GOSUB 740:IF F$=""THEN PO=PO+50:
     GOTO 570
550  IF F1$=""THEN GOSUB 740:IF F$="1 "THEN PO=0:GOTO 57
     0
560  IF PO=>TBTHEN AX=X+DX*C1:AY=Y+DY*C1:GOSUB 740:IF F$
     ="1 "THEN PO=PO-P*2
570  IF PO>TBTHEN TB=PO:TX=X:TY=Y:D=I:C=C1
580  NEXTI
590  IF TB>BPORTB=BPAND(RND(1)>.9OR(TY<YBANDRND(1)>.5))
     THEN BP=TB:XB=TX:YB=TY:CL=C:DB=D
600  NEXTX,Y:P=B%(XB,YB):X1=XB+D%(P,DB,1)*CL:Y1=YB+D%(P,
     DB,2)*CL:IF P=6THEN KX=X1:KY=Y1
610  AX=KX:AY=KY:B%(X1,Y1)=B%(XB,YB):B%(XB,YB)=0:Q=1:
     GOSUB 750:Q=0
620  GOSUB 840
```

Check If a Checkmate; If Yes Then Finish Game

```
630  IF  F$="1 " THEN  PRINT "▣ C H E C K M A T E ":
     END
640  PRINT "▣ ▣ ▣ Y O U R ▲ M O V E ":INPUT  "▣ F R O M
     ";X,Y:IF  X=999 THEN  END
650  INPUT "▲ ▲ T O ";XB,YB
660  IF B%(XB,YB)>0THEN P%(B%(XB,YB))=P%(B%(XB,YB))-1
670  B%(XB,YB)=B%(X,Y)
680  B%(X,Y)=0
690  IF B%(XB,YB)<-1ORYB<8THEN 720
```

```
700  INPUT "P I E C E S ▲ ";A$:FOR I1=1 TO 5:IF A$(I1)
     =A$ THEN B%(XB,YB)=-I1
710  NEXT
720  GOSUB 840
730  GOTO 240
740  PC=B%(X+DX*C1,Y+DY*C1):B%(X+DX*C1,Y+DY*C1)=B%(X,Y):
     B%(X,Y)=0
750  F$="":FOR P1=1 TO 6:FOR I1=1 TO 8:D1=D%(P1,I1,1):D2
     =D%(P1,I1,2):L=1
760  IF AX+D1*L<1ORAX+D1*L>8ORAY+D2*L<1OR AY+D2*L>8
     THEN 800
770  IF P1=1ANDD2<1ANDQ=0THEN 800
780  IF B%(AX+D1*L,AY+D2*L)=-P1THEN F$="1 ":GOTO 810
790  IF P1>2ANDP1<6ANDB%(AX+D1*L,AY+D2*L)=0THEN L=L+1:
     GOTO 760
800  NEXTI1,P1
810  IF X>8THEN 830
820  B%(X,Y)=B%(X+DX*C1,Y+DY*C1):B%(X+DX*C1,Y+DY*C1)=PC
830  RETURN
```

Print Out Chessboard and the Cartesian Co-ordinates

```
840  PRINT :PRINT :PRINT  :PRINT :PRINT :PRINT :PRINT
850  PRINT "█ █ █ █ ▲ ▲ ▲ ▲ ▲ ▲ ▲ ▲ ▲ ▲ ▲ ▲ ▲ ▲ ▲ ▲ 1 2 3 4 5
     6 7 8 █ ":FOR Y=8 TO 1 STEP -1:PRINT "▲ ▲ ▲ ▲ ▲ ▲ ▲ ▲
     ▲ ▲ ▲ █ █ "Y;
860  FOR X=1 TO 8:IF B%(X,Y)<>0THEN 890
870  IF INT((X+Y)/2)*2=X+YTHENPRINT"█ █ ▲ ■";:GOTO 920
880  PRINT"▲";:GOTO 920
890  IF B%(X,Y)<0THEN PRINT "█ ";:GOTO 910
900  PRINT "█ ";
910  PRINT A$(ABS(B%(X,Y)));
920  NEXT:PRINT :NEXT:RETURN
```

ChexSum Tables

10	=	0
20	=	1172
30	=	1365
40	=	4458
50	=	2049
60	=	1878
70	=	1479
80	=	1305
90	=	361
100	=	1372
110	=	4203
120	=	1954
130	=	1583
140	=	2151
150	=	1294
160	=	6204
170	=	131
180	=	1003
190	=	1172
200	=	1172
210	=	1591
220	=	852
230	=	988
240	=	6086
250	=	3667
260	=	1169
270	=	6096
280	=	3803
290	=	1320
300	=	1581
310	=	1326
320	=	1110
330	=	3514
340	=	257
350	=	532
360	=	2848
370	=	4816
380	=	2257
390	=	2237
400	=	3353
410	=	2092
420	=	1978
430	=	532
440	=	899
450	=	2050
460	=	2046
470	=	5216
480	=	3146
490	=	3458
500	=	3394
510	=	2134
520	=	3092
530	=	877
540	=	3394
550	=	2988
560	=	5816
570	=	3297
580	=	206
590	=	7368
600	=	7424
610	=	4899
620	=	306
630	=	1981
640	=	3043
650	=	882
660	=	3448
670	=	1206
680	=	671
690	=	2079
700	=	4088
710	=	131
720	=	306
730	=	525
740	=	5817
750	=	4715
760	=	5120
770	=	1908
780	=	3753
790	=	4804
800	=	441
810	=	808
820	=	4966
830	=	143
840	=	1449
850	=	3878
860	=	2088
870	=	[illegible]
880	=	[illegible]
890	=	1937
900	=	319
910	=	1117
920	=	746
TOTAL	=	213926

Mind Quiz

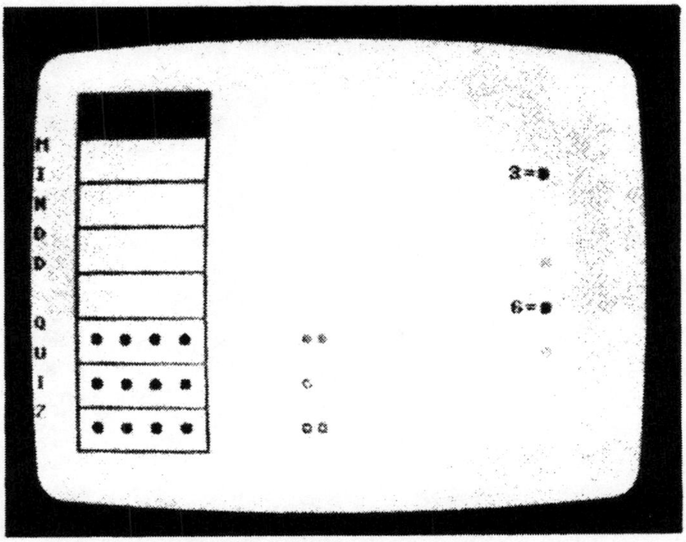

CLASSIFICATION: Logic

The computer or an opponent will generate a sequence of four random numbers in the range of three to eight, represented by the six number keys. You have to guess what the four numbers are by pressing the right sequence of keys. You will get seven chances to guess the numbers. After each guess, the computer will respond by printing a **O** for the right colour in the wrong spot or a ● for the right colour in the right spot.

PROGRAMMING SUGGESTIONS

Add another digit to the number of colours which the player has to guess, giving an extra dimension of complexity.

PROGRAM
Variables

D$	Message 'Instructions Y/N'
A$	Response to input
Y	Flag for end of game and screen position of beads
X	General purpose variable
G$	Response to colour bead input
D%	Array containing random numbers
B%	Array containing input numbers

Listing

```
10    REM MIND QUIZ
20    COLOR4,2,5:COLOR0,2,5:VOL 8:COLOR2,5,6
30    PRINT CHR$(8)CHR$(142):PRINT "▙ "
```

Put Border On Screen; Instructions or Play Computer?

```
40    FOR X=3073 TO 3110:POKE X,64:NEXT
50    FOR X=3112 TO 3992 STEP 40:POKE X,93:NEXT
60    FOR X=3151 TO 4031 STEP 40:POKE X,93:NEXT
70    FOR X=4033 TO 4070:POKE X,64:NEXT
80    POKE 3072,85
90    POKE 3111,73:POKE 4032,74:POKE 4071,75
100   PRINT "▣ ▣ ▣ ▣ ▣ ▲ ▲ ▲ ▲ ▲ ▲ M ▲ ▲ I ▲ ▲ N ▲ ▲ D ▲ ▲
      ▲ ▲ ▲ Q ▲ ▲ U ▲ ▲ I ▲ ▲ Z ▲ ▲ ▲ "
110   DIMA%(4):DIMB%(4):DIMD%(4)
120   D$="▲ ▲ ▲ ▲ ▲ ▲ ▲ ▲ ▲ ▲ ▲ ▲ I N S T R U C T I O N S ▲ Y
       / N ▲ ? ▲ ▲ ▲ ▲ ▲ ▲ ▲ ▲ ▲ "
130   PRINT "▣ ▣ "
140   PRINT "▢ ▣ ▣ ▣ ";D$:FOR X=1 TO 79:NEXT
150   D$=D$+LEFT$(D$,1):D$=MID$(D$,2,36)
160   GETA$:IF A$<>"N "ANDA$<>"Y "THEN 140
170   GOSUB  600
180   PRINT "▣ ▣ "SPC(18)"M ) ▲ P L A Y ▲ M E "CHR$(13)
      SPC(18)"▣ S ) ▲ P L A Y ▲ S O M E O N E ▲ E L S E "
190   GETA$:IF A$<>"M "ANDA$<>"S "THEN 190
200   PRINT "▣ ▣ "SPC(18)"▲ ▲ ▲ ▲ ▲ ▲ ▲ ▲ ▲ ▲ ▲ ▲ "CHR$(13)
      SPC(18)"▣ ▲ ▲ ▲ ▲ ▲ ▲ ▲ ▲ ▲ ▲ ▲ ▲ ▲ ▲ ▲ ▲ ▲ ▲ ▲ ▲ ▲ ▲ ▲ ▲ "
210   IF A$="M "THEN GOSUB 790:GOTO 280
220   R=1
230   FOR X=1 TO 4
240   GETA$:IF A$=CHR$(20)ANDX>1THEN X=X-1:R=R-2:POKE 311
      5+R,160
250   IF VAL(A$)<3ORVAL(A$)>8THEN 240
260   A%(X)=VAL(A$):POKE 3115+R,81
270   R=R+2:NEXT
280   GOSUB 770
290   PRINT "▣ "SPC(32)"▣ ▣ ▣ ▣ ▣ ▣ 3 = ● ▣ ▣ ▣ ▮ ▮ ▮ ◣ 4
       = ● ▣ ▣ ▣ ▮ ▮ ▮ ▣ 5 = ● ▣ ▣ ▣ ▮ ▮ ▮ ▣ 6 = ● ▣ ▣ ▣
      ▮ ▮ ▮ ▣ 7 = ● ▣ ▣ ▣ ▮ ▮ ▮ ▣ 8 = ● ▣ "
300   Y=840:R=1
```

Print Your Guess; Make Sound; Input Player's Colour

```
310   PRINT "▣ "SPC(25)"Y O U R ▲ G U E S S "
320   SOUND 2,19,19
```

```
330   FOR X=1 TO 350:NEXT
340   PRINT "■ "SPC(25)"▲ ▲ ▲ ▲ ▲ ▲ ▲ ▲ ▲ ▲ ▲ ▲ ▲ ▲ ▲ ▲ ▲ "
350   FOR X=1 TO 4:D%(X)=A%(X):NEXT
360   FOR X=1 TO 4
370   GETA$:IF A$=CHR$(20)ANDX>1THEN X=X-1:R=R-2:POKE 311
      5+R+Y,32
380   IF VAL(A$)<3ORVAL(A$)>8THEN 370
390   B%(X)=VAL(A$):POKE 3115+R+Y,81:POKE 2091+R+Y,B%(X)
      -1
400   R=R+2:NEXT
410   FOR X=1 TO 4:IF B%(X)=D%(X)THEN G$=G$+"● ":D%(X)=25
      5:B%(X)=254
420   NEXT
430   IF D%(1)=B%(2)THEN G$=G$+"○ ":D%(1)=255:B%(2)=254
440   IF D%(1)=B%(3)THEN G$=G$+"○ ":D%(1)=255:B%(3)=254
450   IF D%(1)=B%(4)THEN G$=G$+"○ ":D%(1)=255:B%(4)=254
460   IF D%(2)=B%(1)THEN G$=G$+"○ ":D%(2)=255:B%(1)=254
470   IF D%(2)=B%(3)THEN G$=G$+"○ ":D%(2)=255:B%(3)=254
480   IF D%(2)=B%(4)THEN G$=G$+"○ ":D%(2)=255:B%(4)=254
490   IF D%(3)=B%(1)THEN G$=G$+"○ ":D%(3)=255:B%(1)=254
500   IF D%(3)=B%(2)THEN G$=G$+"○ ":D%(3)=255:B%(2)=254
510   IF D%(3)=B%(4)THEN G$=G$+"○ ":D%(3)=255:B%(4)=254
520   IF D%(4)=B%(1)THEN G$=G$+"○ ":D%(4)=255:B%(1)=254
530   IF D%(4)=B%(2)THEN G$=G$+"○ ":D%(4)=255:B%(2)=254
540   IF D%(4)=B%(3)THEN G$=G$+"○ ":D%(4)=255:B%(3)=254
550   PRINT "■ ":FOR X=1 TO ((Y-40)/40):PRINT "■ ";:
      NEXT:PRINT SPC(18)"■ "G$
560   IF G$="● ● ● ● "THEN D$="Y E S ":GOTO 820
570   IF Y=120THEN D$="N O ":GOTO 820
580   Y=Y-120:G$="":R=1
590   GOTO 310
600   IF A$="N "THEN 700
```

Print Instructions; Try Again?

```
610   PRINT "■ ■ ■ ■ ■ ▲ ▲ ▲ ▲ ▲ ▲ ▲ ▲ ▲ ▲ ▲ ▲ ▲ ▲ ▲ ▲ I N S T
      R U C T I O N S ▲ ▲ ▲ ▲ ▲ ▲ ▲ ▲ ▲ ▲ ▲ ▲ ▲ ▲ ▲ ▲ ▲ "
620   PRINT "■ ■ I N ▲ T H I S ▲ G A M E ▲ Y O U ▲ C A N
      ▲ P L A Y ▲ T H E ▲ C O M P U T E R ▲ ▲ ▲ ▲ ▲ ▲ ▲ ▲ ▲
       ▲ O R ▲ A ▲ H U M A N ▲ O P P O N E N T "
630   PRINT "■ ▲ Y O U ▲ H A V E ▲ ■ 7 ■ ▲ C H A N C E S
      ▲ T O ▲ C R A C K ▲ T H E ▲ C O D E "
640   PRINT "■ T O ▲ E N T E R ▲ C O L O U R S ▲ U S E ▲
      K E Y S ▲ ▲ ■ 3 ▲ ■ 4 ▲ ■ 5 ▲ ■ 6 ▲ ■ 7 ▲ ■ 8 ■ "
650   PRINT "■ ▲ ▲ ▲ ▲ P R E S S ▲ D E L ▲ I F ▲ Y O U ▲
      M A K E ▲ A ▲ M I S T A K E "
660   PRINT "▲ ▲ ■ ■ ▲ ● ■ ▲ ▲ M E A N S ▲ R I G H T ▲ C
      O L O U R ▲ R I G H T ▲ S P O T "
```

```
670   PRINT "▲▲ⓊⓇ▲●Ⓒ▲▲MEANS▲RIGHT▲COLOUR▲WRONG▲SPOT"
680   PRINT "ⓈⓊⓊⓊ▲▲▲▲▲▲▲▲▲▲PRESS▲RETURN▲TO▲START▲▲▲▲▲▲▲▲▲▲▲"
690   GETA$:IF A$<>CHR$(13)THEN 690
700   PRINT "Ⓒ ";
710   FOR X=1 TO 8
720   PRINT "Ⓒ▲▲▲┏□□□□□□□┓▲▲▲▲▲▲▲▲▲▲▲▲▲▲▲▲▲▲▲▲▲▲▲▲▲▲▲▲▲▲▲▲▲▲▲▲▲▲□▲▲▲▲▲▲▲▲□"
730   PRINT "▲▲▲□▲▲▲▲▲▲▲▲▲□"
740   NEXT
750   PRINT "▲▲▲□□□□□□□□□□";
760   PRINT "ⓈⓊⓊⓊMⓊⓊ‖IⓊⓊ‖NⓊⓊ‖DⓊⓊ‖▲ⓊⓊ‖QⓊⓊⓊ‖UⓊⓊⓊ‖IⓊⓊ‖Z"
770   FOR X=1 TO 9:FOR Y=0 TO 2:POKE 3074+X+Y*40,160:POKE 2069+X+Y*40,14:NEXTY,X
780   RETURN
790   FOR X=1 TO 4
800   FOR Y=1 TO 3:E=RND(1)*5+3:NEXTY
810   A%(X)=E:NEXT:RETURN
820   FOR X=1 TO 4:POKE 3116+C,81:POKE 2092+C,A%(X):C=C+2:NEXT
830   PRINT "Ⓢ ";:IF D$="NO"THEN PRINT SPC(16)"BAD▲LUCK▲IT▲WAS▲THIS"
840   IF D$="YES"THEN PRINT SPC(16)"GOOD▲ON▲YOU▲YOU▲GOT▲IT"
850   PRINT "ⓈⓊⓊ"SPC(16)"PLAY▲AGAIN▲Y/N▲?"
860   GETA$:IF A$<>"N"ANDA$<>"Y"THEN 860
870   IF A$="N"THEN POKE 0,0:SYS 0
880   RUN
```

ChexSum Tables

10	=	0	310	=	1477	610	=	2938
20	=	1983	320	=	588	620	=	5864
30	=	1439	330	=	979	630	=	3494
40	=	1720	340	=	1398	640	=	3815
50	=	2016	350	=	1762	650	=	3093
60	=	2016	360	=	670	660	=	3447
70	=	1722	370	=	4334	670	=	3458
80	=	533	380	=	1968	680	=	3009
90	=	1750	390	=	3742	690	=	1711
100	=	2294	400	=	770	700	=	435
110	=	1376	410	=	4424	710	=	678
120	=	2568	420	=	131	720	=	4490
130	=	266	430	=	3439	730	=	992
140	=	1693	440	=	3439	740	=	131
150	=	2231	450	=	3441	750	=	2104
160	=	2322	460	=	3439	760	=	2940
170	=	298	470	=	3441	770	=	5071
180	=	4416	480	=	3443	780	=	143
190	=	2322	490	=	3439	790	=	670
200	=	3002	500	=	3441	800	=	2107
210	=	1684	510	=	3443	810	=	935
220	=	312	520	=	3441	820	=	3572
230	=	670	530	=	3443	830	=	3678
240	=	4092	540	=	3443	840	=	3442
250	=	1967	550	=	3301	850	=	1979
260	=	1761	560	=	2862	860	=	2329
270	=	770	570	=	1915	870	=	1366
280	=	303	580	=	1542	880	=	139
290	=	7348	590	=	526	TOTAL	=	198346
300	=	823	600	=	938			

Penetrator

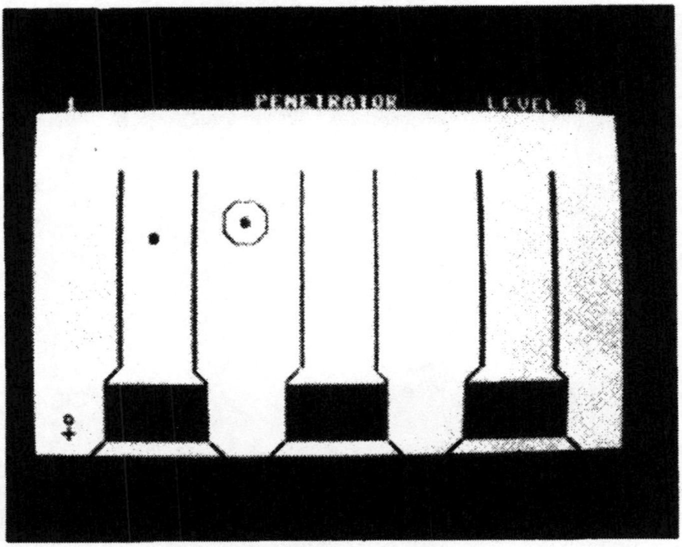

CLASSIFICATION: Shoot Up

You are the pilot of a spaceship which must land and pick up a stranded pilot. In front of your vehicle are three mountains filled with multiplying aliens. You must move your ship up and down with the Q and Z keys to target them, and destroy as many as possible by pressing the SPACE bar.

When the number of aliens gets below five you can land and pick up the pilot — but you must be quick! After picking up the pilot you move onto the next level.

PROGRAMMING SUGGESTIONS

Steadily increase the size of the objects that you must pick up.

Program Variables

S$	Spaceship
T$	Spaceship blanker
D$	Move down a line
B$	Move back a space
BE	Start of screen memory
C	Column position of spaceship
R	Row position of spaceship
PO	Position of multiplying aliens

Listing

```
10    REM PENETRATOR
20    COLOR4,6,3
```

> **Build the Spaceship, Pilot, Backspace Variable, Column Position**

```
30    B$="▌ ":D$="▣ ":S$="/ □ \ "+D$+B$+B$+B$+"▐ ▴ ▐ "+D$
      +B$+B$+B$+"\ □ / "
40    T$="▴ ▴ ▴ ▴ "+D$+B$+B$+B$+B$+"▴ ▴ ▴ ▴ "+D$+B$+B$+B$
      +B$+"▴ ▴ ▴ ▴ " :BE=3072:GOSUB 570
50    GOSUB 450:G$="▣ ▴ ▴ ▀ ":M$="● "+D$+B$+"+ "
60    V$="▴ "+D$+B$+"▴ ":
70    FOR I=1 TO 40:CC$=CC$+"▣ ":NEXT:FOR I=1 TO 25:RR$
      =RR$+"▣ ":NEXT:POKE 208,12:Q=208
80    C(1)=0:C(2)=12:C(3)=24
90    C1(1)=8:C1(2)=20:C1(3)=32
100   C=C(1):R=3:POKE 202,C:POKE 205,R:PRINT "▴ ";S$;:C1
      =C1(1):E=0:LV=LV-.1
110   FOR I=4032 TO 4032+39:POKE I,160:NEXT
120   PRINT "▣ ";LEFT$(CC$,2);LEFT$(RR$,22);M$;
130   FOR I=1 TO 2 STEP 0
140   A=PEEK(Q):IF A=62THEN GOSUB 330
150   IF A=12THEN GOSUB 350:ELSEIF A=60THEN GOSUB 430
160   IF ETHEN GOTO 190
170   GOSUB 380:SOUND 2,4,4
180   Q=198:NEXT
190   C=C(2):C1=C1(2):E=0:CN=0:R=3
200   PRINT "▣ ";LEFT$(CC$,14);LEFT$(RR$,22);M$;:POKE 400
      4,77:Q=208
210   FOR I=1 TO 2 STEP 0:A=PEEK(Q):IF A=62THEN GOSUB 330
220   POKE 4004,77
230   IF A=12THEN GOSUB 350:ELSEIF A=60THEN GOSUB 430
240   Q=198:IF ETHEN 260
250   GOSUB 380:SOUND 2,4,4:NEXT
260   C=C(3):C1=C1(3):E=0:CN=0:R=3:Q=208
270   PRINT "▣ ";LEFT$(CC$,26);LEFT$(RR$,22);M$;
280   FOR I=1 TO 2 STEP 0:A=PEEK(Q):IF A=62THEN GOSUB 330
290   IF A=12THEN GOSUB 350:ELSEIF A=60THEN GOSUB 430
300   IF ETHEN 100
310   Q=198:GOSUB 380:SOUND 2,4,4:NEXT
320   STOP
330   IF R=1THEN RETURN
340   POKE 202,C:POKE 205,R:PRINT T$;:R=R-1:POKE 205,R:
      POKE 202,C:PRINT "▴ "S$;:RETURN
350   IF R=18THEN IF CN<=5THEN GOSUB 610
360   IF R=18THEN RETURN
```

```
370   POKE 202,C:POKE 205,R:PRINT T$;:R=R+1:POKE 205,R:
      POKE 202,C:PRINT "▴ ";S$;:RETURN
380   N=5+INT(RND(1)*LV*10):IF N<5THEN 380
```

Scan the Keyboard; Move Ship Up or Down

```
390   IF N>18THEN RETURN
400   PO=BE+(N*40)+C1:IF PEEK(PO)=32THEN POKE PO,81:CN=CN
      +1:GOSUB 420:SOUND 1,5,5:RETURN
410   RETURN
420   POKE 205,0:POKE 202,0:PRINT "▴ ";:PRINT USING"▣ # #
       ■ ";CN;:RETURN
430   PE=BE+(R*40)+C1:IF PEEK(PE)=81THEN POKE PE,32:CN=CN
      -1:RETURN
440   RETURN
```

Print the Three Mountains; Set the Difficulty Level

```
450   PRINT "◘ ";
460   PRINT "▴ ▴ ▴ ▴ ▴ ▴ ▴ ▴ ▴ ▴ ▴ ▴ ▴ ▴ ▴ ▴ ▴ ▴ ▣ P E N E T R A
      T O R ■ ▴ ▴ ▴ ▣ S C O R E ■ ▴ ▴ ▴ ▴ ▴ ▴ ▴ ▴ "
470   PRINT :PRINT :PRINT
480   PRINT
490   FOR HU=1 TO 13:PRINT "▴ ▴ ▴ ▴ ▴ ▴ ▴ ◻ ▴ ▴ ▴ ▴ ◻ ▴ ▴ ▴
       ▴ ▴ ▴ ◻ ▴ ▴ ▴ ▴ ◻ ▴ ▴ ▴ ▴ ▴ ▴ ▴ ◻ ▴ ▴ ▴ ▴ ◻ ":NEXT
500   PRINT "▴ ▴ ▴ ▴ ▴ / ▴ ▴ ▴ ▴ ▴ \ ▴ ▴ ▴ ▴ ▴ ▴ / ▴ ▴ ▴ ▴
      ▴ \ ▴ ▴ ▴ ▴ ▴ ▴ / ▴ ▴ ▴ ▴ ▴ ▴ \ "
510   PRINT "▴ ▴ ▴ ▴ ▴ ▣ ▴ ▴ ▴ ▴ ▴ ▴ ▴ ▴ ■ ▴ ▴ ▴ ▴ ▴ ▴ ▣ ▴ ▴
      ▴ ▴ ▴ ▴ ▴ ■ ▴ ▴ ▴ ▴ ▴ ▴ ▣ ▴ ▴ ▴ ▴ ▴ ▴ ▴ ▴ ■ "
520   PRINT "▴ ▴ ▴ ▴ ▴ ▣ ▴ ▴ ▴ ▴ ▴ ▴ ▴ ▴ ■ ▴ ▴ ▴ ▴ ▴ ▴ ▣ ▴ ▴
      ▴ ▴ ▴ ▴ ▴ ■ ▴ ▴ ▴ ▴ ▴ ▴ ▣ ▴ ▴ ▴ ▴ ▴ ▴ ▴ ▴ ■ "
530   PRINT "▴ ▴ ▴ ▴ ▴ ▣ ▴ ▴ ▴ ▴ ▴ ▴ ▴ ▴ ■ ▴ ▴ ▴ ▴ ▴ ▴ ▣ ▴ ▴
      ▴ ▴ ▴ ▴ ▴ ■ ▴ ▴ ▴ ▴ ▴ ▴ ▣ ▴ ▴ ▴ ▴ ▴ ▴ ▴ ▴ ■ "
540   PRINT "▴ ▴ ▴ ▴ ▴ ▣ ▴ ▴ ▴ ▴ ▴ ▴ ▴ ▴ ■ ▴ ▴ ▴ ▴ ▴ ▴ ▣ ▴ ▴
      ▴ ▴ ▴ ▴ ▴ ■ ▴ ▴ ▴ ▴ ▴ ▴ ▣ ▴ ▴ ▴ ▴ ▴ ▴ ▴ ▴ ■ "
550   PRINT "▴ ▴ ▴ / ▴ ▴ ▴ ▴ ▴ ▴ ▴ ▴ \ ▴ ▴ ▴ / ▴ ▴ ▴ ▴ ▴
      ▴ ▴ \ ▴ ▴ ▴ / ▴ ▴ ▴ ▴ ▴ ▴ ▴ ▴ \ "
560   RETURN
570   SCNCLR:PRINT "D I F F I C U L T Y ▴ L E V E L ▴ 1 -
       H A R D E S T ▴ 9 - E A S I E S T ";
580   GETWE$:IF WE$=""THEN 580
590   IF WE$<"1 "ORWE$>"9 "THEN 580
600   LV=VAL(WE$):RETURN
610   REM
620   IF C1=8THEN PRINT "▣ ";LEFT$(CC$,2);LEFT$(RR$,22);V
      $;
630   IF C1=20THEN POKE 3966,32:POKE 4006,32
```

```
640   IF C1=32THEN PRINT "▣ ";LEFT$(CC$,26);LEFT$(RR$,22)
      ;V$;
650   PRINT "▣ ";LEFT$(CC$,10);LEFT$(RR$,2);"P I L O T ▲
      R E S C U E D ";
660   FOR HJ=1 TO 999‡NEXT
670   PRINT "▣ ";LEFT$(CC$,10);LEFT$(RR$,2);"▲ ▲ ▲ ▲ ▲ ▲
      ▲ ▲ ▲ ▲ ▲ ▲ ▲ ▲ ";
680   SC=SC+100
690   PRINT "▣ ";LEFT$(CC$,33);LEFT$(RR$,0);"▣ ";‡
      PRINT USING"# # # # ";SC;‡PRINT "■ ";
700   VE=1‡FOR I=1 TO 3
710   PRINT "▣ ";LEFT$(CC$,VE);LEFT$(RR$,R);T$;‡CN=0‡E=1‡
      VE=VE+12
720   NEXT
730   FOR BV=5 TO 18‡DF=BE+(BV*40)+C1‡POKE DF,32‡NEXT
740   RETURN
```

ChexSum Tables

10	= 0	260	= 2889	510	= 2461
20	= 486	270	= 2035	520	= 2461
30	= 6464	280	= 2702	530	= 2461
40	= 6083	290	= 2280	540	= 2461
50	= 2946	300	= 537	550	= 2958
60	= 1379	310	= 1582	560	= 143
70	= 5178	320	= 145	570	= 3635
80	= 1639	330	= 762	580	= 1394
90	= 1819	340	= 4005	590	= 1751
100	= 4726	350	= 1892	600	= 1028
110	= 2053	360	= 824	610	= 0
120	= 1961	370	= 4065	620	= 2706
130	= 886	380	= 2634	630	= 1884
140	= 1681	390	= 820	640	= 2847
150	= 2280	400	= 5336	650	= 3193
160	= 923	410	= 143	660	= 1053
170	= 857	420	= 2771	670	= 2527
180	= 629	430	= 4286	680	= 829
190	= 2382	440	= 143	690	= 3606
200	= 3168	450	= 435	700	= 1143
210	= 2702	460	= 3136	710	= 3944
220	= 525	470	= 585	720	= 131
230	= 2280	480	= 153	730	= 3256
240	= 1070	490	= 3879	740	= 143
250	= 1062	500	= 2961	TOTAL	= 154194

Dragon's Lair

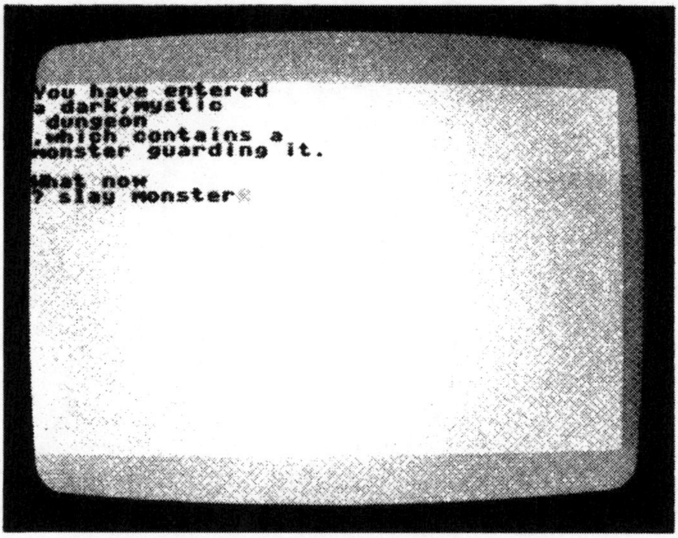

CLASSIFICATION: Adventure

Move through the Dragon's Lair in search of treasure but be careful, a fire breathing nasty is wandering around this place and he isn't too fussy about what or who he eats. You have a number of commands to move to move through this world. They are:

COMMAND	FUNCTION
go left	Move left one location
go right	Move right one location
go forward	Move forward one location
pick-up 'object'	Pick up given object
examine 'object'	Tells you the name of the object
drop 'object'	You guessed it!!
recover treasure	Adds treasure to your hoards
slay monster	Only if you have a weapon
spell monster	Only if you have a magic staff
gaze-into palantir	Reveals important information

PROGRAM
Variables

O%	Number of weapons
O$	Weapons
PO	Strength
TR	Treasure
D	Place
C	Object
N$, V$	Input instructions
P	Flag number of words input

Listing

```
10      COLOR4,8,3: COLOR0,13,3:PRINT CHR$(14)
20      PO=15:DIMO%(3),O$(3):TR=0
```

Read in Objects; Generate a Random Environment

```
30      FOR I=0 TO 3:READO$(I):NEXT
40      DATASWORD,STAFF,PALANTIR,TALISMAN
50      O%(INT(RND(1)*2))=1
60      PRINT "█ █ █O U ▲ H A V E ▲ E N T E R E D ":
        PRINT "A ▲ ";
70      D=INT(RND(1)*4):IF D=0THEN PRINT "█N ▲ E V I L ▲ S
         M E L L I N G "
80      IF D=1THEN PRINT "H O M E L Y "
90      IF D=2THEN PRINT "D A N K ▲ A N D ▲ W E T "
100     IF D=3THEN PRINT "D A R K , M Y S T I C "
110     D=INT(RND(1)*4+1):IF D=1THEN PRINT "▲ B A R N "
120     IF D=2THEN PRINT "▲ D U N G E O N "
130     IF D=3THEN PRINT "▲ C A S T L E "
140     IF D=4THEN PRINT "▲ T O W E R "
150     C=INT(RND(1)*6):PRINT ", W H I C H ▲ C O N T A I N
        S ▲ A ":C1=C
160     IF C=0THEN PRINT "M Y S T E R I O U S ▲ O B J E C T
         . ":O=INT(RND(1)*4)
170     IF C=1THEN PRINT "B O O K ▲ O F ▲ S P E L L S . "
180     IF C=2THEN PRINT "H O R D E ▲ O F ▲ T R E A S U R E
        . "
190     IF C=3THEN PRINT "S M A L L ▲ A N I M A L ▲ R U M A
         G I N G ▲ I N ▲ T H E ▲ C O R N E R . "
200     IF C=4THEN PRINT "M O N S T E R ▲ G U A R D I N G ▲
         I T . "
210     IF C=5THEN PRINT "D R A G O N ▲ B L O C K I N G ▲ Y
         O U R ▲ W A Y . "
220     IF C<3ANDRND(1)>.6THEN PRINT "█ H E R E ▲ I S ▲ A L
         S O ▲ A ▲ ▲ ▲ ▲ ▲ ▲ ▲ ▲ M O N S T E R . ":C1=3
230     IF PO<1THEN PRINT "◣ █ H O U ▲ A R T ▲ S L A I N █
        ":GOTO 1010
240     IF PO<15THEN PO=PO+O%(3)
250     FOR I=0 TO 3:IF RND(1)>.9THEN PO=PO-O%(I)
260     NEXT
```

Input a Response From Player; Check What He Did and Counter

```
270     PRINT :PRINT "● H A T ▲ N O W ":INPUT A$
280     V$="":N$="":P=1:FOR I=1 TO LEN(A$)
```

```
290   IF MID$(A$,I,1)="▲ "THEN P=2:GOTO 320
300   IF P=1THEN V$=V$+MID$(A$,I,1)
310   IF P=2THEN N$=N$+MID$(A$,I,1)
320   NEXTI
330   PRINT "◣ "V$"▲ "N$"■ "
340   IF V$="S L A Y "THEN 560
350   IF V$="G O "THEN 620
360   IF V$="P I C K - U P "THEN 650
370   IF V$="E X A M I N E "THEN 680
380   IF V$="D R O P "THEN 720
390   IF V$="G A Z E - I N T O "THEN 750
400   IF V$="S P E L L "THEN 830
410   IF V$="R E C O V E R "THEN 920
420   IF V$="R E A D "THEN 970
430   IF V$="I N V E N T O R Y "THEN 1010
440   PRINT "◣ █ ▲ D O N ' T ▲ U N D E R S T A N D . ■ ":
      GOTO 230
450   IF C>3ANDRND(1)>.7THEN C1=C1+1
460   FOR I=1 TO 750:NEXT
```

Print the Countering Message From the Computer

```
470   IF C1=1ANDRND(1)>.9THEN PRINT "█ H E ▲ R O O F ▲ F
      A L L S ▲ I N ! ":PO=PO-2:GOTO 230
480   IF C1=2ANDRND(1)>.9THEN PRINT "█ O U ▲ F E L L ▲ D
      O W N ▲ A ▲ P I T ▲ I N ▲ T H E ▲ F L O O R . ":PO
      =PO-3:GOTO 230
490   IF C1=3THEN PRINT "█ H E ▲ A N I M A L ▲ K E E P S
      ▲ I T S ▲ ▲ D I S T A N C E . "
500   IF C1=4ANDRND(1)>.6THEN PRINT "█ H E ▲ M O N S T E
      R ▲ A D V A N C E S . "
510   IF C1>5THEN C1=5
520   IF C1<5ORRND(1)<.7THEN 230
530   IF RND(1)>.7THEN PRINT "█ E ▲ K I L L S ▲ Y O U ! "
      :PO=0:GOTO 1010
540   GOTO 230
550   PRINT "█ H E ▲ M O N S T E R ▲ A T T A C K S ▲ ▲ ▲
      Y O U . ":PO=PO-INT(RND(1)*4)
560   IF C1<3THEN PRINT "█ H E R E ▲ I S ▲ N O ▲ M O N S
      T E R . ":GOTO 450
570   IF O%(0)=0THEN PRINT "■ █ O U ▲ H A V E ▲ N O ▲ W E
       A P O N S ! ■ ":GOTO 450
580   PO=PO-INT(RND(1)*3)
590   IF C=5ANDRND(1)>.6THEN PRINT "█ H E ▲ D R A G O N ▲
       L I V E S . ":GOTO 450
600   PRINT "█ H E ▲ B E A S T ▲ I S ▲ D E A D . ":C1=0
610   GOTO 450
```

```
620  IF C1>2ANDRND(1)<C1/7THEN PRINT "▜ H E ▲ M O N S T
     E R ▲ W O N ' T ▲ L E T ▲ Y O U . "$GOTO 450
630  IF N$<>"L E F T "ANDN$<>"R I G H T "ANDN$<>"F O R W
     A R D S "THEN 390
640  PRINT "▛ K "$GOTO 60
650  IF N$<>O$(O)THEN PRINT "▜ H E R E ▲ I S ▲ N O ▲ "N$
     $GOTO 450
660  O%(O)=O%(O)+1$PRINT "▛ K "
670  GOTO 450
680  IF C1>3THEN PRINT "▜ H I S ▲ A N G E R S ▲ T H E ▲
     B E A S T . "$C1=C1+1$GOTO 460
690  IF C>0THEN PRINT "▜ H E R E ▲ I S ▲ N O T H I N G ▲
     T O ▲ ▲ ▲ E X A M I N E . "$GOTO 450
700  PRINT "▜ H E ▲ O B J E C T ▲ T U R N S ▲ O U T ▲ ▲
     T O ▲ B E ▲ A ▲ "O$(O)". "
710  GOTO 450
720  FOR I=0 TO 3$IF N$=O$(I)ANDO%(I)=0THEN PRINT "▚ O U
     ▲ D O N ' T ▲ H A V E ▲ A ▲ "N$$GOTO 450
730  IF N$=O$(I)THEN O%(I)=O%(I)-1$O=I$PRINT "▛ K "
740  NEXT$GOTO 450
750  IF N$<>"▜ A L A N T I R "THEN PRINT "▚ O U ▲ C A N
     ' T ▲ G A Z E ▲ A T ▲ T H A T . "$GOTO 450


760  IF O%(2)=0THEN PRINT "▚ O U ▲ D O N ' T ▲ H A V E ▲
     A ▲ ▲ ▲ ▲ ▲ ▲ ▲ ▜ A L A N T I R . "$GOTO 450
770  IF RND(1)>.3THEN 810
780  IF RND(1)>.5THEN PRINT "▜ H E ▲ G L O B E ▲ R E M A
     I N S ▲ B L A N K . "$GOTO 450
790  IF RND(1)>.5THEN PRINT  "▚ O U ▲ F I N D ▲ A ▲ M O
     N S T E R ▲ L U R K I N G ▲ I N ▲ T H E ▲ S H A D
     O W S . "$C1=3$GOTO 490
800  PRINT "▚ O U ▲ S E E ▲ A ▲ G
     T R E A S U R E ▲ I N ▲ Y O U R ▲ ▲ ▲ ▲ ▲ ▲ ▚ O U R
     N E Y S . "$GOTO 230
810  PRINT "▚ O U ▲ F E E L ▲ W E A K E R . "
820  PO=PO-1$GOTO 450
830  IF O%(1)=0THEN PRINT "▚ O U ▲ H A V E N ' T ▲ T H E
     ▲ M E A N S ▲ T O ▲ C A S T ▲ S P E L L S . "$
     GOTO 230
840  IF N$<>"M O N S T E R "THEN PRINT "▚ O U ▲ C A N '
     T ▲ S P E L L ▲ T H A T . "$GOTO 450
850  IF C1<3THEN PRINT "▜ H E R E ▲ I S ▲ N O ▲ M O N S
     T E R . "$GOTO 230
860  IF RND(1)<.8THEN 890
870  PRINT "▚ O U R ▲ S P E L L ▲ F A I L E D . "$
     PRINT "▚ T ▲ H A S ▲ A N G E R E D ▲ T H E ▲ ▲ ▲ ▲
     B E A S T . "$$C1=C1+1$GOTO 460
880  GOTO 450
890  PRINT "▜ H E ▲ S P E L L ▲ W O R K E D . "$C1=0
```

```
900   IF RND(1)>.6THEN PRINT "▯U T ▲ Y O U R ▲ S T A F F
       ▲ S N A P P E D ▲ W I T H ▲ T H E ▲ S T R A I N .
      "↕O%(1)=O%(1)-1
910   GOTO 230
920   IF C<>2THEN PRINT "▯H E R E ▲ I S ▲ N O T H I N G
      ▲ T O ▲ ▲ ▲ R E C O V E R . "↕GOTO 450
930   IF N$<>"T R E A S U R E "THEN PRINT "T H A T ▲ C A
      N N O T ▲ B E ▲ ▲ ▲ ▲ ▲ ▲ ▲ ▲ ▲ R E C O V E R E D . "
      ↕GOTO 400
940   IF C1>2ANDRND(1)>.3THEN PRINT "▯H E ▲ M O N S T E
      R ▲ W O N ' T ▲ L E T ▲ Y O U . "↕C1=C1+1↕GOTO 460
950   TR=TR+INT(RND(1)*101)+100
960   PRINT "▯ K "↕↕GOTO 230
970   IF C<>1THEN PRINT "▯H E R E ▲ I S ▲ N O ▲ B O O K
      . "↕GOTO 450
980   IF N$<>"B O O K "THEN 440
990   PRINT "▯O U ▲ F E E L ▲ F A I N T "↕PO=PO-2
1000  GOTO 230
1010  PRINT "▯O U ▲ H A V E "PO"S T R E N G T H "
1020  PRINT "▯O U ▲ H A V E "TR"S I L V E R "↕PRINT "C O
       I N S . "
1030  PRINT "▯O U ▲ H A V E "↕FOR I=0 TO 3↕PRINT O%(I)O$
      (I);
1040  IF O%(I)<>1THEN PRINT "S ";
1050  PRINT ↕NEXT
1060  IF PO>0THEN 450
```

ChexSum Tables

10	= 1780	370	= 1422	730	= 3023
20	= 1716	380	= 1215	740	= 719
30	= 1356	390	= 1557	750	= 4675
40	= 2545	400	= 1296	760	= 4486
50	= 1299	410	= 1447	770	= 1108
60	= 2332	420	= 1195	780	= 3984
70	= 3567	430	= 1688	790	= 6524
80	= 1330	440	= 2648	800	= 5475
90	= 1750	450	= 2117	810	= 1565
100	= 1740	460	= 964	820	= 1352
110	= 2707	470	= 4932	830	= 5169
120	= 1462	480	= 6515	840	= 4313
130	= 1384	490	= 3676	850	= 3286
140	= 1330	500	= 3729	860	= 1105
150	= 3315	510	= 1036	870	= 6537
160	= 3558	520	= 1640	880	= 530
170	= 2000	530	= 3509	890	= 2134
180	= 2266	540	= 528	900	= 6245
190	= 3964	550	= 4076	910	= 528
200	= 2497	560	= 3292	920	= 4353
210	= 2894	570	= 3541	930	= 5121
220	= 4637	580	= 1516	940	= 5629
230	= 3113	590	= 3832	950	= 1994
240	= 1748	600	= 2162	960	= 1190
250	= 2759	610	= 530	970	= 3163
260	= 131	620	= 5091	980	= 1366
270	= 1539	630	= 4264	990	= 2248
280	= 2440	640	= 1074	1000	= 528
290	= 2196	650	= 3212	1010	= 1959
300	= 1943	660	= 1625	1020	= 2671
310	= 1920	670	= 530	1030	= 2742
320	= 206	680	= 4255	1040	= 1430
330	= 867	690	= 4132	1050	= 342
340	= 1216	700	= 3119	1060	= 874
350	= 1033	710	= 530	TOTAL	= 310526
360	= 1421	720	= 5160		

Crash Barrier

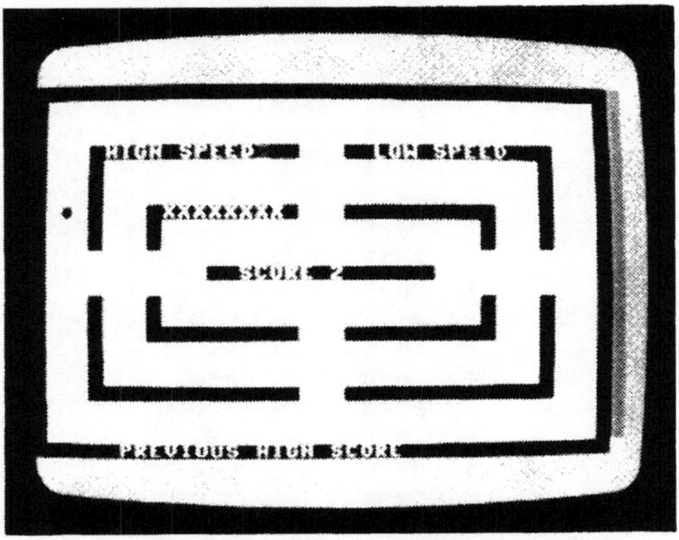

CLASSIFICATION: Evasion COLOUR ILLUSTRATION OBC

Test your skills as a high speed driver. Race around the track swapping lanes whenever you feel like it. Use the I, P, Q and Z keys to move the car around the race track. The longer you can move around the track, the more points you score. Periodically a barrier will appear between the lanes and you will have to swerve to avoid it. The longer you survive, the more frequently crash barriers appear.

PROGRAMMING SUGGESTIONS

Adding a gear stick to the controls of the game would give players more choice of play. Also throw obstacles such as mud slicks into the outer lanes to make the driver's life even more torturous.

PROGRAM
Variables

SC	Start of screen memory
CO	Start of color memory
PO	Car's position on screen
E	Flag to indicate end of game
R	Row position of car
C	Column position of car
QL	Number of barrier to erect (1-17)
R1	Row vector of barrier
C1	Column vector of barrier
PT	Position on screen of barrier
FL	Random flag to place barrier on screen

Listing

Scan Keyboard, Move the Car

```
10     REM CRASH BARRIER
20     DZ$="▣ ":FOR I=1 TO 12:DZ$=DZ$+"▣ ":NEXT
30     FOR I=1 TO 19:DZ$=DZ$+"▮ ":NEXT
40     COLOR4,7,6:COLOR0,2,6:COLOR1,6,2:GOSUB 740:VOL 8
50     DIM C1(25),D1(25),R1(25)
60     FOR I=1 TO 18:READC1(I),R1(I),D1(I):NEXT
70     OA=0:PRINT "▣ ";:GOSUB 430
80     COLOR4,7,5:COLOR0,2,7:COLOR1,6,2:SC=3072:CO=2048:C
       =2:R=2:D=2:E=0:GOSUB 370
90     PRINT "▣ ":POKE PO,81:POKE CC,6
100    A=PEEK(198):IF A=64THEN GOSUB 380
110    IF A=62THEN GOSUB 180:D=1
120    IF A=12THEN GOSUB 200:D=2
130    IF A=33THEN GOSUB 220:D=4
140    IF A=41THEN GOSUB 240:D=8
150    FL=INT(RND(1)*3):IF FL=1THEN GOSUB 260:IF E=1
       THEN GOSUB 350:GOTO 70
160    IF E=1THEN GOSUB 350:GOTO 70
170    SL=SL+.25:PRINT DZ$;"▣ ■ ";INT(SL);"▀ ";:GOTO 100
180    POKE PO,32:POKE CC,2:R=R-1:GOSUB 370:IF PEEK(PO)>
       =128THEN E=1:RETURN
190    POKE CC,6:POKE PO,81:RETURN
200    POKE PO,32:POKE CC,2:R=R+1:GOSUB 370:IF PEEK(PO)>
       =128THEN E=1:RETURN
210    POKE CC,6:POKE PO,81:RETURN
220    POKE PO,32:POKE CC,2:C=C-1:GOSUB 370:IF PEEK(PO)>
       =128THEN E=1:RETURN
230    POKE CC,6:POKE PO,81:RETURN
240    POKE PO,32:POKE CC,2:C=C+1:GOSUB 370:IF PEEK(PO)>
       =128THEN E=1:RETURN
250    POKE CC,6:POKE PO,81:RETURN
```

Erect a Barrier Between Two Walls; Check for Collision

```
260    IF OA=1GOTO 320
270    QL=INT(RND(1)*21)
280    R1=R1(QL):C1=C1(QL):D1=D1(QL)
290    ON D1GOTO 300,310:RETURN
300    R1=R1+1:PT=3072+(R1*40)+C1:FOR J=PT TO PT+80
        STEP 40:POKE J,160:NEXT:OA=1:RETURN
310    C1=C1+1:PT=3072+(R1*40)+C1:FOR J=PT TO PT+2:POKE J,
       160:NEXT:OA=1:RETURN
```

```
320   ON D1GOTO 330,340:RETURN
330   FOR J=PT TO PT+80 STEP 40:POKE J,32:NEXT:OA=0:
      RETURN
340   FOR J=PT TO PT+2:POKE J,32:NEXT:OA=0:RETURN
350   FOR I=1 TO 16:FOR J=1 TO 99:NEXT:COLOR4,I,5:
      SOUND 1,17,8:SOUND 2,8,4:NEXT
360   RETURN
370   PO=3072+(R*40)+C:CC=2048+(R*40)+C:RETURN
380   IF D=1THEN A=62:RETURN
390   IF D=2THEN A=12:RETURN
400   IF D=4THEN A=33:RETURN
410   IF D=8THEN A=41:RETURN
420   RETURN
430   REM
```

Draw the Race Track and Instructions For Game; Data for Barriers

```
440   PRINT "◙ ■ ";
450   PRINT "▣ ▲ ▲ ▲ ▲ ▲ ▲ ▲ ▲ ▲ ▲ ▲ ▲ ▲ ▲ ▲ ▲ ▲ ▲ ▲ ▲ ▲ ▲
      ▲ ▲ ▲ ▲ ▲ ▲ ▲ ▲ ▲ ▲ ▲ ▲ ▲ ▲ ▲ ▲ ▲ ▲ ◘ ▲ ▬ ";
460   PRINT "▣ ■ ▲ ▬ ▲ ▲ ▲ ▲ ▲ ▲ ▲ ▲ ▲ ▲ ▲ ▲ ▲ ▲ ▲ ▲ ▲ ▲ ▲
      ▲ ▲ ▲ ▲ ▲ ▲ ▲ ▲ ▲ ▲ ▲ ▲ ▲ ▲ ▲ ▲ ▲ ▲ ▣ ▲ ◘ ▲ ▬ ";
470   PRINT "▣ ■ ▲ ▬ ▲ ▲ ▲ ▲ ▲ ▲ ▲ ▲ ▲ ▲ ▲ ▲ ▲ ▲ ▲ ▲ ▲ ▲ ▲
      ▲ ▲ ▲ ▲ ▲ ▲ ▲ ▲ ▲ ▲ ▲ ▲ ▲ ▲ ▲ ▲ ▲ ▣ ■ ▲ ◘ ▲ ▬ "
      ;
480   PRINT "▣ ■ ▲ ▬ ▲ ▲ ▲ ▲ ▲ ▲ ▲ ▲ ▲ ▲ ▲ ▲ ▲ ▲ ▲ ▲ ▲ ▲ ▲
      ▲ ▲ ▲ ▲ ▲ ▲ ▲ ▲ ▲ ▲ ▲ ▲ ▲ ▲ ▲ ▲ ▲ ▲ ▣ ▲ ◘ ▲ ▬ ";
490   PRINT "▣ ■ ▲ ▬ ▲ ▲ ▲ ▣ ■ ▲ H I G H ▲ S P E E D ◩ ▲
      ■ ▲ ▲ ▬ ▲ ▲ ▲ ▣ ■ ▲ ▲ L O W ▲ S P E E D ◩ ▲ ■ ▲ ▲ ▬
      ▲ ▲ ▲ ▣ ■ ▲ ◘ ▲ ▬ ";
500   PRINT "▣ ■ ▲ ▬ ▲ ▲ ▲ ▣ ▲ ▬ ▲ ▲ ▲ ▲ ▲ ▲ ▲ ▲ ▲ ▲ ▲ ▲
      ▲ ▲ ▲ ▲ ▲ ▲ ▲ ▲ ▲ ▲ ▲ ▲ ▲ ▲ ▲ ▲ ▣ ▲ ▬ ▲ ▲ ▲ ▣ ▲ ◘
      ▲ ▬ ";
510   PRINT "▣ ■ ▲ ▬ ▲ ▲ ▲ ▣ ■ ▲ ▬ ▲ ▲ ▲ ▲ ▲ ▲ ▲ ▲ ▲ ▲ ▲
      ▲ ▲ ▲ ▲ ▲ ▲ ▲ ▲ ▲ ▲ ▲ ▲ ▲ ▲ ▲ ▲   ▣ ■ ▲ ▬ ▲ ▲ ▲ ▣
      ■ ▲ ◘ ▲ ▬ ";
520   PRINT "▣ ■ ▲ ▬ ▲ ▲ ▲ ▣ ▲ ▬ ▲ ▲ ▲ ▲ ▲ ▲ ▲ ▲ ▲ ▲ ▲ ▲
      ▲ ▲ ▲ ▲ ▲ ▲ ▲ ▲ ▲ ▲ ▲ ▲ ▲ ▲ ▲ ▲ ▣ ▲ ▬ ▲ ▲ ▲ ▣ ▲ ◘
      ▲ ▬ ";
530   PRINT "▣ ■ ▲ ▬ ▲ ◩ ▲ ▲ ▣ ■ ▲ ▬ ▲ ◩ ▲ ▲ ▣ ■ ▲ X X X
      X X X X X ▲ ▬ ▲ ▲ ▲ ▣ ▲ ▲ ▲ ▲ ▲ ▲ ▲ ▲ ▲ ▲ ▲ ▲ ▬ ▲ ◩ ▲ ▲
      ▣ ■ ▲ ▬ ▲ ◩ ▲ ▲ ▣ ■ ▲ ◘ ▲ ▬ ";
540   PRINT "▣ ■ ▲ ▬ ▲ ▲ ▲ ▣ ▲ ▬ ▲ ▲ ▲ ▣ ▲ ▬ ▲ ▲ ▲ ▲ ▲ ▲
      ▲ ▲ ▲ ▲ ▲ ▲ ▲ ▲ ▲ ▲ ▲ ▲ ▲ ▲ ▲ ▣ ▲ ▬ ▲ ▲ ▲ ▣ ▲ ▬ ▲ ▲
      ▲ ▣ ▲ ◘ ▲ ▬ ";
550   PRINT "▣ ■ ▲ ▬ ▲ ◩ ▲ ▲ ▣ ■ ▲ ▬ ▲ ◩ ▲ ▲ ▣ ■ ▲ ▬ ▲ ◩
      ▲ ▲ ▲ ▲ ▲ ▲ ▲ ▲ ▲ ▲ ▲ ▲ ▲ ▲ ▲ ▲ ▲ ▲ ▲ ▲ ▣ ■   ▬ ▲ ◩
      ▲ ▲ ▣ ■ ▲ ▬ ▲ ◩ ▲ ▲ ▣ ■ ▲ ◘ ▲ ▬ ";
```

```
560   PRINT "▣ ■ ▲ ▀ ▲ ▲ ▲ ▲ ▲ ▲ ▲ ▲ ▲ ▲ ▲ ▲ ▲ ▲ ▲ ▲ ▲ ▲ ▲ ▲ ▲ ▲ ▲ ▲
      ▲ ▲ ▲ ▲ ▲ ▲ ▲ ▲ ▲ ▲ ▲ ▲ ▲ ▲ ▲ ▲ ▲ ▲ ▲ ▲ ▲ ▲ ▲ ▲ ▲ ▣ ▲ ⊏ ▲ ▀ ";
570   PRINT "▣ ■ ▲ ▀ ▲ ▛ ▲ ▲ ▲ ▲ ▲ ▲ ▲ ▲ ▲ ▲ ▲ ▲ ▲ ▲ ▣ ■ ▲ ▲ S C
      O R E ▲ ▲ ▲ ▲ ▲ ▲ ▲ ▲ ▲ ▲ ▀ ▲ ▛ ▲ ▲ ▲ ▲ ▲ ▲ ▲ ▲ ▲ ▲ ▲ ▲ ▲ ▲ ▣ ■
       ▲ ⊏ ▲ ▀ ";
580   PRINT "▣ ■ ▲ ▀ ▲ ▲ ▲ ▲ ▲ ▲ ▲ ▲ ▲ ▲ ▲ ▲ ▲ ▲ ▲ ▲ ▲ ▲ ▲ ▲ ▲ ▲ ▲ ▲
      ▲ ▲ ▲ ▲ ▲ ▲ ▲ ▲ ▲ ▲ ▲ ▲ ▲ ▲ ▲ ▲ ▲ ▲ ▲ ▲ ▲ ▲ ▲ ▲ ▲ ▣ ▲ ⊏ ▲ ▀ ";
590   PRINT "▣ ■ ▲ ▀ ▲ ▛ ▲ ▲ ▣ ■ ▲ ▀ ▲ ▛ ▲ ▲ ▣ ■ ▲ ▀ ▲ ▛
      ▲ ▲ ▲ ▲ ▲ ▲ ▲ ▲ ▲ ▲ ▲ ▲ ▲ ▲ ▲ ▲ ▲ ▲ ▲ ▲ ▲ ▲ ▲ ▲ ▲ ▲ ▣ ■   ▀ ▲ ▛
       ▲ ▲ ▣ ■ ▲ ▀ ▲ ▛ ▲ ▲ ▣ ■ ▲ ⊏ ▲ ▀ ";
600   PRINT "▣ ■   ▀ ▲ ▲ ▲ ▣ ▲ ▀ ▲ ▲ ▲ ▣ ▲ ▀ ▲ ▲ ▲ ▲ ▲ ▲ ▲
      ▲ ▲ ▲ ▲ ▲ ▲ ▲ ▲ ▲ ▲ ▲ ▲ ▲ ▲ ▲ ▲ ▲ ▲ ▲ ▲ ▣   ▀ ▲ ▲ ▲ ▣ ▲ ▀ ▲ ▲
       ▲ ▣ ▲ ⊏ ▲ ▀ ";
610   PRINT "▣ ▚ ▲ ▀ ▲ ▛ ▲ ▲ ▣ ■ ▲ ▀ ▲ ▛ ▲ ▲ ▣ ■   ▲ ▲ ▲
      ▲ ▲ ▲ ▲ ▲ ▲ ▲ ▀ ▲ ▲ ▲ ▣ ▲ ▲ ▲ ▲ ▲ ▲ ▲ ▲ ▲ ▲ ▲ ▲ ▲ ▀ ▲ ▛ ▲ ▲
       ▣ ■ ▲ ▀ ▲ ▛ ▲ ▲ ▣ ■ ▲ ⊏ ▲ ▀ ";
620   PRINT "▣ ■ ▲ ▀ ▲ ▲ ▲ ▣ ▲ ▀ ▲ ▲ ▲ ▲ ▲ ▲ ▲ ▲ ▲ ▲ ▲ ▲ ▲ ▲ ▲
      ▲ ▲ ▲ ▲ ▲ ▲ ▲ ▲ ▲ ▲ ▲ ▲ ▲ ▲ ▲ ▲ ▲ ▲ ▲ ▲ ▲ ▲ ▣ ▲ ▀ ▲ ▲ ▲ ▣ ▲ ⊏
       ▲ ▀ ";
630   PRINT "▣ ■ ▲ ▀ ▲ ▛ ▲ ▲ ▣ ■ ▲ ▀ ▲ ▛ ▲ ▲ ▲ ▲ ▲ ▲ ▲ ▲ ▲ ▲ ▲
      ▲ ▲ ▲ ▲ ▲ ▲ ▲ ▲ ▲ ▲ ▲ ▲ ▲ ▲ ▲ ▲ ▲ ▲ ▲ ▲ ▲ ▲ ▲ ▲ ▲ ▲ ▣ ■ ▲ ▀ ▲ ▛
       ▲ ▲ ▣ ■ ▲ ⊏ ▲ ▀ ";
640   PRINT "▣ ■ ▲ ▀ ▲ ▲ ▲ ▣ ▲ ▀ ▲ ▲ ▲ ▲ ▲ ▲ ▲ ▲ ▲ ▲ ▲ ▲ ▲ ▲ ▲
      ▲ ▲ ▲ ▲ ▲ ▲ ▲ ▲ ▲ ▲ ▲ ▲ ▲ ▲ ▲ ▲ ▲ ▲ ▲ ▲ ▲ ▲ ▣ ▲ ▀ ▲ ▲ ▲ ▣ ▲ ⊏
       ▲ ▀ ";
650   PRINT "▣ ■ ▲ ▀ ▲ ▛ ▲ ▲ ▣ ■ ▲ ▲ ▲ ▲ ▲ ▲ ▲ ▲ ▲ ▲ ▲ ▲ ▲ ▲ ▲ ▲
      ▲ ▲ ▀ ▲ ▲ ▲ ▣ ▲ ▲ ▲ ▲ ▲ ▲ ▲ ▲ ▲ ▲ ▲ ▲ ▲ ▲ ▲ ▲ ▲ ▀ ▲ ▛ ▲ ▲
       ▣ ■ ▲ ⊏ ▲ ▀ ";
660   PRINT "▣ ■ ▲ ▀ ▲ ▲ ▲ ▲ ▲ ▲ ▲ ▲ ▲ ▲ ▲ ▲ ▲ ▲ ▲ ▲ ▲ ▲ ▲ ▲ ▲ ▲ ▲ ▲
      ▲ ▲ ▲ ▲ ▲ ▲ ▲ ▲ ▲ ▲ ▲ ▲ ▲ ▲ ▲ ▲ ▲ ▲ ▲ ▲ ▲ ▲ ▲ ▲ ▲ ▣ ▲ ⊏ ▲ ▀ ";
670   PRINT "▣ ■ ▲ ▀ ▲ ▛ ▲ ▲ ▲ ▲ ▲ ▲ ▲ ▲ ▲ ▲ ▲ ▲ ▲ ▲ ▲ ▲ ▲ ▲ ▲ ▲ ▲
      ▲ ▲ ▲ ▲ ▲ ▲ ▲ ▲ ▲ ▲ ▲ ▲ ▲ ▲ ▲ ▲ ▲ ▲ ▲ ▲ ▲ ▲ ▲ ▲ ▲ ▲ ▣ ■ ▲ ⊏ ▲ ▀
       ";
680   PRINT "▣ ■ ▲ ▀ ▲ ▲ ▲ ▲ ▲ ▲ ▲ ▲ ▲ ▲ ▲ ▲ ▲ ▲ ▲ ▲ ▲ ▲ ▲ ▲ ▲ ▲ ▲ ▲
      ▲ ▲ ▲ ▲ ▲ ▲ ▲ ▲ ▲ ▲ ▲ ▲ ▲ ▲ ▲ ▲ ▲ ▲ ▲ ▲ ▲ ▲ ▲ ▲ ▲ ▣ ▲ ⊏ ▲ ▀ ";
690   PRINT "▣ ■ ▲ ▲ ▲ ▲ ▲ ▲ ▲ P R E V I O U S ▲ H I G H ▲
      S C O R E ▲ ▲ ▲ ▲ ▲ ▲ ▲ ▲ ▲ ▲ ▲ ▲ ▲ ▲ ▲ ▲ ▲ ⊏ ▙ ";
700   PRINT  "▙ "
710   C=0:R=0
720   GETA$:IF A$=""THEN 720
730   RETURN
740   PRINT "▚ ▤ ▤ ▤ ▤ ▤ ▤ ▤ ▤ ▤ ▤ ▤ ▤ ";
750   PRINT "D O ▲ Y O U ▲ W A N T ▲ I N S T R U C T I O
      N S ▲ ( Y / N ) ▲ : ▲ ";
760   GETA$:IF A$=""THEN 760
770   IF A$="N "THEN RETURN
780   IF A$<>"Y "THEN GOTO 760
790   PRINT "▚ ":PRINT "▲ ▲ ▲ ▲ ▲ ▲ ▲ ▲ ▲ ▲ ▲ ▲ ▲ ▣ C R A S
       H ▲ B A R R I E R ▀ "
800   PRINT :PRINT :PRINT
```

```
810   PRINT "▲▲▲▲▲▲▲▲▲STEER▲THE▲CAR▲
      ROUND▲THE▲MAZE"
820   PRINT "▲▲▲▲▲▲▲▲▲FOR▲AS▲LONG▲AS
      ▲POSSIBLE▲USING"
830   PRINT "▲▲▲▲▲▲▲▲▲THE▲-"
840   PRINT :PRINT "▲▲▲▲▲▲▲▲▲▲▲▲▲▲▲▲▲▲▲▲▲▲I
      ▲-▲LEFT▲"
850   PRINT "▲▲▲▲▲▲▲▲▲▲▲▲▲▲▲▲▲▲▲P▲-▲
      RIGHT"
860   PRINT "▲▲▲▲▲▲▲▲▲▲▲▲▲▲▲▲▲▲▲Q▲-▲
      UP"
870   PRINT "▲▲▲▲▲▲▲▲▲▲▲▲▲▲▲▲▲▲▲Z▲-▲
      DOWN"
880   PRINT :PRINT :PRINT "▲▲▲▲▲▲▲▲▲PRESS▲A
      NY▲KEY▲TO▲START";
890   GETA$:IF A$=""THEN 890
900   RETURN
910   DATA16,0,1,21,0,1,0,10,2,0,14,2,34,14,2,34,10,2,17,
      20,1,21,20,1
920   DATA4,10,2,4,14,2,17,16,1,21,16,1,30,14,2,30,10,2,1
      7,4,1,21,4,1,17,8,1
930   DATA21,8,1,17,13,1,21,13,1
```

ChexSum Tables

10	= 0	320	= 1236	630	= 4269
20	= 2554	330	= 2878	640	= 3221
30	= 1931	340	= 2479	650	= 3855
40	= 2370	350	= 3803	660	= 2771
50	= 1248	360	= 143	670	= 3131
60	= 2233	370	= 3298	680	= 2771
70	= 1282	380	= 1184	690	= 3037
80	= 5041	390	= 1180	700	= 244
90	= 1280	400	= 1180	710	= 682
100	= 1782	410	= 1187	720	= 1216
110	= 1365	420	= 143	730	= 143
120	= 1364	430	= 0	740	= 755
130	= 1368	440	= 584	750	= 2766
140	= 1365	450	= 2406	760	= 1216
150	= 3916	460	= 2771	770	= 901
160	= 1483	470	= 2962	780	= 1525
170	= 3164	480	= 2771	790	= 2596
180	= 4000	490	= 5083	800	= 585
190	= 1135	500	= 3221	810	= 2953
200	= 4000	510	= 3885	820	= 3074
210	= 1135	520	= 3221	830	= 836
220	= 3986	530	= 5437	840	= 1967
230	= 1135	540	= 3647	850	= 1752
240	= 3986	550	= 5727	860	= 1470
250	= 1135	560	= 2771	870	= 1678
260	= 1070	570	= 3833	880	= 3025
270	= 1239	580	= 2771	890	= 1211
280	= 2355	590	= 5727	900	= 143
290	= 1232	600	= 3903	910	= 3383
300	= 5724	610	= 5293	920	= 4024
310	= 5337	620	= 3221	930	= 1332
				TOTAL	= 221692

Hangman

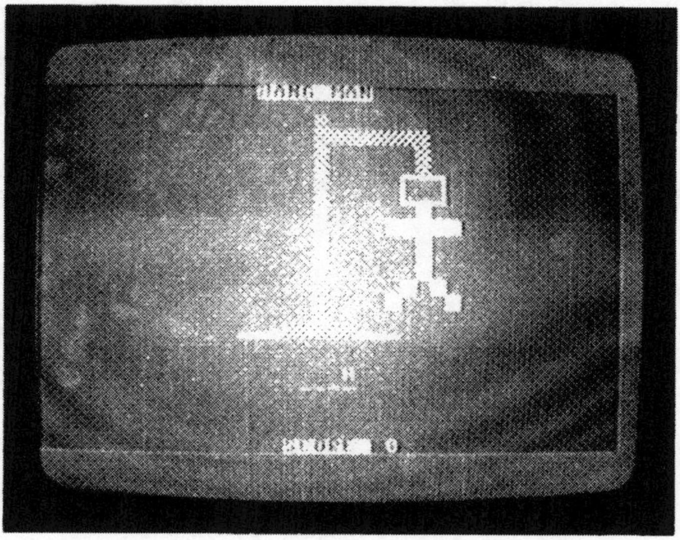

CLASSIFICATION: Educational

The classic word-guessing game in brilliant colour. Guess the word before the computer hangs you.

The computer will print out a line of dashes, each dash representing a letter of the unknown word. Guess a letter by pressing a key. If you guessed correctly, the computer will replace a dash or dashes with the letter. If you were wrong, the computer will begin to build the scaffold and start the execution. Hint: the most common letters in English are E and T.

PROGRAMMING SUGGESTIONS

Add more words to the word bank. Design an edit mode which allows you to change, add or delete words quickly without writing DATA statements. Kids can use this editor to test their parents on their most commonly misspelt words.

Program Variables

W	Pointer to random word
RR$	Move cursor down rows
LE	Length of word
LC	Letter count
CC$	Move cursor across columns
N	Number of words in word bank
W$ ( )	Array for word bank
W$	Word

Listing

```
10    COLOR0,3,3:COLOR4,7,4 :VOL 8:PRINT "■ ";
20    FOR I=1 TO 40:CC$=CC$+"■ ":NEXT:FOR I=1 TO 25:RR$
      =RR$+"■ ":NEXT:N=73:GOSUB 340
30    DIMW$(N):FOR I=0 TO N:READW$(I):NEXT
40    SCNCLR:M$="■ H A N G ▲ M A N ■ ":PRINT TAB((40-
      LEN(M$))/2);M$:LC=0
50    PRINT LEFT$(RR$,23);SPC(17);"■ S C O R E ▲ ■ ";SC;
60    W=INT(RND(1)*N):W$=W$(W):LE=LEN(W$):PE=(40-LE)/2:LV
      =10
70    PRINT "■ ";LEFT$(RR$,20);
80    PRINT SPC(PE);:FOR I=1 TO LE:PRINT "- ";:NEXT:CN=0:
      PT$="0 0 0 0 0 0 0 0 0 0 0 0 0 0 0 0 0 0 0 0 0 0 0 0
      "
```

Enter the Letters of the Word One by One

```
90    F=0:GETKEYA$
100   IF A$<"A "ORA$>"Z "THEN GOTO 90
110   PRINT "■ ";LEFT$(RR$,19);:F=0
120   FOR I=1 TO LE:L$=MID$(W$,I,1):IF L$=A$THEN IF
      MID$(PT$,I,1)<>"1 "THEN GOSUB 300
130   NEXT
140   IF CN=LE THEN GOSUB 290:GOTO 40
150   IF F=0THEN GOSUB 170
160   GOTO 90
170   IF LC=10THEN GOSUB 310:GOTO 40
180   LC=LC+1:LV=LV-1
```

Print One More Section of the Hangman; Decrement Score

```
190   IF LC=1THEN PRINT "■ ";LEFT$(RR$,16);SPC(14);Y$(1);
      :SOUND 2,7,7:RETURN
200   IF LC=2THEN PRINT "■ ";LEFT$(RR$,15);SPC(19);Y$(2);
      :SOUND 2,9,8:RETURN
210   IF LC=3THEN PRINT "■ ";LEFT$(RR$,3);SPC(19);Y$(3);:
      SOUND 1,5,5:RETURN
220   IF LC=4THEN PRINT "■ ";LEFT$(RR$,3);SPC(26);Y$(4);:
      SOUND 2,6,5:RETURN
230   IF LC=5THEN PRINT "■ ";LEFT$(RR$,6);SPC(25);Y$(5);:
      SOUND 2,5,6:RETURN
240   IF LC=6THEN PRINT "■ ";LEFT$(RR$,8);SPC(26);Y$(6);:
      SOUND 1,8,8:RETURN
250   IF LC=7THEN PRINT "■ ";LEFT$(RR$,9);SPC(24);Y$(7);:
      SOUND 1,6,9:RETURN
```

```
260   IF LC=8THEN PRINT "▣ ";LEFT$(RR$,9);SPC(27);Y$(8);:
      SOUND 1,6,6:RETURN
270   IF LC=9THEN PRINT "▣ ";LEFT$(RR$,12);SPC(26);Y$(9);
      :SOUND 1,6,6:RETURN
280   IF LC=10THEN PRINT "▣ ";LEFT$(RR$,12);SPC(26);Y$(10
      );:SOUND 2,7,6:RETURN
290   PRINT "▣ ";"▮ G O O D ▴ G U E S S ▬ ";:FOR I=1
       TO 100:GETA$:NEXT:SC=SC+LV:RETURN
300   POKE 202,0:PRINT SPC(PE+I-1);L$;:F=1:CN=CN+1:MID$(P
      T$,I,1)="1 ":RETURN
310   PRINT "▣ ";LEFT$(RR$,18);
320   K$="▮ ▣ T H E ▴ W O R D ▴ W A S ▴ "+W$+"▬ ▬ ":KE=
      LEN(K$):TA=(40-KE)/2:PRINT SPC(TA);K$;
330   FOR I=1 TO 50:GETA$:SOUND 1,5,6:SOUND 2,9,2:NEXT:
      RETURN
```

Build the Scaffolding, the Noose and the Hangman

```
340   Y$(1)="□ □ □ ※ ※ ※ ※ ※ □ □ □ "
350   Y$(2)="※ □ ▮ ※ □ ▮ ※ □ ▮ ※ □ ▮ ※ □ ▮ ※ □ ▮ ※ □ ▮ ※
      □ ▮ ※ □ ▮ ※ □ ▮ ※ □ ▮ ※ ▮ □ ※ ▮ □ ※ "
360   Y$(3)="※ ※ ※ ※ ※ ※ ※ ※ "
370   Y$(4)="※ ▣ ▮ ※ ▣ ▮ ※ "
380   Y$(5)="┌ □ ┐ ▣ ▮ ▮ ▮ └ □ ┘ "
390   Y$(6)="▣ ▴ ▣ ▮ ▴ ▣ ▮ ▴ ▣ ▮ ▴ ▬ "
400   Y$(7)="▣ ▴ ▴ ▬ "
410   Y$(8)="▣ ▴ ▴ ▬ "
420   Y$(9)="▣ ▴ ▮ ▮ ▣ ▴ ▮ ▮ ▣ ▴ ▮ ▮ ▣ ▬ "
430   Y$(10)="▣ ▴ ▣ ▴ ▣ ▴ ▬ "
440   RETURN
450   DATA DOOR,HOUSE,WALL,BRICK,RETURN,COMPUTER
460   DATA TABLE,KEY,CHAIR,POWER,CURTAIN,CASSETTE,TAPE,CO
      LOR,DATA,STABLE,RUN
470   DATA RECORD,SUPPLY,DEMAND,TREASURE,TITANIC,MELBOURN
      E,PERTH,ECONOMIC
480   DATA CALCULATOR,HELP,HEAD,HIGH,BATTLE,BEEF,BECAUSE,
      EAT,EEL,ETCH,GOLD
490   DATA GATE,GET,JUMP,JUSTICE,JAIL,KILL,KEEPER,LOOK,LE
      ACH,KENNEDY,MORRISON
500   DATA ZEBRA,TEETH,UNIVERSITY,ZOO,CUPBOARD,PERCEPTION
      ,CLARITY,FENCE,VENTILATOR
510   DATA SWITCH,LIGHT,PAPER,PLATE,BRACKET,BUTTON,MACHIN
      E,CURSOR,PLUG
520   DATA CARPET,BAG,RING,LORD,STAR,STATISTICS,CHIP,INTE
      RGRATE,BOTTLE
```

ChexSum Tables

10	=	1942	180	=	1524	350	=	7379
20	=	4935	190	=	3399	360	=	1937
30	=	1968	200	=	3411	370	=	1428
40	=	3744	210	=	3358	380	=	2240
50	=	2367	220	=	3345	390	=	1447
60	=	4623	230	=	3346	400	=	801
70	=	1067	240	=	3370	410	=	806
80	=	4419	250	=	3366	420	=	1884
90	=	897	260	=	3361	430	=	972
100	=	1939	270	=	3405	440	=	143
110	=	1440	280	=	3499	450	=	3372
120	=	4786	290	=	4394	460	=	6162
130	=	131	300	=	4537	470	=	6167
140	=	1654	310	=	1066	480	=	5934
150	=	925	320	=	5720	490	=	6246
160	=	480	330	=	2637	500	=	6800
170	=	1612	340	=	2497	510	=	5668
						520	=	5690
						TOTAL	=	160240

Looney Landa

CLASSIFICATION: Simulation

You have a high-technology exploratory spacecraft at your disposal. Your mission is to land the craft softly on the blue landing pads on the moon. Thrust can be varied up to five without exceeding the safety limits and, in emergencies, you can retro up to nine, risking engine burn-out. Lateral control is achieved by rolling the craft either left or right and thrusting. If you succeed in your mission, you will be given a more difficult task.

The controls are: increase thrust with Z, reduce it with Q, roll left or right with I or P.

PROGRAMMING SUGGESTIONS

Design new environments: create orbiting junk to avoid, different planets with higher gravity and different planetary surfaces. Increase fuel and mass of craft to make manoeuvres more difficult. Invent a new mission — take-off and dock with the mother ship, or land on an asteroid.

PROGRAM
Variables

TL	Toll value
TH	Thrust
FU	Fuel level
M	Mass value
LV	Level
G	Gravity
TM	Timer interval

Listing

Select Graphics Mode and Initialise Game

```
10    COLOR0,1:COLOR4,1:COLOR2,7:COLOR3,10,2:COLOR1,6,5:
      GRAPHIC3,1:VOL 8
20    GOSUB 320:B=1:TL=16:GOSUB 410
30    TH=0:FU%=1000:M=1000:VX=0:VY=0:SX=9600:SY=1080:G=10
      :TM=.1:BO=0
40    CHAR1,34,0,"R O L L ":CHAR1,34,6,"F U E L ":CHAR1,3
      4,10,"V E R T ":CHAR1,34,15,"H O R Z ":COLOR1,4,5
```

Get Player's Input, Update Screen

```
50    GETA$:CHAR1,34,8,STR$(FU%)+"▲ "
60    CHAR1,34,13,STR$(INT(VY))+"▲ "
70    CHAR1,34,19,STR$(INT(VX))+"▲ "
80    IF SX>9120ANDSX<10560ANDSY>16200THEN 450
90    BOX0,INT(SX/120),INT(SY/120)-5,INT(SX/120)+4,INT(SY
      /120),INT(TL*360/32)
100   IF A$<>"P "THEN 130
110   GOSUB 400:TL=TL+1:IF TL>31THEN TL=0
120   B=1:GOSUB 410
130   IF A$<>"I "THEN 160
140   GOSUB 400:TL=TL-1:IF TL<0THEN TL=31
150   B=1:GOSUB 410
160   IF FU%=0THEN GOSUB 200:GOTO 50
170   IF A$="Q "THEN TH=TH-1:IF TH<0THEN TH=0
180   IF A$="Z "THEN TH=TH+1:IF TH>9-BOTHEN TH=9-BO
190   IF TH>FU%THEN TH=FU%
```

Calculate New Position and Velocities
Did Space Craft Crash?

```
200   QY=((TH*9000)/(M+FU%))*COS(((TL-16)*π)/32)
210   QX=((TH*9000)/(M+FU%))*SIN(((TL-16)*π)/32)
220   SX=SX+VX+.005*QX:SY=SY+VY+.005*QY:VY=VY+G-QY:VX=VX
      +QX:FU%=FU%-TH
230   IF (PEEK(8192+INT(SY/960)*320+INT(SX/960)*16+((
      INT(SY/120))AND7))AND30)>0THEN 460
240   IF (PEEK(8196+INT(SY/960)*320+INT(SX/960)*16+((
      INT(SY/120))AND7))AND30)>0THEN 460
250   BOX1,INT(SX/120),INT(SY/120)-5,INT(SX/120)+4,INT(SY
      /120),INT(TL*360/32)
260   IF TH=0THEN 50
```

```
270   SOUND 3,500+30*TH,80:IF TH>5-BOTHEN SOUND 1,990,10
280   IF TH+BO-5<=0ORRND(0)>(TH+BO-5)/30THEN 50
290   BO=BO+1:SOUND 3,1020,20:IF TH>9-BOTHEN TH=TH-1
300   IF BO=9THEN CHAR1,0,22,"R E T R O ▲ F A I L U R E ! !"
310   GOTO 50
```

Scenery Information

```
320   DRAW3,0,0 TO 0,159 TO 131,159 TO 131,0
330   DRAW3,0,0 TO 4,8 TO 6,16 TO 7,24 TO 8,32 TO 9,40 TO 10,48 TO 12,56 TO 7,64 TO 13,72 TO 14,80
340   DRAW3 TO 16,88 TO 14,96 TO 10,104 TO 6,112 TO 8,120 TO 8,128 TO 10,136 TO 12,144 TO 14,152 TO 18,157
350   DRAW3,37,157 TO 47,152 TO 50,144 TO 52,136 TO 56,128 TO 64,120 TO 72,128 TO 76,136 TO 80,136
360   DRAW3 TO 78,136 TO 90,136 TO 94,130 TO 94,126 TO 90,120 TO 86,115 TO 85,108 TO 90,104 TO 96,95
370   DRAW3 TO 105,90 TO 112,95 TO 116,88 TO 124,80 TO 125,66 TO 118,60 TO 115,48 TO 126,22 TO 128,7 TO 131,0
380   DRAW3,18,157 TO 27,130 TO 37,157:DRAW2,78,135 TO 90,135:PAINT3,1,9
390   RETURN
400   B=0
410   DRAWB,147+9*COS(((TL-16)*π)/16),26+18*SIN(((TL-16)*π)/16)
420   DRAWB TO 147-9*COS(((TL-16)*π)/16),26-18*SIN(((TL-16)*π)/16)
430   DRAWB,147,26 TO 147+9*SIN(((TL-16)*π)/16),26-18*COS(((TL-16)*π)/16)
440   RETURN
450   IF TL=16ANDABS(VX)<=10ANDVY<=10THEN END
460   SOUND 3,900,300:FOR I=1 TO 16:COLOR3,I,4:FOR J=1 TO 200:NEXTJ,I
```

ChexSum Tables

10	=	3367	170	=	2757	330	=	4700
20	=	1588	180	=	3563	340	=	5386
30	=	5652	190	=	1425	350	=	4981
40	=	5720	200	=	3795	360	=	5001
50	=	1804	210	=	3795	370	=	5773
60	=	1766	220	=	7314	380	=	3556
70	=	1764	230	=	5861	390	=	143
80	=	2763	240	=	5865	400	=	296
90	=	5529	250	=	5530	410	=	4995
100	=	1129	260	=	813	420	=	5116
110	=	2388	270	=	3138	430	=	5606
120	=	664	280	=	3547	440	=	143
130	=	1125	290	=	3515	450	=	2909
140	=	2391	300	=	2655	460	=	3552
150	=	664	310	=	476	TOTAL	=	148100
160	=	1608	320	=	1972			

2D Maze

CLASSIFICATION: Evasion

You are placed randomly within a maze and must work your way through to the end.

You can turn left or right with the I and P keys, or move forward to the next junction by hitting the SPACE bar. The end of the maze is a flashing wall of colour.

PROGRAMMING SUGGESTIONS

Put a time limit on solving the maze. Introduce random teleporters which change your position and orientation; once triggered, they disappear. Increase the size of the maze. Have nasty things chase you! Add secret, invisible passageways that change your position but can only be found accidentally.

PROGRAM
Variables

MZ	Maze array
J%	Current junction
D%	Actual orientation
N%	Next junction
M	Number of moves

Listing

Initialise Game and Define Maze

```
10    PRINT "♥ W A I T ":COLOR1,1:DX=9:DY=9:XF=5:YF=9
20    DIMMZ%(DX,DY)
30    RESTORE
40    FOR I=0 TO DY:FOR J=0 TO DX:READMZ%(J,I):NEXTJ,I
50    DATA15,3,4,7,5,7,5,5,15,5,11,14,5,13,5,13,5,3,10,6,
      14,11,6,5,5,5,7,11,8,10
60    DATA10,8,10,6,3,6,11,12,7,9,12,5,9,8,6,12,15,5,13,3
      ,5,5,3,6,15,3,10,2,6,13
70    DATA7,5,9,10,10,12,9,10,12,5,14,7,5,9,12,5,5,15,5,1
      ,11,14,5,7,7,5,3,10,4,5
80    DATA11,8,4,9,8,4,9,12,7,5
90    DEFFNL(X)=((X*2)AND15)+INT((XAND8)/8)
100   DEFFNR(X)=INT(X/2)+(XAND1)*8
110   X=INT(RND(0)*6+2):Y=INT(RND(0)*5):D%=2↑INT(RND(0)
      *4):GRAPHIC2,0:GOSUB 210
```

Get Player's Input; Move Player, Rotate Left or Rotate Right

```
120   GETA$:IF A$<>"I "ANDA$<>"P "ANDA$<>"▲ "THEN 120
130   IF A$="I "THEN D%=FNR(D%):GOSUB 210:GOTO 120
140   IF A$="P "THEN D%=FNL(D%):GOSUB 210:GOTO 120
150   IF (D%ANDMZ%(X,Y))=1THEN X=X-1:IF X<0THEN X=DX
160   IF (D%ANDMZ%(X,Y))=2THEN Y=Y+1:IF Y>DYTHEN Y=0
170   IF (D%ANDMZ%(X,Y))=4THEN X=X+1:IF X>DXTHEN X=0
180   IF (D%ANDMZ%(X,Y))=8THEN Y=Y-1:IF Y<0THEN Y=DY
190   GOSUB 210:IF X=XFANDY=YFTHEN GRAPHIC0:END
200   GOTO 120
```

Draw Player's View; End Game

```
210   SCNCLR:XN=X:YN=Y:IF (D%ANDMZ%(X,Y))=0THEN RETURN
220   IF (D%ANDMZ%(X,Y))=1THEN XN=X-1:IF XN<0THEN XN=DX
230   IF (D%ANDMZ%(X,Y))=2THEN YN=Y+1:IF YN>DYTHEN YN=0
240   IF (D%ANDMZ%(X,Y))=4THEN XN=X+1:IF XN>DXTHEN XN=0
250   IF (D%ANDMZ%(X,Y))=8THEN YN=Y-1:IF YN<0THEN YN=DY
260   DRAW1,0,0 TO 87,57:DRAW1,0,159 TO 87,130:DRAW1,319,
      0 TO 232,57:DRAW1,319,159 TO 232,130
270   IF (MZ%(XN,YN)ANDD%)=0THEN 300
280   BOX1,157,103,162,107:DRAW1,157,103 TO 130,85:DRAW1,
      162,103 TO 189,85
```

```
290   DRAW1,157,107 TO 130,116:DRAW1,162,107 TO 189,116:
      GOTO 310
300   DRAW1,130,85 TO 189,85:DRAW1,130,116 TO 189,116
310   IF (MZ%(XN,YN)ANDFNR(D%))=0THEN 340
320   DRAW1,87,57 TO 87,130:DRAW1,130,85 TO 87,85:DRAW1,1
      30,116 TO 87,116
330   IF (MZ%(XN,YN)ANDD%)>0THEN DRAW1,130,85 TO 130,116
340   IF (MZ%(XN,YN)ANDFNL(D%))=0THEN 370
350   DRAW1,232,57 TO 232,130:DRAW1,189,85 TO 232,85:
      DRAW1,189,116 TO 232,116
360   IF (MZ%(XN,YN)ANDD%)>0THEN DRAW1,189,85 TO 189,116
370   IF (MZ%(XN,YN)ANDFNL(D%))>0THEN 400
380   DRAW1,232,57 TO 189,85:DRAW1,232,130 TO 189,116
390   IF (MZ%(XN,YN)ANDD%)=0THEN DRAW1,189,85 TO 189,116
400   IF (MZ%(XN,YN)ANDFNR(D%))>0THEN 430
410   DRAW1,87,57 TO 130,85:DRAW1,87,130 TO 130,116
420   IF (MZ%(XN,YN)ANDD%)=0THEN DRAW1,130,85 TO 130,116
430   IF XN=XFANDYN=YFTHEN CHAR1,18,11,"H O M E "
440   RETURN
```

ChexSum Tables

10	=	3085	160	=	3286	310	=	2229
20	=	807	170	=	3284	320	=	3669
30	=	141	180	=	3328	330	=	2914
40	=	2902	190	=	2244	340	=	2215
50	=	4511	200	=	527	350	=	3882
60	=	4500	210	=	3077	360	=	2920
70	=	4520	220	=	3625	370	=	2208
80	=	1252	230	=	3604	380	=	2567
90	=	2764	240	=	3602	390	=	2922
100	=	2229	250	=	3634	400	=	2226
110	=	4926	260	=	4807	410	=	2494
120	=	3210	270	=	1801	420	=	2916
130	=	2600	280	=	3813	430	=	2715
140	=	2589	290	=	3332	440	=	143
150	=	3318	300	=	2561	TOTAL	=	125899

Blackjack

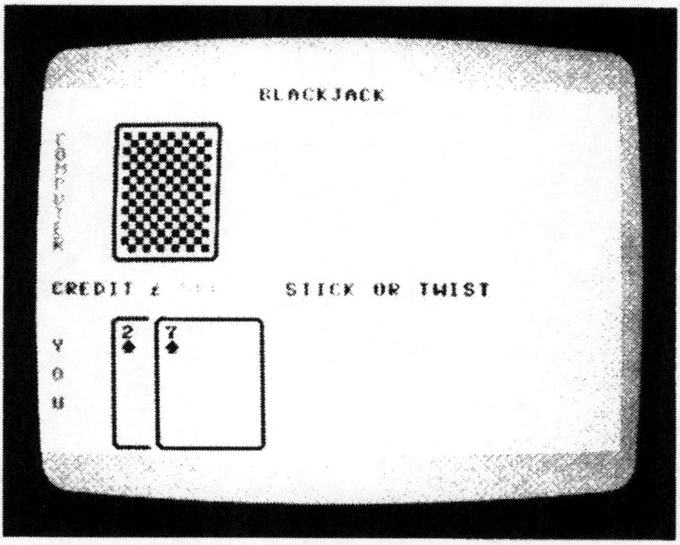

CLASSIFICATION: Gambling

Play Blackjack, the player versus the computer. You start with $50 and can bet up to your credit on one hand.

Enter your bet and hit return, then wait for the computer to deal your card (face down). Use key S to stick, if you think your hand is good enough, or T to twist a new card over. You bust if the total exceeds 21. Try D to double your stake if you feel lucky.

PROGRAM
Variables

CD$	Array of names of cards (A, 2, 3, J, Q, K)
SS$	Suits of deck
CR	Money
CV	Computer's total card value
PV	Player's total card value
NC	Number of cards computer has
NP	Number of cards player has
B	Amount of bet
DT$	Next card
SQ	Stake
DB	Flag of doubling stake
CO%	Computer's card
P%	Player's card
CN%	Array which indicates which cards dealt
C1$, C2$	Computer's first and second cards

Listing

Initialise Game Variables
Draw Screen; Deal First Cards Face Down

```
10   BL$="▚ ▚ ▚ ▚ ▚ ▚ ◙ ▮▮ ▮▮ ▮▮ ▮▮ ▮▮ ▮▮ "⇕CL$="▲ ▲ ▲ ▲ ▲ ▲ ◙
     ▮▮ ▮▮ ▮▮ ▮▮ ▮▮ ▮▮ "⇕CN$="◙ ◙ ◙ ◙ ◙ ◙ ◙ ◙ ◙ ◙ ◙ ◙ ◙ ◙ ◙ ◙ "
20   CA$="◙ ◙ ◙ ◙ ◙ ◙ ◙ ◙ ◙ ◙ ◙ ◙ ◙ ◙ ◙ ◙ ◙ ◙ ◙ ◙ "⇕NL$="▲ ▲ ▲
     ▲ ▲ ▲ ▲ ▲ ▲ ▲ ▲ ▲ ▲ ▲ ▲ ▲ ▲ ▲ ▲ ▲ ▲ ▲ ▲ ▲ ▲ ▲ ▲ "
30   C$="▬ ▬ ▬ ▬ ▬ ▬ "⇕D$="▚ ◙ ▮▮ ▚ ◙ ▮▮ ▚ ◙ ▮▮ ▚ ◙ ▮▮ ▚ ◙ ▮▮
     ▚ ◙ ▮▮ ▚ ◙ ▮▮ ▚ "⇕CR=500⇕DC$="◙ ◙ "
40   VOL 8⇕DIMSS$(3)⇕DIMPC(9)⇕DIMCC(9)
50   DIMCD$(12)⇕DIMCN%(12)⇕FOR I=0 TO 12⇕READCD$(I)⇕CD$(
     I)=CD$(I)+"▲ "⇕CN%(I)=15⇕NEXTI
60   DATAA,2,3,4,5,6,7,8,9,10,J,Q,K
70   CD$(9)="1 0 "⇕SS$(0)="◙ ♥ "⇕SS$(1)="◙ ◆ "⇕SS$(2)="■
     ♣ "⇕SS$(3)="■ ♠ "
80   PRINT "◙ ◙ ▲ ▲ ▲ ▲ ▲ ▲ ▲ ▲ ▲ ▲ ▲ ▲ ▲ ▲ ▲ ▲ ▲ ▲ ▲ ▲ B L A C K
     J A C K "
90   PRINT "◙ ◙ ◙ ◙ C ◙ ▮▮ O ◙ ▮▮ M ◙ ▮▮ P ◙ ▮▮ U ◙ ▮▮ T ◙ ▮▮
     E ◙ ▮▮ R ◙ ◙ ◙ ◙ ◙ ◙ ◙ ◙ ▮▮ ▬ Y ◙ ▮▮ ▲ ◙ ▮▮ O ◙ ▮▮ ▲ ◙ ▮▮ U
     "
100  L=0⇕CX$="◙ ◙ ◙ ◙ "⇕SQ=0⇕B=0⇕CN=-1⇕PN=-1⇕DB=0⇕S=0
110  CY$=CN$+DC$⇕GOSUB 320⇕P1$=DT$⇕PS=X⇕PN=0⇕PC(PN)=Y⇕
     GOSUB 420
120  CY$=DC$⇕GOSUB 320⇕C1$=DT$⇕CS1=X⇕CN=0⇕CC(CN)=Y
130  GOSUB 560⇕CY$=CN$+DC$⇕DT$=P1$⇕X=PS⇕GOSUB 380⇕RC$=CX
     $⇕RP$=CX$
```

Flip Over Player's First Card and Enter Bet
Deal Next Two Cards

```
140  PRINT CN$;CA$;"◙ E N T E R ▲ B E T ■ ";⇕INPUT B
150  PRINT CN$;CA$;NL$
160  IF B<1ORB>CRTHEN 140
170  GOSUB 550
180  CY$=CN$+DC$⇕GOSUB 320⇕PN=PN+1⇕PC(PN)=Y⇕P1$=DT$⇕PS
     =X
190  CY$=DC$⇕CX$=RC$⇕GOSUB 320⇕C2$=DT$⇕CS2=X⇕CN=CN+1⇕CC(
     CN)=Y
200  CY$=CN$+DC$⇕CX$=RP$⇕DT$=P1$⇕X=PS⇕GOSUB 380⇕GOSUB 42
     0
210  IF PV=21THEN 290
220  PRINT CN$;CA$;"◙ S T I C K ▲ O R ▲ T W I S T ";
230  GETA$⇕IF A$=""THEN 230
240  IF A$<>"S "ANDA$<>"T "ANDA$<>"D "THEN PRINT CN$;CA$
     ;NL$⇕SOUND 1,350,5⇕GOTO 210
```

```
250   IF A$="T "THEN GOSUB 320:PN=PN+1:PC(PN)=Y:GOSUB 380
      :GOSUB 420:GOSUB 600:GOTO 210
260   IF A$<>"D "ORDB>0ORB>CRTHEN 280
270   GOSUB 550:DB=1:GOTO 210
280   IF A$<>"S "ORPV<12THEN 210
```

Player Sticks, So Reveal Computer's Hand and Play

```
290   S=1:GOSUB 570:GOSUB 480
300   GOSUB 600
310   GOSUB 320:CN=CN+1:CC(CN)=Y:GOSUB 380:GOSUB 480:
      GOTO 300
320   SOUND 3,700,5:Y=INT(RND(0)*13):IF CN%(Y)=0THEN 320
```

Determine Next Card's Value and Suit; Draw Face Down; Flip Card Over

```
330   DT$=CD$(Y):X=INT(RND(0)*4)
340   IF (CN%(Y)AND(2↑X))=0THEN 320
350   CN%(Y)=CN%(Y)-2↑X
360   PRINT "▣ ■ ";CY$;CX$;"▨ ";C$;"▧ ▣ ▮▮ ";D$;"▣ ";CY$;C
      X$;"▣ ";D$;"▣ ▮▮ ▧ ";C$;"▨ ";
370   PRINT "▣ ";CY$;CX$;"▣ ▮ ";BL$;BL$;BL$;BL$;BL$;BL$;B
      L$;BL$;:FOR I=1 TO 100:NEXT:RETURN
380   CC$=LEFT$(SS$(X),1)
390   FOR I=1 TO 500:NEXT:PRINT "▣ ";CY$;CX$;"▣ ▮ ";CC$;D
      T$;"▴ ▴ ▴ ▴ ▣ ▮▮ ▮▮ ▮▮ ▮▮ ▮▮ ▮▮ ";SS$(X);"▴ ▴ ▴ ▴ ▴ ▣ ▮▮ ▮▮
       ▮▮ ▮▮ ▮▮ ▮▮ ";
400   PRINT CL$;CL$;CL$;CL$;CL$;CL$;:CX$=CX$+"▮ ▮ ▮ "
410   SOUND 1,1000,3:FOR I=1 TO 500:NEXT:RETURN
```

Calculate Player's Hand; Calculate Computer's Hand

```
420   PV=0:AC=0:FOR I=0 TO PN:PV=PV+PC(I)+1:IF PC(I)=0
      THEN PV=PV+10:AC=AC+1
430   IF PC(I)>9THEN PV=PV-PC(I)+9
440   NEXT
450   IF PV>21ANDAC>0THEN PV=PV-10:AC=AC-1:GOTO 450
460   IF PV>21THEN L=1
470   RETURN
480   IF CN<0THEN RETURN
490   CV=0:AC=0:FOR I=0 TO CN:CV=CV+CC(I)+1:IF CC(I)=0
      THEN CV=CV+10:AC=AC+1
500   IF CC(I)>9THEN CV=CV-CC(I)+9
510   NEXT
520   IF CV>21ANDAC>0THEN CV=CV-10:AC=AC-1:GOTO 520
530   IF CV>21THEN L=-1
540   RETURN
```

Draw Credit and Stake

```
550 SQ=SQ+B:PRINT CN$;"▚ ◙ ▐ S T A K E ▲ ▲ £ ▲ ▲ ▲ ▲ ▲ ▲ ▲ ▲ ▲ ▮▮ ▮▮ ▮▮ ▮▮ ▮▮ ▮▮ ▮▮ ▮▮ ▩ ";SQ:CR=CR-B
560 PRINT CN$;"▚ ▐ C R E D I T ▲ £ ▲ ▲ ▲ ▲ ▲ ▲ ▲ ▲ ▲ ▮▮ ▮▮ ▮▮ ▮▮ ▮▮ ▮▮ ▮▮ ▮▮ ▩ ";CR:RETURN
570 PRINT "◙ ◙ ◙ ◙ ▐ ▐ ▐ ▐ ▐ ";C1$;"◙ ▮▮ ▮▮ ";SS$(CS1);"▲ ◙ ▮▮ ▮▮ ▲ ▲ ◙ ▮▮ ▮▮ ▲ ▲ ◙ ▮▮ ▮▮ ▲ ▲ ◙ ▮▮ ▮▮ ▲ ▲ ◙ ▮▮ ▮▮ ▲ ▲ ◙ ▮▮ ▮▮ ▲ ▲ "
580 SOUND 1,1000,3
590 CY$=DC$:CX$=RC$:DT$=C2$:X=CS1:GOSUB 380:GOSUB 480:RETURN
```

Determine Winner and Amount Won or Lost

```
600 IF L=1THEN PRINT CN$;CA$;"▩ ▲ ▲ Y O U ▲ ▮▮ B U S T E D ! ▬ ▲ ▲ ▲ ":SOUND 1,800,10:SOUND 1,700,20:GOTO 780
610 IF L<>-1THEN 640
620 PRINT CN$;CA$;NL$;CN$;CA$;"▜ ▲ ▲ ▲ I ▲ B U S T E D ":CR=CR+2*SQ
630 SOUND 1,800,10:FOR I=1 TO 50:NEXT:SOUND 1,900,10:GOTO 790
640 IF CV<>21ORCN<>1THEN 670
650 PRINT CN$;CA$;"■ ▮▮ I ▲ G O T ▲ B L A C K J A C K ! ▬ ":SOUND 1,900,20:IF PV=21ANDPN=1THEN CR=CR-3*SQ
660 FOR I=1 TO 10:SOUND 1,800+10*I,10:NEXT:CR=CR-SQ:GOTO 790
670 IF S=0THEN RETURN
680 IF PV<>21ORPN<>1THEN 710
690 PRINT CN$;CA$;"■ ▮▮ Y O U ▲ G O T ▲ B L A C K J A C K ! ▬ ":CR=CR+3*SQ:GOSUB 570
700 FOR I=1 TO 30:SOUND 1,300+10*I,10:SOUND 2,420+10*I,10::FOR J=1 TO 50:NEXTJ:NEXTI:GOTO 790
710 IF CV<17THEN PRINT CN$;CA$;"▛ ▲ ▲ ▲ ▲ I ▲ T W I S T . . . ▲ ▲ ▲ ▲ ":RETURN
720 IF CV<PVTHEN 740
730 PRINT CN$;CA$;"▩ ▲ ▲ ▲ ▲ Y O U ▲ L O S E . . . ":SOUND 1,700,10:FOR I=1 TO 50:NEXT:SOUND 1,600,25:GOTO 790
740 PRINT CN$;CA$;"▛ ▲ ▲ ▲ ▲ I ▲ L O S E . . . ▲ ▲ ▲ ▲ ▲ "
750 FOR I=1 TO 10:SOUND 1,900+10*I,10:FOR J=1 TO 50:NEXTJ:SOUND 1,1000-10*I,10:NEXT
760 CR=CR+2*SQ
770 GOTO 790
780 GOSUB 570
```

```
790   GOSUB 560:PRINT CN$;"▣ ▥ ";NL$;CN$;CA$;"▣ ▣ ▲ A N O
       T H E R ▲ G A M E ▲ ? "
800   GETA$:IF A$=""THEN 800
810   IF A$="N "THEN END
820   IF CR>0THEN 80
830   PRINT CN$;CA$;"▣ ▥ ▲ ▲ ▲ ▲ B A N K R U P T ! ▬ ":
      END
```

ChexSum Tables

10	= 6108	290	= 1067	570	= 5388
20	= 2532	300	= 298	580	= 635
30	= 6598	310	= 3279	590	= 3495
40	= 1924	320	= 3113	600	= 5046
50	= 5345	330	= 1965	610	= 1155
60	= 1682	340	= 1750	620	= 3982
70	= 5225	350	= 1450	630	= 3029
80	= 1897	360	= 4995	640	= 1882
90	= 4377	370	= 5023	650	= 6228
100	= 4092	380	= 1162	660	= 3884
110	= 4303	390	= 6940	670	= 762
120	= 3533	400	= 2948	680	= 1905
130	= 4527	410	= 1920	690	= 4433
140	= 2124	420	= 6113	700	= 5669
150	= 844	430	= 2235	710	= 3046
160	= 1392	440	= 131	720	= 996
170	= 303	450	= 3661	730	= 5235
180	= 4349	460	= 1088	740	= 1941
190	= 4733	470	= 143	750	= 4780
200	= 3668	480	= 831	760	= 1069
210	= 940	490	= 6061	770	= 538
220	= 2128	500	= 2194	780	= 303
230	= 1215	510	= 131	790	= 3470
240	= 5092	520	= 3634	800	= 1211
250	= 4542	530	= 1244	810	= 895
260	= 2311	540	= 143	820	= 809
270	= 1372	550	= 5617	830	= 2370
280	= 1784	560	= 3683	TOTAL	= 235915

Dungeon

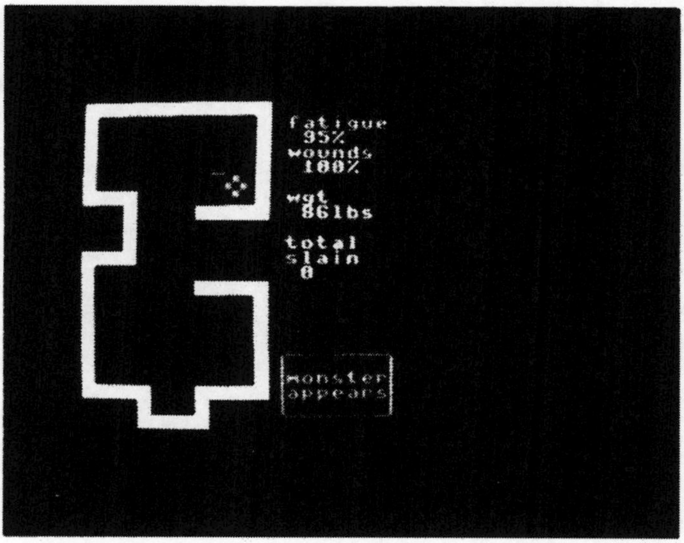

CLASSIFICATION: Adventure

You have been placed in a chamber with a monster and have the following attributes:

- Fatigue
- Wounds
- Weight

You are the red object — explore the rooms and battle the evil monsters. Your controls are R to turn your man right and L to turn your man left. The keys 1 to 9 move you forward the corresponding number of places. The T key thrusts the sword at the monster, but be careful, he fights back. Your wound tolerance must not reach zero or you will die.

PROGRAMMING SUGGESTIONS

Alter the game so if a player stays too long in one position a monster will come after him. Also give the player and the monster more than just the one weapon they currently have. Weapons like a spear or a mace would be useful tools to have.

Program Variables

SC	Screen start
RO	Room number
FA	Fatigue value
X, Y	Player's co-ordinates
MX, MY	Monster's co-ordinates
D	Direction
R$	Room
WO	Wounds value
TS	Total slain
WE	Weight value
V	Steps of movement forward
M	Monster flag

Listing

```
10    REM  DUNGEON
20    DIMR$(4)
```

Define Cursor Movement Variables; Set Colours, Data For Mazes

```
30    Y$="{HOME}{DOWN}{DOWN}{DOWN}{DOWN}{DOWN}{DOWN}{DOWN}{DOWN}{DOWN}{DOWN}{DOWN}{DOWN}{DOWN}{DOWN}{DOWN}{DOWN}{DOWN}{DOWN}{DOWN}{DOWN}{DOWN}{DOWN}"
      :X$="{RIGHT}{RIGHT}{RIGHT}{RIGHT}{RIGHT}{RIGHT}{RIGHT}{RIGHT}{RIGHT}{RIGHT}{RIGHT}{RIGHT}{RIGHT}{RIGHT}{RIGHT}{RIGHT}{RIGHT}{RIGHT}{RIGHT}{RIGHT}{RIGHT}{RIGHT}{RIGHT}{RIGHT}"
40    COLOR4,6,4:COLOR0,7,5:PRINT CHR$(14):SC=3072
60    SR=INT(RND(1)*11+10)
70    DE=INT(RND(1)*11+10):WE=75+INT(RND(1)*25)
80    TS=0:RO=0:FA=100:WO=100:D=1:X=3:Y=15
90    FOR I=0 TO 4:READR$(I):NEXT
100   DATAO93D7L5ED5R1O4D7L4D2L4U2L4U9R3U4L3U6
110   DATAD1OR5E4O3D991L4U9D9L8U9E4O6
120   DATAO3D5RE5U1O4R4D7E4O92L93U994
130   DATAO6D7U7R6D8L2D5R2D8L4E4O4U91R6D4U4L6U1E4OR2L2U6
140   DATAO93D9L9R6D9L1D3L1E4O3U993
150   ON ROGOTO 170,180,190,200
160   MX=10:MY=3:GOTO 210
170   MX=4:MY=3:GOTO 210
180   MX=3:MY=10:GOTO 210
190   MX=10:MY=18:GOTO 210
200   MX=2:MY=18:GOTO 210
210   M=0:IF RND(1)>.5THEN M=INT(RND(1)*3+1):MS=INT(RND(1
      )*10)+5
220   GOSUB 1060:V=0:F=0:GOTO 260
```

Move Your Player Forward, Rotate Him Left or Right

```
230   GETA$:V=VAL(A$):IF V=0THEN 480
240   FA=FA-INT((V/200)*(100-WO)+(V/200)*WE+.5)
250   GOSUB 970:IF M=1ANDRND(1)>.2THEN F=1
260   SW=0:FOR I=1 TO V:PRINT LEFT$(Y$,Y+1);LEFT$(X$,X)"{UP}
      {UP}{DOWN}{RVS}{RVS}{UP}{UP}"
270   X1=X+(D=3)-(D=1):Y1=Y+(D=0)-(D=2)
310   IF  PEEK(SC+Y1*40+X1)<>32ORPEEK(SC+Y1*40+X1+1)<>32
      THEN I=V:GOTO 410
320   IF  PEEK(SC+Y1*40+X1+40)<>32ORPEEK(SC+Y1*40+X1+41)
      <>32THEN I=V:GOTO 410
340   X=X1:Y=Y1:IF X>0ANDX<11ANDY>0ANDY<20THEN 410
350   RO=RO+(X=0)-(X=11)+((Y=20)-(Y=0))*2
360   IF X=0THEN X=10
370   IF X=11THEN X=1
380   IF Y=0THEN Y=19
390   IF Y=20THEN Y=1
```

```
400   GOTO 150
410   PRINT LEFT$(Y$,Y+1);LEFT$(X$,X)"▣ ";
420   ON D+1GOTO 430,440,450,460
430   PRINT "▣ ▴ ▣ ▮▮ ▮▮ ▣ ▣ □ ▮▮ ";:GOTO 470
440   PRINT "▣ ▣ ▬ ▣ ▣ ▮▮ ▮▮ ▣ ▣ ▬ ▴ ▮▮ ";:GOTO 470
```

Print the Player and the Monster

```
450   PRINT "▣ ▣ ▣ ▣ ▮▮ ▮▮ ▬ ▴ ▣ ▮▮ ▮▮ ";:GOTO 470
460   PRINT "▴ ▣ ▣ ▮▮ ▮▮ ▣ ▣ □ ▮▮ ▮▮ ";
470   IF V>0THEN NEXTI
480   IF A$<>"L "ANDA$<>"R "THEN 540
490   IF FA<100THEN FA=FA+1:GOSUB 970
500   SW=0:D=D+(A$="L ")-(A$="R "):IF D<0THEN D=3
510   IF D>3THEN D=0
520   A$=""
530   V=0:GOTO 410
540   IF A$<>"T "THEN 620
550   SW=3:FA=FA-2
560   PRINT LEFT$(Y$,Y+1);LEFT$(X$,X+1);"▣ ";:IF D=0
      THEN PRINT "▣ ":GOTO 600
570   IF D=1THEN PRINT "▣ □ ":GOTO 600
580   IF D=2THEN PRINT "▣ ▮▮ □ ":GOTO 600
590   PRINT "▮▮ □ "
600   X1=X:Y1=Y:X1=X1+((D=3)-(D=1))*2:Y1=Y1+((D=0)-(D=2))
      *2
610   F=1
620   IF SW>0THEN SW=SW-1:IF SW=0THEN GOSUB 970:A$="":
      GOTO 410
630   IF M=0THEN 930
640   IF MS>=SRANDRND(1)>.7THEN F=1
650   IF F=0THEN 770
660   PRINT LEFT$(Y$,MY+1);LEFT$(X$,MX)"▴ ▴ ▣ ▮▮ ▮▮ ▴ ▴ ";:
      IF SM>0ANDMX>=XTHEN PRINT "□ □ ▮▮ ▮▮ ▮▮ ▴ "
690   SM=0:DY=MY+(MY>Y)-(MY<Y):IF PEEK(SC+DY*40+MX)<>32
      ORPEEK(SC+DY*40+MX+1)<>32THEN 730
700   IF PEEK(SC+DY*40+MX+40)<>32ORPEEK(SC+DY*40+MX+41)
      <>32THEN 730
720   MY=DY
730   DY=MX+(MX>X+2)-(MX<X-1):IF ABS(DY-X)<=1THEN DY=DY
      +(DY>1)*2
740   IF PEEK(SC+MY*22+DY)<>32ORPEEK(SC+MY*22+DY+1)<>32
      THEN 770
750   IF PEEK(SC+MY*22+DY+22)<>32ORPEEK(SC+MY*22+DY+23)
      <>32THEN 770
760   MX=DY
770   PRINT LEFT$(Y$,MY+1);LEFT$(X$,MX)"▣ ▣ ▣ ▬ ▣ ▣ ▮▮ ▮▮ ▣
       ";:IF SW=0THEN 820
780   IF  ABS(X1-MX)>1 OR ABS(Y1-MY)>1 THEN  820
```

```
790   SW=1:S=SR/4:S=S+(S*DE)/100:MS=MS-INT(S+.5):IF MS>0
      THEN 820
800   PRINT LEFT$(Y$,MY+1);LEFT$(X$,MX)"▲ ▲ ◙ ▌▌ ▌▌ ▲ "
810   TS=TS+1:M=0:GOTO 930
820   IF SM>0ORRND(1)>.5ORF=0THEN 890
830   X2=MX:Y2=MY
840   PRINT LEFT$(Y$,MY+1);LEFT$(X$,MX);:IF MX<XTHEN
      PRINT "◙ ◘ ▣ □ ";:Y2=Y2+1:X2=X2+1:GOTO 880
850   IF MX=0THEN 930
860   IF PEEK(SC+MY*22+MX-1)=160THEN 930
870   PRINT "▌▌ □ ▣ □ ";:X2=X2-1
880   SM=4
890   IF SM=0THEN 930
900   SM=SM-1
910   IF ABS(X2-X)>1ORABS(Y2-Y)>1THEN 930
920   SW=1:S=MS:S=S+(S*2*M)/100:WO=WO-INT(S+.5)
930   IF WO>0ANDFA>0THEN 230
940   FOR I=1 TO 1000:NEXT:PRINT "◘ ◙ ◙ ◙ ▣ T H O U ▲ A R
       T ":PRINT "▲ ▲ ▲ ▲ S L A I N ":M=0
950   GOSUB 970:PRINT "□ □ ";:POKE 198,0:END
960   IF D1=3THEN PRINT "▌▌ ";
970   PRINT LEFT$(Y$,2);LEFT$(X$,14)"◣ F A T I G U E ▣ ◙
      ▌▌ ▌▌ ▌▌ ▌▌ ▌▌ ▌▌ ▌▌ "FA"▌▌ % ▲ "
980   PRINT TAB(14)"◣ W O U N D S ◙ ▌▌ ▌▌ ▌▌ ▌▌ ▌▌ ▌▌ ▣ "WO"▌▌ %
       ▲ "
990   PRINT TAB(14)"◙ ◣ W G T ◙ ▌▌ ▌▌ ▌▌ ▣ "WE"▌▌ L B S ◙ "
1000  PRINT TAB(14)"◣ T O T A L ◙ ▌▌ ▌▌ ▌▌ ▌▌ ▌▌ S L A I N ▣ ◙
       ▌▌ ▌▌ ▌▌ ▌▌ ▌▌ "TS
1010  PRINT LEFT$(Y$,17);LEFT$(X$,14)"◥ □ □ □ □ □ □ □ ◙ ▌▌
       ▌▌ ▌▌ ▌▌ ▌▌ ▌▌ ▌▌ ▌▌ □ ▲ ▲ ▲ ▲ ▲ ▲ ▲ ▲ □ ◙ ▌▌ ▌▌ ▌▌ ▌▌ ▌▌ ▌▌ ▌▌
      ▌▌ ";
1020  PRINT "□ ▲ ▲ ▲ ▲ ▲ ▲ ▲ ▲ □ ◙ ▌▌ ▌▌ ▌▌ ▌▌ ▌▌ ▌▌ ▌▌ ▌▌ □ ▲ ▲
      ▲ ▲ ▲ ▲ ▲ □ ◙ ▌▌ ▌▌ ▌▌ ▌▌ ▌▌ ▌▌ ▌▌ ▌▌ □ ▲ ▲ ▲ ▲ ▲ ▲ ▲ ▲ □ "
      ;
1030  PRINT "◙ ▌▌ ▌▌ ▌▌ ▌▌ ▌▌ ▌▌ ▌▌ ▌▌ □ □ □ □ □ □ □ □ □ □ □ ▌▌ ▌▌
      ▌▌ ▌▌ ▌▌ ▌▌ ";
1040  IF  M>0 THEN  PRINT "◙ ▌▌ M O N S T E R ◙ ▌▌ ▌▌ ▌▌ ▌▌ ▌▌
      ▌▌ ▌▌ A P P E A R S "
1050  RETURN
1060  PRINT "◘ ▣ ";:D1=1: FOR I=1 TO LEN(R$(RO))
1070  S$=MID$(R$(RO),I,1):IF VAL(S$)>0THEN FOR J=1 TO
      VAL(S$):GOSUB 1150:NEXT
1080  IF S$="U "THEN D1=0
1090  IF S$="L "THEN D1=3
1100  IF S$="D "THEN D1=2
1110  IF S$="R "THEN D1=1
1120  IF S$="E "THEN PRINT "▀ ";
1130  IF S$="O "THEN  PRINT "◘ ";
1140  NEXT:PRINT "▣ ":GOSUB 970:RETURN
1150  PRINT "▲ ▌▌ ";
```

```
1160  IF D1=0THEN PRINT "▢ ";
1170  IF D1=1THEN PRINT "▙ ";
1180  IF D1=2THEN PRINT "▣ ";
1190  IF D1=3THEN PRINT "▌▌ ";
1200  RETURN
1210  IF S$="O "THEN  PRINT "▚ ";
```

ChexSum Tables

10	= 0	440	= 2338	850	= 890
20	= 400	450	= 2308	860	= 2490
30	= 2820	460	= 1667	870	= 1695
40	= 2383	470	= 836	880	= 393
60	= 1558	480	= 1981	890	= 882
70	= 3210	490	= 1910	900	= 735
80	= 3299	500	= 3439	910	= 2570
90	= 1367	510	= 919	920	= 4045
100	= 2802	520	= 359	930	= 1463
110	= 2040	530	= 920	940	= 3842
120	= 2019	540	= 1132	950	= 1696
130	= 3664	550	= 1181	960	= 1123
140	= 1848	560	= 4034	970	= 4198
150	= 1500	570	= 1656	980	= 2958
160	= 1540	580	= 1810	990	= 2406
170	= 1502	590	= 549	1000	= 3615
180	= 1551	600	= 5274	1010	= 6868
190	= 1591	610	= 300	1020	= 5552
200	= 1550	620	= 3767	1030	= 4377
210	= 4283	630	= 790	1040	= 3385
220	= 1735	640	= 2144	1050	= 143
230	= 1885	650	= 773	1060	= 2354
240	= 3701	660	= 5599	1070	= 4207
250	= 2158	690	= 8163	1080	= 1166
260	= 3641	700	= 5195	1090	= 1160
270	= 3346	720	= 508	1100	= 1151
310	= 5600	730	= 5637	1110	= 1166
320	= 5979	740	= 4856	1120	= 1226
340	= 3454	750	= 5193	1130	= 1106
350	= 3425	760	= 507	1140	= 1031
360	= 1018	770	= 4120	1150	= 481
370	= 1019	780	= 2733	1160	= 1117
380	= 1020	790	= 5240	1170	= 993
390	= 1021	800	= 2410	1180	= 991
400	= 526	810	= 1733	1190	= 1123
410	= 1793	820	= 2194	1200	= 143
420	= 1648	830	= 1060	1210	= 1106
430	= 2106	840	= 5837	TOTAL	= 262921

Warlock

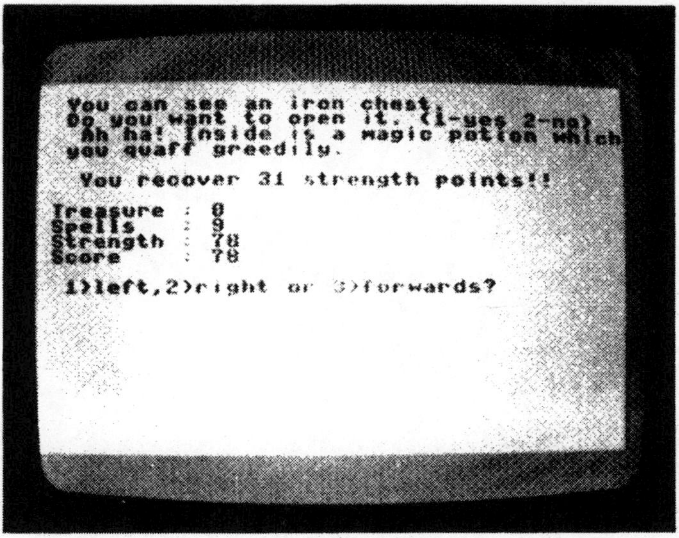

CLASSIFICATION: Adventure

You have been cast into the world of the warlock, a time of dungeons and dragons. The objective of the game is to live as long as possible but at the same time gather as much treasure as you can. You will be confronted with monsters and creatures of all sorts and you will have one of three alternatives: attack, retreat or use a spell. Beware, spells are not always effective against creatures of the night.

PROGRAM
Variables

S	Strength
SP	Spells
TR	Player's treasures
M	Monsters
CO	Colours of monsters
HA	Next event
Z	Up or down stairs
D	Silently or noisily
E	Angry, friendly or dumb looking
MH	Advance or stop
MT	Coins taken by the monster
SS	Metal spikes
TT	Silver or gold
T	Monster's treasure

Listing

```
10    COLOR4,7,3:COLOR0,2,5:S=100:SP=8+INT(RND(1)*4):TR
      =0
20    PRINT CHR$(14)"▚ ▩ ▲ ▲ ▲ ▲ ▲ ▲ ▲ ▲ ▲ ▲ ▲ - = * ▲ ● ♠ ▚
      ▙ ▛ ▦ ▨ ▲ * = - "
30    PRINT :PRINT "▲ ▲ ▲ ▐ O U ′ V E ▲ B E E N ▲ T R A N
       S P O R T E D ▲ T O ▲ S O M E W H E R E "
40    PRINT "▲ W I T H I N ▲ T H E ▲ ● A R L O C K ′ S ▲
      C A V E S . "
50    PRINT :PRINT "▲ ▲ ▲ L I V E ▲ A S ▲ L O N G ▲ A S ▲
       P O S S I B L E ▲ G A I N I N G "
60    PRINT "▲ T R E A S U R E ▲ A N D ▲ K I L L I N G ▲
      M O N S T E R S . "
70    PRINT :PRINT :PRINT :PRINT "▲ ▲ ▲ ▜ L E A S E ▲ P R
       E S S ▲ A N Y ▲ K E Y ▲ T O ▲ S T A R T . "
80    GETA$:IF A$=""THEN 80
90    PRINT "▚ "
```

Print Message; Press Any Key to Start

```
100   S=S-INT(RND(1)*5)+1:IF S<1THEN 760
110   PRINT :PRINT "▲ ▐ R E A S U R E ▲ : "TR:PRINT "▲ ♥
      P E L L S ▲ ▲ ▲ : "SP:PRINT "▲ ♥ T R E N G T H ▲ :
      "S
120   PRINT "▲ ♥ C O R E ▲ ▲ ▲ ▲ : "TR*10+S:POKE 198,0
130   M=INT(RND(1)*13)+1
140   T=INT(RND(1)*20)+1
150   CO=INT(RND(1)*7)+1
160   HA=INT(RND(1)*6)+1
170   PRINT :PRINT "▲ ▲ 1 ) L E F T , 2 ) R I G H T ▲ O R
       ▲ 3 ) F O R W A R D S ? "
180   GETA$:IF A$=""ORA$<>"1 "ANDA$<>"2 "ANDA$<>"3 "
      THEN 180
190   PRINT "▚ "
200   IF RND(1)<.15THEN GOTO 160
210   ON HAGOTO 220,340,460,460,1010,1370
220   PRINT "▲ ▲ ▲ ▐ O U ▲ C A N ▲ S E E ▲ A ▲ F L I G H
      T ▲ O F ▲ S T A I R S ▲ G O I N G "
```

Check If You Want to Use the Stairs or Move Into a Room

```
230   Z=INT(RND(1)*2)+1
240   IF Z=1THEN PRINT "▲ ▲ U P W A R D S ▲ I N T O ▲ T H
       E ▲ G L O O M . "
```

```
250   IF Z=2THEN PRINT "▲ ▲ D O W N ▲ I N T O ▲ B L A C K
       N E S S . "
260   PRINT :PRINT "▲ ▲ ▲ ▒ O ▲ Y O U ▲ W I S H ▲ T O ▲ U
       S E ▲ T H E M ? ":PRINT "▲ ▲ ▲ ▲ ▲ ▲ ▲ ▲ ▲ 1 - Y E S
       ▲ 2 - N O "
270   GETA$:IF A$=""ORA$<>"1 "ANDA$<>"2 "THEN 270
280   IF A$="2 "ORRND(1)<.8THEN 100
290   PRINT :PRINT "▲ ▲ ▲ * * W H O O P S * * "
300   FOR I=1 TO 1000:NEXT
310   PRINT :PRINT "▲ ▲ ▒ O U ▲ F E L L ▲ D O W N ▲ T H E
       ▲ S T A I R S ! "
320   PRINT :PRINT "▲ ▲ 5 ▲ S T R E N G T H ▲ P O I N T S
       ▲ T A K E N ▲ A W A Y . "
330   S=S-5:GOTO 100
340   PRINT "▲ ▲ ▒ O U ▲ C A N ▲ S E E ▲ A ▲ D O O R . "
350   PRINT "▲ ▲ ▒ O ▲ Y O U ▲ W A N T ▲ T O ▲ O P E N ▲
      I T ▲ ( 1 - Y E S ▲ 2 - N O ) ? "
360   GETA$:IF A$=""ORA$<>"1 "ANDA$<>"2 "THEN 360
370   IF A$="2 "THEN 100
380   PRINT :PRINT "▲ ▲ ▒ H E ▲ D O O R ▲ O P E N S ";
390   D=INT(RND(1)*2)+1
400   IF D=1THEN PRINT "▲ S I L E N T L Y . "
410   IF D=2THEN PRINT "▲ W I T H ▲ A ▲ L O U D ▲ C R E A
       K I N G . "
420   FOR I=1 TO 500:NEXT
430   IF RND(1)<.7THEN 450
440   GOTO 100
```

Print 'Behind a Door You Can See a Creature of Some Sort'

```
450   PRINT "▲ ▲ ▒ E H I N D ▲ T H E ▲ D O O R - "
460   PRINT "▲ ▲ ▒ O U ▲ C A N ▲ S E E ▲ A ";
470   E=INT(RND(1)*3)+1
480   IF E=1THEN PRINT "N ▲ A N G R Y "
490   IF E=2THEN PRINT "▲ F R I E N D L Y "
500   IF E=3THEN PRINT "▲ D U M B "
510   PRINT "▲ ▲ L O O K I N G ▲ ";
520   ON COGOSUB 1300,1310,1320,1330,1340,1350,1360,1370
530   ON MGOSUB 1160,1170,1180,1190,1200,1210,1220,1230,1
      240,1250,1260,1270,1280,1290
540   MH=INT(RND(1)*2)+1
550   IF MH=1THEN PRINT :PRINT "▲ ▲ ▒ E ▲ A D V A N C E S
       ! "
560   IF MH=2THEN PRINT :PRINT "▲ ▲ ▒ E ▲ S T O P S ! "
570   PRINT :PRINT "▲ ▲ 1 ) A T T A C K , 2 ) R E T R E A
       T ▲ O R ▲ 3 ) U S E ▲ A ▲ S P E L L "
580   GETA$:IF A$<>"1 "ANDA$<>"2 "ANDA$<>"3 "THEN 580
590   IF A$<>"2 "THEN 640
```

```
600   PRINT :PRINT "▲▲▲▲▲▒▒▒▒▒▒/!!"
610   FOR I=1 TO 800:NEXT
620   IF RND(1)<.8THEN 100
630   PRINT :PRINT :PRINT "▲▲▒E▲DOESN'T▲LE
      T▲YOU▲ANYHOW!":GOTO 570
640   IF A$="1 "THEN 730
650   IF SP=0THEN PRINT "▲▲▒OU▲HAVE▲NONE.
      ":GOTO 570
660   IF RND(1)<.35THEN 700
670   PRINT : PRINT "▒▲▲▒HE▲SPELL▲WORKE
      D.":PRINT
680   SP=SP-1:IF SP<5THEN PRINT "▲▲▒UT▲YOU'RE
      ▲SHORT▲ON▲THEM▲NOW."
690   GOTO 910
700   PRINT :PRINT "▒▲▲▒HE▲SPELL▲DIDN'T
      ▲WORK."
710   PRINT "▲▲▒T▲JUST▲MADE▲HIM▲ANG
      RY."
720   GOTO 570
730   IF RND(1)<.31ANDINT(RND(1)*10)*10<SORRND(1)<.28
      THEN 900
740   IF RND(1)<.8THEN 790
750   PRINT "▒"
760   PRINT :PRINT "▲▲▒OU'RE▲▒▒♦▒!!"
770   PRINT :PRINT "▲▲▲▲▲♥▒┌▒▒▲:"TR*10+S
780   END
```

'You Are Dead'; 'You Are Wounded'; 'You Have Lost Your Strength'

```
790   PRINT : PRINT "▒▲▲▒OU'VE▲BEEN▲WOU
      NDED▲AND▲YOUR▲STRENGTH":
      PRINT "▲▲HAS▲BEEN▲HALVED."
800   S=INT(S/2)
810   IF INT(RND(1))<.4ORSS<>0THEN 100
820   IF RND(1)<.4THEN 870
830   MT=INT(TR/INT(RND(1)*7)):PRINT "▲▲ALSO▲THE
      ▲MONSTER▲STOLE"MT"COINS▲FRO
      M"
840   PRINT "▲▲YOUR▲PURSE..."
850   TR=TR-MT
860   TR=0:GOTO 100
870   PRINT "▲▲┌H▲NO!▲▒HE▲MONSTER▲S
      TOLE▲ALL▲YOUR"
880   PRINT "▲▲COINAGE.▲▒AD▲LUCK."
890   TR=0:GOTO 100
900   PRINT "▒"
910   PRINT "▲▲●ELL▲DONE!!"
```

```
920   PRINT ⬍PRINT "▲ ▲ ▲ ▙ O U ▲ K I L L E D ▲ H I M , "
      ;
930   PRINT "▲ A N D ▲ H I S ";
940   TT=INT(RND(1)*2)+1
950   PRINT T"C O I N S ▲ O F "
960   IF TT=1THEN PRINT "▲ ▲ S I L V E R ";
970   IF TT=2THEN PRINT "▲ ▲ G O L D ";
980   PRINT "▲ A R E ▲ N O W ▲ Y O U R S . "
990   TR=TR+T
1000  GOTO 100
1010  IF RND(1)<.3THEN 100
1020  PRINT "▲ ▲ * * W H O O P S * * "
1030  FOR I=1 TO 1000⬍NEXT
1040  PRINT ⬍PRINT "▲ ▲ ▙ O U ▲ F E L L ▲ D O W N ▲ A ▲ P
       I T ! "
1050  PRINT "▲ ▲ ◆ T ▲ T H E ▲ B O T T O M ";
1060  HN=INT(RND(1)*4)
1070  ON HNGOTO 1080,1090,1110,1130,1130
1080  GOTO 460
1090  PRINT "▲ I S ▲ N O T H I N G . "
1100  GOTO 100
1110  PRINT "▲ I S ▲ A ▲ P O O L ▲ O F ▲ A C I D ! ! "
1120  GOTO 760
1130  SS=INT(RND(1)*10)+1
1140  PRINT "A R E "SS"M E T A L ▲ S P I K E S ! ! "
1150  GOTO 790
1160  PRINT "D E M O G O R G O N ! "⬍RETURN
1170  PRINT "H Y D R A ! "⬍RETURN
1180  PRINT "S E R P E N T ! "⬍RETURN
1190  PRINT "G I A N T ! "⬍RETURN
1200  PRINT "D R A G O N ! "⬍RETURN
1210  PRINT "J U B I L E X ! "⬍RETURN
1220  PRINT "Z O M B I E ! "⬍RETURN
1230  PRINT "W R A I T H ! "⬍RETURN
1240  PRINT "M I N O T A U R ! "⬍RETURN
1250  PRINT "D E V I L ! "⬍RETURN
1260  PRINT "W E R E W O L F ! "⬍RETURN
1270  PRINT "O R C ! "⬍RETURN
1280  PRINT "W A R L O C K ! "⬍RETURN
1290  PRINT "▣ W H I T E ▲ ";⬍RETURN
1300  PRINT "▣ B L A C K ▲ ▣ ";⬍RETURN
1310  PRINT "C O L O U R L E S S ▲ ";⬍RETURN
1320  PRINT "▣ R E D ▲ ▣ ";⬍RETURN
1330  PRINT "▦ Y E L L O W ▲ ▣ ";⬍RETURN
1340  PRINT "▣ G R E E N ▣ ▲ ";⬍RETURN
1350  PRINT "▨ P U R P L E ▲ ▣ ";⬍RETURN
1360  PRINT "▣ B L U E ▲ ▣ ";⬍RETURN
1370  PRINT "▲ ▲ ▙ O U ▲ C A N ▲ S E E ▲ A ";
1380  Z=INT(RND(1)*2+1)
1390  IF Z=1THEN PRINT "▲ W O O D E N ";
```

```
1400 IF Z=2THEN PRINT "N▲I R O N ";
1410 PRINT "▲C H E S T . "
1420 PRINT "▲▲▓O▲Y O U▲W A N T▲T O▲O P E N▲
     I T .▲( 1 - Y E S▲2 - N O ) "
1430 GETA$:IF A$=""ORA$<>"1 "ANDA$<>"2 "THEN 1430
1440 IF A$="2 "THEN 100
1450 Z=INT(RND(1)*10+1)
1460 IF Z=1THEN ? "▲▲┌H▲D E A R !▲▓T▲W A S▲B
      O O B Y▲T R A P P E D ! ":? "▲▲▓O U▲C H O K
      E▲O N▲P O I S O N▲G A S . ":S=S-10
1470 IF Z<3THEN 100
1480 IF Z<8THEN PRINT "▲▲▓T▲W A S▲E M P T Y . ":
     GOTO 100
1490 PRINT "▲▲▲♠H▲H A !▲▓N S I D E▲I S▲A▲
     M A G I C▲P O T I O N▲W H I C H "
1500 PRINT "▲▲Y O U▲Q U A F F▲G R E E D I L Y . "
1510 Z=INT(RND(1)*20+16)
1520 PRINT :PRINT "▲▲▲▓O U▲R E C O V E R "Z"S T R
     E N G T H▲P O I N T S ! ! ":S=S+Z:GOTO 100
```

ChexSum Tables

10	= 3629	290	= 1287	570	= 3340
20	= 3229	300	= 1021	580	= 3162
30	= 3938	310	= 2665	590	= 1104
40	= 2585	320	= 2955	600	= 2204
50	= 3435	330	= 1187	610	= 971
60	= 2770	340	= 1874	620	= 1106
70	= 3716	350	= 3163	630	= 3616
80	= 1149	360	= 2942	640	= 916
90	= 372	370	= 908	650	= 2956
100	= 2472	380	= 1826	660	= 1176
110	= 4756	390	= 1316	670	= 2405
120	= 2283	400	= 1622	680	= 4646
130	= 1389	410	= 2618	690	= 534
140	= 1396	420	= 964	700	= 2589
150	= 1407	430	= 1120	710	= 2265
160	= 1401	440	= 525	720	= 532
170	= 2804	450	= 1648	730	= 3747
180	= 3744	460	= 1449	740	= 1110
190	= 372	470	= 1317	750	= 372
200	= 1551	480	= 1396	760	= 2125
210	= 2084	490	= 1545	770	= 2560
220	= 3541	500	= 1225	780	= 129
230	= 1338	510	= 952	790	= 6417
240	= 2868	520	= 2612	800	= 846
250	= 2634	530	= 4820	810	= 2174
260	= 4119	540	= 1408	820	= 1113
270	= 2941	550	= 2331	830	= 5915
280	= 1709	560	= 2067	840	= 1323

850	=	863
860	=	1007
870	=	3290
880	=	1785
890	=	1007
900	=	372
910	=	1196
920	=	1938
930	=	821
940	=	1428
950	=	918
960	=	1608
970	=	1419
980	=	1341
990	=	778
1000	=	525
1010	=	1103
1020	=	994
1030	=	1021
1040	=	2213
1050	=	1510
1060	=	1174
1070	=	2010
1080	=	531
1090	=	1074
1100	=	525
1110	=	1611
1120	=	531
1130	=	1482
1140	=	1806
1150	=	538
1160	=	1272
1170	=	866
1180	=	1045
1190	=	854
1200	=	925
1210	=	1033
1220	=	944
1230	=	951
1240	=	1138
1250	=	857
1260	=	1116
1270	=	702
1280	=	1028
1290	=	948
1300	=	960
1310	=	1379
1320	=	811
1330	=	1222
1340	=	976
1350	=	1224
1360	=	896
1370	=	1449
1380	=	1337
1390	=	1456
1400	=	1379
1410	=	709
1420	=	3190
1430	=	3002
1440	=	908
1450	=	1402
1460	=	7880
1470	=	796
1480	=	2777
1490	=	3723
1500	=	1841
1510	=	1463
1520	=	4723
TOTAL	=	279355

Reel Thing

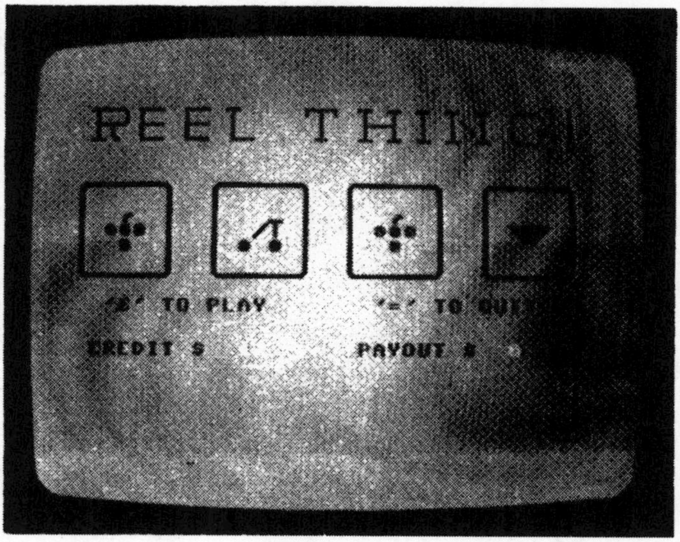

CLASSIFICATION: Gambling

Play a four wheel poker machine. You start with ten dollars and can win up to $2000. There are five different symbols — cherries, grapes, pine-apples, watermelons and, for big dollars, dollar signs. Spin the wheels and try your luck. There are different combinations in every game. Controls are £ to spin wheels and = to exit.

PROGRAMMING SUGGESTIONS

The odds of the wheels can be adjusted in this game. New symbols could be designed. Finally, the payout could be changed, for example, if cherry, cherry, dollar, dollar was to pay $3Ø, then this could be inserted after line 63:

If R(Ø) = Ø and R(1) = Ø and R(2) = 4 and
R(3) = 4 then W = 3Ø

Program Variables

WH	Weighting of each symbol on each wheel
R	Symbol currently showing
SC	Screen memory
CL	Colour memory
CR	Money
W	Amount won
WT	Weighting of wheel
FT	Random function to select symbol

Listing

Initialise Game and Draw Title Screen

```
10    VOL 8:COLOR0,2,6:COLOR4,2,6:COLOR1,14,4
20    PRINT "▙ ▣ ▲ ▲ ▲ ▲ ┬ ═ ╗ ┌ ═ ▲ ┌ ═ ▲ ┬ ▲ ▲ ▲ ▲ ▲ ┌ ┬
      ╝ ▲ ┬ ▲ ┬ ▲ ┬ ▲ ┬ ▲ ┬ ▲ ╔ ═ ╗ ▲ ║ "
30    PRINT "▲ ▲ ▲ ▲ ├ ┬ ╝ ├ ═ ▲ ├ ═ ▲ ║ ▲ ▲ ▲ ▲ ▲ ▲ ║ ▲ ▲
      ├ ═ ┤ ▲ ║ ▲ ║ \ ║ ▲ ║ ▲ ┬ ▲ ║ "
40    PRINT "▲ ▲ ▲ ▲ ┴ ╚ ▲ ╚ ═ ▲ ╚ ═ ▲ ╚ ═ ▲ ▲ ▲ ▲ ▲ ▲ ┴ ▲ ▲
      ┴ ▲ ┴ ▲ ┴ ▲ ┴ ▲ ┴ ▲ ╚ ═ ╝ ▲ ● "
50    DIMWH(3,4):DIMR(3):SC=1024:CL=55296:CR=10:W=0:
      GOSUB 680:FOR I=0 TO 3:R(I)=0:NEXT
60    COLOR1,2,3:PRINT "▣ ▣ ▲ ▲ ▲ ╔ ═ ═ ═ ═ ═ ╗ ▲ ▲ ╔ ═ ═
      ═ ═ ═ ╗ ▲ ▲ ╔ ═ ═ ═ ═ ═ ╗ ▲ ▲ ╔ ═ ═ ═ ═ ═ ╗ "
70    PRINT "▣ ▣ ▣ ║ ▚ ▚ ▚ ▚ ▚ ║ ▲ ▲ ║ ▚ ▚ ▚ ▚ ▚ ║ ▲ ▲ ║
      ▚ ▚ ▚ ▚ ▚ ║ ▲ ▲ ║ ▚ ▚ ▚ ▚ ▚ ║ "
80    PRINT "▣ ▣ ▣ ║ ▚ ▚ ▚ ▚ ▚ ║ ▲ ▲ ║ ▚ ▚ ▚ ▚ ▚ ║ ▲ ▲ ║
      ▚ ▚ ▚ ▚ ▚ ║ ▲ ▲ ║ ▚ ▚ ▚ ▚ ▚ ║ "
90    PRINT "▣ ▣ ▣ ║ ▚ ▚ ▚ ▚ ▚ ║ ▲ ▲ ║ ▚ ▚ ▚ ▚ ▚ ║ ▲ ▲ ║
      ▚ ▚ ▚ ▚ ▚ ║ ▲ ▲ ║ ▚ ▚ ▚ ▚ ▚ ║ "
100   PRINT "▣ ▣ ▣ ║ ▚ ▚ ▚ ▚ ▚ ║ ▲ ▲ ║ ▚ ▚ ▚ ▚ ▚ ║ ▲ ▲ ║
      ▚ ▚ ▚ ▚ ▚ ║ ▲ ▲ ║ ▚ ▚ ▚ ▚ ▚ ║ "
110   PRINT "▣ ▣ ▣ ║ ▚ ▚ ▚ ▚ ▚ ║ ▲ ▲ ║ ▚ ▚ ▚ ▚ ▚ ║ ▲ ▲ ║
      ▚ ▚ ▚ ▚ ▚ ║ ▲ ▲ ║ ▚ ▚ ▚ ▚ ▚ ║ "
120   PRINT "▣ ▣ ▣ ╚ ═ ═ ═ ═ ═ ╝ ▲ ▲ ╚ ═ ═ ═ ═ ═ ╝ ▲ ▲ ╚
      ═ ═ ═ ═ ═ ╝ ▲ ▲ ╚ ═ ═ ═ ═ ═ ╝ "
130   PRINT :COLOR1,2,4:PRINT "▣ ▣ ▲ ▲ ▲ ' £ ' ▲ T O ▲ P
      L A Y ▲ ▲ ▲ ▲ ▲ ▲ ▲ ▲ ' = ' ▲ T O ▲ Q U I T "
140   GOSUB 210:GOSUB 240
```

Get input

```
150   GETA$:IF A$=""THEN 150
160   IF A$="= "THEN 200
170   IF A$<>"£ "THEN 150
180   CR=CR-1:GOSUB 210:GOSUB 240:GOSUB 280:GOSUB 580:
      IF CR=0THEN 200
190   GOTO 150
```

End Game

```
200   COLOR1,6:PRINT "{HOME}{DOWN}{DOWN}{DOWN}{DOWN}{DOWN}{DOWN}{DOWN}{DOWN}{DOWN}{DOWN}{DOWN}{DOWN}{DOWN}{DOWN}{DOWN}{DOWN}{DOWN}
      {DOWN}{DOWN}{DOWN}{RIGHT}{RIGHT}{RIGHT}{RIGHT}{RIGHT}{RIGHT}W E L L , ▲T H A N K ▲Y O U ▲
      F O R ▲P L A Y I N G ! ":END
```

Print Credit Rating

```
210   COLOR1,13,4:PRINT "{HOME}{DOWN}{DOWN}{DOWN}{DOWN}{DOWN}{DOWN}{DOWN}{DOWN}{DOWN}{DOWN}{DOWN}{DOWN}{DOWN}{DOWN}{DOWN}{DOWN}{DOWN}
      {DOWN}{DOWN}▲▲▲▲C R E D I T ▲$▲▲▲▲▲▲▲{LEFT}{LEFT}{LEFT}{LEFT}{LEFT}
      {LEFT}";CR
220   COLOR1,8:PRINT "{HOME}{DOWN}{DOWN}{DOWN}{DOWN}{DOWN}{DOWN}{DOWN}{DOWN}{DOWN}{DOWN}{DOWN}{DOWN}{DOWN}{DOWN}{DOWN}{DOWN}{DOWN}
      {RIGHT}{RIGHT}{RIGHT}{RIGHT}{RIGHT}{RIGHT}{RIGHT}{RIGHT}{RIGHT}{RIGHT}{RIGHT}{RIGHT}{RIGHT}";CR
230   RETURN
```

Print Payout

```
240   COLOR1,13,4:PRINT "{HOME}{DOWN}{DOWN}{DOWN}{DOWN}{DOWN}{DOWN}{DOWN}{DOWN}{DOWN}{DOWN}{DOWN}{DOWN}{DOWN}{DOWN}{DOWN}{DOWN}{DOWN}
      {DOWN}{DOWN}{RIGHT}{RIGHT}{RIGHT}{RIGHT}{RIGHT}{RIGHT}{RIGHT}{RIGHT}{RIGHT}{RIGHT}{RIGHT}{RIGHT}{RIGHT}{RIGHT}{RIGHT}{RIGHT}{RIGHT}{RIGHT}{RIGHT}{RIGHT}{RIGHT}{RIGHT}{RIGHT}P A
      Y O U T ▲$▲▲▲▲▲▲{LEFT}{LEFT}{LEFT}{LEFT}{LEFT}{LEFT}"
250   RETURN
260   COLOR1,8:PRINT "{HOME}{DOWN}{DOWN}{DOWN}{DOWN}{DOWN}{DOWN}{DOWN}{DOWN}{DOWN}{DOWN}{DOWN}{DOWN}{DOWN}{DOWN}{DOWN}{DOWN}{DOWN}
      {RIGHT}{RIGHT}{RIGHT}{RIGHT}{RIGHT}{RIGHT}{RIGHT}{RIGHT}{RIGHT}{RIGHT}{RIGHT}{RIGHT}{RIGHT}{RIGHT}{RIGHT}{RIGHT}{RIGHT}{RIGHT}{RIGHT}{RIGHT}{RIGHT}{RIGHT}{RIGHT}{RIGHT}{RIGHT}
      {RIGHT}{RIGHT}{RIGHT}{RIGHT}{RIGHT}{RIGHT}";W
270   RETURN
```

Spin Wheels

```
280   FOR I=1 TO 4:COLOR1,10
290   PRINT "{HOME}{DOWN}{DOWN}{DOWN}{DOWN}{DOWN}{DOWN}{DOWN}{DOWN}";:FOR K=1 TO 5:FOR J=1
       TO 4:IF I<=JTHEN PRINT "▬{RIGHT}{RIGHT}{RIGHT}{RIGHT}▚▚▚▚▚";:
      GOTO 310
300   PRINT "{RIGHT}{RIGHT}{RIGHT}{RIGHT}{RIGHT}{RIGHT}{RIGHT}{RIGHT}{RIGHT}{RIGHT}";
310   NEXTJ:PRINT :NEXTK
320   PRINT "{HOME}{DOWN}{DOWN}{DOWN}{DOWN}{DOWN}{DOWN}{DOWN}{DOWN}";:FOR K=1 TO 5:FOR J=1
       TO 4:IF I<=JTHEN PRINT "▬{RIGHT}{RIGHT}{RIGHT}{RIGHT}▚▚▚▚▚";:
      GOTO 340
330   PRINT "{RIGHT}{RIGHT}{RIGHT}{RIGHT}{RIGHT}{RIGHT}{RIGHT}{RIGHT}{RIGHT}{RIGHT}";
340   NEXTJ:PRINT :NEXTK
350   IF I=1THEN PRINT "{HOME}{DOWN}{DOWN}{DOWN}{DOWN}{DOWN}{DOWN}{DOWN}{DOWN}{RIGHT}{RIGHT}{RIGHT}";:
      GOSUB 410
360   IF I=2THEN PRINT "{HOME}{DOWN}{DOWN}{DOWN}{DOWN}{DOWN}{DOWN}{DOWN}{DOWN}{RIGHT}{RIGHT}{RIGHT}{RIGHT}{RIGHT}{RIGHT}{RIGHT}{RIGHT}{RIGHT}
       {RIGHT}{RIGHT}{RIGHT}{RIGHT}";:GOSUB 410
370   IF I=3THEN PRINT "{HOME}{DOWN}{DOWN}{DOWN}{DOWN}{DOWN}{DOWN}{DOWN}{DOWN}{RIGHT}{RIGHT}{RIGHT}{RIGHT}{RIGHT}{RIGHT}{RIGHT}{RIGHT}{RIGHT}
       {RIGHT}{RIGHT}{RIGHT}{RIGHT}{RIGHT}{RIGHT}{RIGHT}{RIGHT}{RIGHT}{RIGHT}{RIGHT}{RIGHT}{RIGHT}{RIGHT}";:GOSUB 410
380   IF I=4THEN PRINT "{HOME}{DOWN}{DOWN}{DOWN}{DOWN}{DOWN}{DOWN}{DOWN}{DOWN}{RIGHT}{RIGHT}{RIGHT}{RIGHT}{RIGHT}{RIGHT}{RIGHT}{RIGHT}{RIGHT}
       {RIGHT}{RIGHT}{RIGHT}{RIGHT}{RIGHT}{RIGHT}{RIGHT}{RIGHT}{RIGHT}{RIGHT}{RIGHT}{RIGHT}{RIGHT}{RIGHT}{RIGHT}{RIGHT}{RIGHT}{RIGHT}{RIGHT}{RIGHT}{RIGHT}{RIGHT}{RIGHT}{RIGHT}";:
      GOSUB 410
```

```
390   SOUND 1,200,5:NEXTI
400   RETURN
```

Select and Draw Symbol

```
410   WT=0:FOR J=0 TO 4:WT=WT+WH(I-1,J):NEXT
420   FT=INT(RND(0)*WT+1):J=0
430   FT=FT-WH(I-1,J):IF FT<=0THEN R(I-1)=J:GOTO 470
440   J=J+1:IF J<4THEN 430
450   R(I-1)=4
460   PRINT "▣▲▲▲▲▲◙▌▌▌▌▌▌▌▌▌▌▲▧✚▧▲◙▌▌▌▌▌▌▌▌
      ▌▌▲▧✚▧▲◙▌▌▌▌▌▌▌▌▌▌▌▌▲▧✚▧▲◙▌▌▌▌▌▌▌▌▌▌▲▲▲
      ▲▲":RETURN
470   IF J>0THEN 500
480   COLOR1,10,4:PRINT "▲▲▲▲▲◙▌▌▌▌▌▌▌▌▌▌▲▲▲□▲
      ◙▌▌▌▌▌▌▌▌▌▌▲▲/▧▲";
490   COLOR1,3,4:PRINT "◙▌▌▌▌▌▌▌▌▌▌▲●▲●▲◙▌▌▌▌▌▌▌▌▌▌
      ▲▲▲▲▲":RETURN
500   IF J>1THEN 530
510   COLOR1,10,4:PRINT "▲▲▲▲▲◙▌▌▌▌▌▌▌▌▌▌▲▲▧▲▲
      ";
520   COLOR1,5,4:PRINT "◙▌▌▌▌▌▌▌▌▌▌▲●●●▲◙▌▌▌▌▌▌▌▌▌▌
      ▲▲●▲▲◙▌▌▌▌▌▌▌▌▌▌▲▲▲▲▲":RETURN
530   IF J>2THEN 560
540   COLOR1,6,4:PRINT "▲▲▲▲▲◙▌▌▌▌▌▌▌▌▌▌▲▧V▧▲"
      ;
550   COLOR1,9,4:PRINT "◙▌▌▌▌▌▌▌▌▌▌▲▲✱▲▲◙▌▌▌▌▌▌▌▌▌▌
      ▲▲✱▲▲◙▌▌▌▌▌▌▌▌▌▌▲▲▲▲▲▲":RETURN
560   COLOR1,3,6:PRINT "▲▲▲▲▲◙▌▌▌▌▌▌▌▌▌▌▲□□□▲"
      ;
570   COLOR1,16,4:PRINT "◙▌▌▌▌▌▌▌▌▌▌▲◥◙▲▬◤▲◙▌▌▌▌
      ▌▌▌▌▌▌▲▲□▲▲◙▌▌▌▌▌▌▌▌▌▌▲▲▲▲▲▲":RETURN
```

Calculate Payout

```
580   W=0
590   IF R(0)=0THEN W=W+1:IF R(1)=0THEN W=W+1:IF R(2)=0
      THEN W=W+4:IF R(3)=0THEN W=W+17
600   IF R(0)=1ANDR(1)=1THEN W=W+3:IF R(2)=1THEN W=W+13:
      IF R(3)=1THEN W=W+80
610   IF R(0)=2ANDR(1)=2THEN W=W+4:IF R(2)=2THEN W=W+60:
      IF R(3)=2THEN W=W+80
620   IF R(0)=3ANDR(1)=3ANDR(2)=3THEN W=W+176:IF R(3)=3
      THEN W=W+154
630   IF R(0)=4ANDR(1)=4ANDR(2)=4THEN W=W+120:IF R(3)=4
      THEN W=W+2000
640   GOSUB 260:P=W
```

```
650    IF W>10THEN FOR J=1 TO INT(P/10):CR=CR+10:W=W-10:
       GOSUB 220:SOUND 1,990,1:NEXT
660    IF W>0THEN FOR J=1 TO W:CR=CR+1:W=W-1:GOSUB 220:
       SOUND 1,1000,1:NEXT
670    RETURN
```

Establish Weighting of Wheels

```
680    WH(0,0)=8:WH(0,1)=8:WH(0,2)=5:WH(0,3)=3:WH(0,4)=1
690    WH(1,0)=4:WH(1,1)=4:WH(1,2)=3:WH(1,3)=3:WH(1,4)=1
700    WH(2,0)=3:WH(2,1)=4:WH(2,2)=3:WH(2,3)=4:WH(2,4)=2
710    WH(3,0)=2:WH(3,1)=4:WH(3,2)=3:WH(3,3)=5:WH(3,4)=1
720    RETURN
```

ChexSum Tables

10	= 2040	250	= 143	490	= 3514
20	= 5176	260	= 3062	500	= 778
30	= 4948	270	= 143	510	= 2387
40	= 4709	280	= 1179	520	= 5044
50	= 5489	290	= 5352	530	= 779
60	= 7613	300	= 567	540	= 2539
70	= 6157	310	= 697	550	= 4673
80	= 6157	320	= 5223	560	= 2570
90	= 6157	330	= 567	570	= 5030
100	= 6157	340	= 697	580	= 316
110	= 6157	350	= 1670	590	= 6033
120	= 6661	360	= 1944	600	= 5293
130	= 3334	370	= 2402	610	= 5293
140	= 672	380	= 2962	620	= 4503
150	= 1212	390	= 858	630	= 4556
160	= 919	400	= 143	640	= 725
170	= 1141	410	= 2975	650	= 4905
180	= 3207	420	= 1921	660	= 4196
190	= 526	430	= 3786	670	= 143
200	= 4714	440	= 1443	680	= 3673
210	= 3984	450	= 718	690	= 3680
220	= 2028	460	= 7048	700	= 3681
230	= 143	470	= 777	710	= 3684
240	= 5181	480	= 3756	720	= 143
				TOTAL	= 222653

Road Patrol

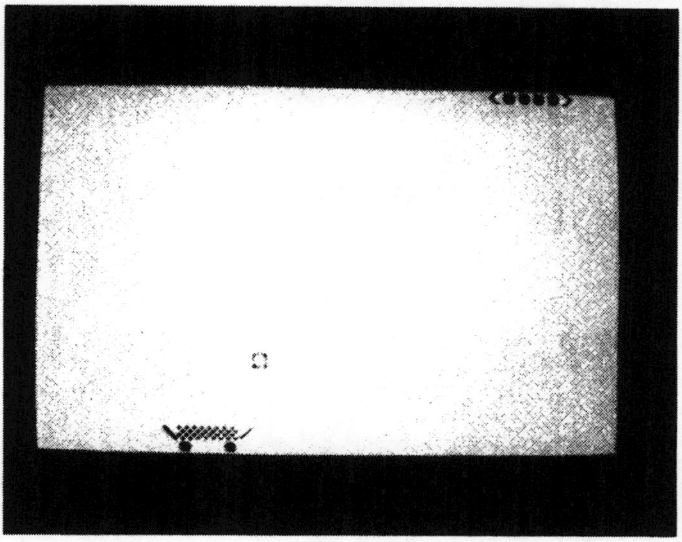

CLASSIFICATION: Shoot Up

Move your vehicle left and right along the bottom of the screen, avoiding the aliens' bombs descending upon you. You can fire at the aliens by pressing the SPACE bar. Move left and right using the I and P keys.

PROGRAMMING SUGGESTIONS

Increase the speed of the missiles so that the player's reactions have to be swifter. Occasionally place barriers around the patrol car so that it is paralyzed.

PROGRAM
Variables

PA$	Patrol car
SA$	Alien ship
MS	Missile in flight flag
SV	Start of screen
SC	Score
K1	Start of machine language routine
E	Flag to indicate end of game

Listing

```
10    REM ROAD PATROL
20    RESTORE:FOR I=1 TO 40:LN$=LN$+"▴ ":NEXT:PA$="╲ ✲ ✲
      ✲ ✲ ⁄ ◙ ▮▮ ▮▮ ▮▮ ▮▮ ▮▮ ▮▮ ▴ ● ▴ ▴ ● ":LT$="◙ "
30    FOR I=1 TO 23:LT$=LT$+"◙ ":NEXT
40    FOR I=1 TO 40:J$=J$+"◙ ":NEXT:FOR I=1 TO 25:H$=H$
      +"◙ ":NEXT
50    RT$="▴ ▴ ▴ ▴ ▴ ▴ ":K1=12000:SV=3072
```

Read In Machine Language Program; Define the Ship and Alien

```
60    FOR I=0 TO 10:READA:POKE 12000+I,A:NEXT
70    PRINT "◙ ";:GOSUB 420:SA$="▴ < ● ● ● ● > ▴ "
80    GOSUB 490:PRINT "◙ ";
90    PRINT "◙ ";:E=0:PO=17:PRINT LT$;LEFT$(LN$,PO);PA$;:
      F=0:F1=0:RO=2
100   MS=0:ML=0
110   PRINT "◙ ";"S C O R E : ▴ ";:PRINT USING"# # # ";SC
      ;:A=PEEK(198):IF A=33THEN GOSUB 190
```

Main Logic Loop; Move Your Ship Backwards and Forwards

```
120   IF A=41THEN GOSUB 220
130   IF A=60THEN F=1
140   IF FTHEN GOSUB 250:IF ETHEN GOTO 90
150   GOSUB 310
160   JC=INT(RND(1)*LV):IF JC=1THEN F1=1
170   IF F1THEN GOSUB 330:IF ETHEN 90
180   GOTO 110
190   PRINT LT$;:SYS K1
200   IF PO>1THEN PO=PO-1
210   PRINT LEFT$(LN$,PO);PA$;:RETURN
220   PRINT LT$;:SYS K1
230   IF PO<35THEN PO=PO+1:PRINT LEFT$(LN$,PO);PA$;:
      RETURN
240   RETURN
250   IF MS=1THEN 270
260   PT=PO+2:R=20:MS=1
270   POKE TM,32:TM=(SV+(R*40)+PT)
280   IF PEEK(TM)<>32THEN GOSUB 390:E=1:MS=0:RETURN
290   IF R=0THEN MS=0:POKE TM,32:F=0:RETURN
300   POKE TM,209:R=R-1:RETURN
310   IF CO=30THEN GOSUB 570
320   PRINT "◙ ";LEFT$(H$,RO);LEFT$(J$,CO);SA$;:CO=CO+1:
      RETURN
```

Alien Drops Bombs On You; You Fire Up at Alien, Check for Crash

```
330  IF ML=1THEN 350
340  ZN=CO+2:PF=RO+1:ML=1
350  POKE RD,32:RD=SV+(PF*40)+ZN
360  IF PEEK(RD)<>32THEN GOSUB 540:E=1:RETURN
370  IF PF=24THEN ML=0:F1=0:RETURN
380  POKE RD,209:PF=PF+1:RETURN
390  FOR I=1 TO 15:FOR J=1 TO 20:COLOR4,I,4:NEXT:NEXT:E
     =1
400  FOR I=990 TO 1023:SOUND 3,I,5:NEXT
410  SC=SC+20:COLOR4,1,3:COLOR0,4,5:RETURN
420  PRINT "▣ ";TAB(13);"P A T R O L ▲ C A R "
430  PRINT :PRINT :PRINT "A V O I D ▲ T H E ▲ A L I E N
     ▲ U S I N G ▲ T H E ▲ I ▲ K E Y ▲ T O ▲ M O V E ":
     PRINT
440  PRINT "L E F T , ▲ T H E ▲ P ▲ K E Y ▲ T O ▲ M O V
     E ▲ R I G H T ▲ A N D ▲ T H E ▲ ":PRINT
450  PRINT "S P A C E B A R ▲ T O ▲ F I R E ▲ A T ▲ T H
     E ▲ A L I E N . G O O D ▲ L U C K ! ":PRINT :
     PRINT :PRINT
460  PRINT TAB(8);"P R E S S ▲ R E T U R N ▲ T O ▲ S T A
      R T ";
470  GETA$:IF A$<>CHR$(13)THEN 470
480  RETURN
490  PRINT "▣ E N T E R ▲ L E V E L ▲ O F ▲ D I F F I C
     U L T Y ▲ 8 - E A S Y ▲ 1 - H A R D ";
500  GETA$:IF A$=""THEN 500
510  IF A$<"0 "ORA$>"9 "THEN 500
520  LV=VAL(A$):RETURN
530  DATA162,79,169,32,157,152,15,202,208,250,96
540  PRINT "▣ ";TAB(12);"▮ P A T R O L ▲ C A R ▲ D E S T
      R O Y E D ▬ ";:SC=SC-10
550  FOR I=1 TO 10:SOUND 1,5,8:SOUND 2,5,4:NEXT:FOR I=1
      TO 1000:NEXT:COLOR0,2,5:COLOR0,4,5
560  PRINT "▣ ";TAB(12);"▲ ▲ ▲ ▲ ▲ ▲ ▲ ▲ ▲ ▲ ▲ ▲ ▲ ▲ ▲ ▲ ▲ ▲ ▲ ▲
      ▲ ▲ ▲ ▲ ";:RETURN
570  PRINT "▣ ";LEFT$(H$,RO);LEFT$(J$,CO);RT$;
580  RO=INT(RND(1)*20):IF RO<=1THEN 580:ELSECO=1
590  RETURN
```

ChexSum Tables

10	=	0	210	=	1402	410	=	2154
20	=	6267	220	=	770	420	=	1764
30	=	1914	230	=	3159	430	=	4225
40	=	3636	240	=	143	440	=	3485
50	=	2030	250	=	878	450	=	4251
60	=	2122	260	=	1656	460	=	2394
70	=	2476	270	=	2199	470	=	1707
80	=	824	280	=	2644	480	=	143
90	=	4485	290	=	2170	490	=	3682
100	=	855	300	=	1399	500	=	1212
110	=	4004	310	=	1067	510	=	1530
120	=	975	320	=	3192	520	=	936
130	=	973	330	=	872	530	=	2301
140	=	1639	340	=	2026	540	=	3869
150	=	295	350	=	2195	550	=	4361
160	=	2447	360	=	2158	560	=	2126
170	=	1309	370	=	1809	570	=	2084
180	=	526	380	=	1557	580	=	3113
190	=	770	390	=	2992	590	=	143
200	=	1459	400	=	1766	TOTAL	=	120540

Letterbox

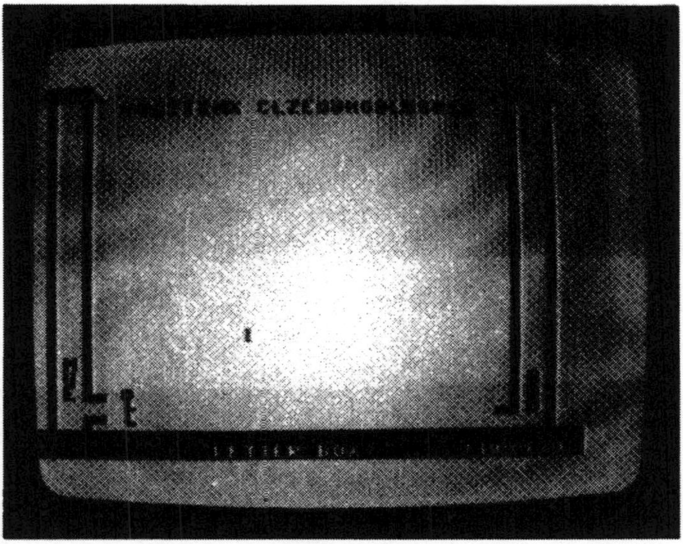

CLASSIFICATION: Educational

Catch the falling letters and post them in the letterbox on the left. If you do not catch them, they will go into the dead-letter box on the right. If you fill the good-letter box before the dead-letter box, then you will go to the next of the five floors. However, should the dead-letter box be filled first, you will go back to the previous floor. The letters fall faster for each higher floor.

Move the mailman left and right with the left and right cursor keys prior to the letter falling. When the letter is falling the mailman can only be moved right by pressing the key that matches the letter that is falling. To move the mailman left, use the same key and the shift key.

PROGRAMMING SUGGESTIONS

Have more than one letter falling to the ground and award bonus points if the player catches the letters.

PROGRAM
Variables

A$(24)	Random letter table
A$(0)	Used for mailman movement with cursor key
C$	Colour table
LM$	Left facing mailman
RM$	Right facing mailman
LV	Floor level
S	Sound register
SL	Good letter stack (number from top)
SR	Missed letter stack (number from top)
X4	Horizontal location of mailman
DX	Direction of mailman
N	Number of dropped letters
K	Row number of dropped letters
M$	Key pressed
M	ASC value of pressed key
K1	Screen location for stacking letters
F	Colour of dropped letters

Listing

```
10     REM LETTER BOX
```

Define Variables; Draw the Post Office

```
20     VOL 8
30     DN$="▣ ⊡ ⊡ ⊡ ⊡ ⊡ ⊡ ⊡ ⊡ ⊡ ⊡ ⊡ ⊡ ⊡ ⊡ ⊡ ⊡ ⊡ ⊡ ⊡ ⊡
       ⊡ "
40     BL$="▀ ■ ■ ■ ■ ■ ▲ ▲ ▲ ▲ ▲ ▲ ▲ ▲ ▲ ▲ ▲ ▲ ▲ ▲ ▲ ▲ ▲ ▲ ▲ ▲ ▲ ▲ ▲ ▲ ▲ ▲ ▲ ▲ ▲ ▲ ▲ ▲ ▲ ▲ ▲ ▲ ▲ ▲ ▲ ▲ ▲ ▲ ▲ ▲ ▲ "
50     RT$="▣ ■ ■ ■ ■ ■ ■ ■ ■ ■ ■ ■ ■ ■ ■ ■ ■ ■ ■ ■ ■ ■ ■ ■ ■ ■ ■ ■ ■ ■ ■ ■ ■ ■ ■ ■ ■ ■ ■ ■ ■ ■ ■ "
60     DIMA$(24):A$(0)="■ ":C$="▣ ◣ ▣ ▣ ▣ ▣ ▣ ▣ ⊗ "
70     LM$="■ ● ▲ ⊡ ▮▮ ▮▮ ┤ ▲ ⊡ ▮▮ ▮▮ ▦ ▲ ":RM$="■ ▲ ● ⊡ ▮▮ ▮▮ ▲
       ├ ⊡ ▮▮ ▮▮ ▲ ▦ ":LV=1
80     SL=20:SR=21:X1=INT(RND(.)*8)+10:DX=1
90     IF LV<1THEN LV=1
100    IF LV>5THEN LV=5
110    GOSUB 340
120    FOR L=1 TO 24:A$(L)=CHR$(INT(RND(.)*26+65)):NEXT
130    PRINT LEFT$(DN$,21)RIGHT$(RT$,X1)RM$;
140    E=INT(RND(.)*4)+1:F=E+6-LV
150    FOR J=E TO F:PRINT "▣ ■ ■ ■ ■ ■ ▲ ▲ ▲ ▲ ▲ ▲ ▲ ▲ ▲ ▲ ▲ ▲ ▲ ▲ ▲ ▲ ▲ ▲ ▲ ▲ ▲ ▲ ▲ ▲ ▲ ▲ ▲ ▲ ▲ ▲ ▲ ▲ ▲ ▲ ▲ ▲ ▲ ▲ ▲ ▲ ▲ ▲ ▲ ▲ ▲ "
160    N=0:FOR I=1 TO 24
170    GOSUB 440
180    PRINT "▣ ⊡ "MID$(C$,J,1)TAB(I+5)A$(I);
190    NEXT:NEXT
200    PRINT "▣ ";:N=INT(RND(.)*24)+1
210    FOR K=1 TO 22
220    PRINT LEFT$(DN$,K)TAB(5+N)"▲ ⊡ ▮▮ "MID$(C$,F,1)A$(N)
       "▮▮ ";
230    FOR T=1 TO 85-(LV*12):NEXT:GOSUB 440
240    IF SL=0THEN LV=LV+1:N=SR:GOSUB 700:GOTO 80
250    IF K=23THEN 120
260    NEXT
270    FOR T=4+N TO 32
280    IF T=X1THEN GOSUB 510:T=T+1:GOTO 300
290    PRINT TAB(T)"▲ "MID$(C$,F)A$(N):PRINT "□ ";
300    NEXT
310    GOSUB 760
320    IF SR=0THEN LV=LV-1:N=SL:GOSUB 730:GOTO 80
330    GOTO 120
340    COLOR0,7,5:COLOR4,7,5:PRINT "▣ "
350    PRINT "▣ ▣ ▣ ◤ ▲ ▲ ▲ ◥ ▀ ▲ ▲ ▲ ▲ ▲ ▲ ▲ ▲ ▲ ▲ ▲ ▲ ▲ ▲ ▲ ▲ ▲ ▲ ▲ ▲ ▲ ▲ ▲ ▲ ▲ ▲ ▲ ▲ ▲ ▲ ▲ ▲ ▲ ▲ ⊠ ⊗ ◤ ▲ ▲ ▲ ◥ "
```

```
360   FOR I=1 TO 22
370   PRINT "▜■▐▜▚▐▀▲▲▲▲▲▲▲▲▲▲▲▲▲▲▲
      ▲▲▲▲▲▲▲▲▲▲▲▲▲▲▲▐▜▚▐▀"
380   NEXT
390   PRINT "▚■▲▲▲▲▲▲▲▲▲▲▲▲▲▲▲▲▲▲▲
      ▲▲▲▲▲▲▲▲▲▲▲▲▲▲▲▲▲"
400   PRINT "▚■▲▲▲▲▲▲▲▲▲▲▲▲▲▲L E T T E R▲B
      O X▲▲▲▲▲▲▲▲F L O O R▲▲▲▌▌▌"LV"▚"
410   PRINT LEFT$(DN$,21)"▜▜▜▜▜▄▜▌▌▲▜▚▄";
420   PRINT LEFT$(BL$,29)"□▌▌▄"
430   RETURN
```

Move Mailman Left or Right, Depending on Key Pressed

```
440   REM MOVE MAILMAN
450   GETM$:IF M$=""THEN 540
460   IF M$="▌"THEN PRINT "▚":END
470   IF M$=A$(N)THEN MM$=RM$:DX=1:GOTO 510
480   M=ASC(M$):M=M-128
490   IF M=ASC(A$(N)+CHR$(0))THEN MM$=LM$:DX=-1:GOTO 510
500   M$="":GOTO 540
510   PRINT LEFT$(DN$,21)RIGHT$(RT$,X1)MM$;
520   X1=X1+DX:IF X1<5THEN X1=5
530   IF X1>29THEN X1=29
540   IF K<20ORK>22THEN RETURN
550   IF DX=-1AND(X1<(N+3)ORX1>(N+5))THEN RETURN
560   IF DX=1AND(X1<(N+4)ORX1>(N+6))THEN RETURN
570   FOR T=5+N TO 5 STEP -1
580   PRINT LEFT$(DN$,22)TAB(T)MID$(C$,F)A$(N)"□"LM$
590   NEXT
600   FOR T=5 TO 2 STEP -1
610   PRINT LEFT$(DN$,22)TAB(T)MID$(C$,F)A$(N)"▲"
620   NEXT
630   PRINT LEFT$(DN$,22)TAB(5)"□"LM$
640   REM GOT LETTER STACK
650   FOR K1=3074+SL*40 TO 3074+20*40 STEP 40
660   POKE K1,PEEK(K1+40)
670   NEXT
680   POKE K1,32:SL=SL-1
690   N=1:GOSUB 700:K=23:X1=5:RETURN
```

Make Sound for Dead and Live Stacks; Put Letter in Dead Stack

```
700   REM SOUND
710   SOUND 1,25,25
720   RETURN
730   REM SOUND
740   SOUND 2,50,15
```

```
750     RETURN
760     REM MISSED LETTER STACK
770     FOR K1=3105+SR*40 TO 3105+21*40 STEP 40
780     POKE K1,PEEK(K1+40)
790     NEXT
800     POKE K1,32:SR=SR-1
810     N=1:GOSUB 730:RETURN
```

ChexSum Tables

10	=	0	280	=	2318	550	=	3050
20	=	277	290	=	1981	560	=	2853
30	=	1061	300	=	131	570	=	1327
40	=	2317	310	=	303	580	=	2576
50	=	2115	320	=	2939	590	=	131
60	=	2588	330	=	527	600	=	1069
70	=	4790	340	=	1528	610	=	2229
80	=	3110	350	=	3171	620	=	131
90	=	1126	360	=	710	630	=	1565
100	=	1128	370	=	2957	640	=	0
110	=	299	380	=	131	650	=	2599
120	=	3090	390	=	2111	660	=	1039
130	=	1826	400	=	3765	670	=	131
140	=	2327	410	=	1859	680	=	1252
150	=	2418	420	=	1529	690	=	1780
160	=	1116	430	=	143	700	=	0
170	=	302	440	=	0	710	=	586
180	=	1888	450	=	1232	720	=	143
190	=	320	460	=	1435	730	=	0
200	=	1767	470	=	2647	740	=	584
210	=	710	480	=	1421	750	=	143
220	=	3059	490	=	3667	760	=	0
230	=	2037	500	=	994	770	=	2609
240	=	2921	510	=	1833	780	=	1039
250	=	839	520	=	1946	790	=	131
260	=	131	530	=	1197	800	=	1284
270	=	984	540	=	1380	810	=	878
						TOTAL	=	117530

Ganymede

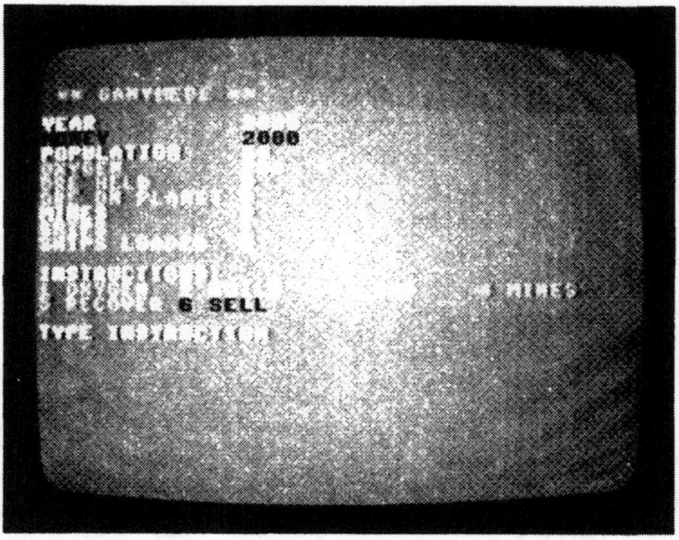

CLASSIFICATION: Strategy

The purpose of this game is to run a small moon base on Jupiter's satellite, Ganymede. You must attempt to set up a mine on Jupiter's surface and collect the valuable ore deposited there.

This treasure means life to you as you must sell it to Earth to obtain money to buy supplies and the vital oxygen which your people need. You must also build more mines as they can be destroyed by storms on Jupiter's surface. Can you sell enough ore to Earth to buy the oxygen you need, or will you suffocate?

Commands are:

1. Import oxygen from earth.
2. Build spaceships.
3. Load spaceships with mining equipment and personnel.
4. Send your loaded ship to set up mines.
5. Recover some mined ore from the surface of Jupiter.
6. Sell recovered ore to Earth.

PROGRAM
Variables

MI	Mines
M	Money
S	Ships
L	Ships loaded
OB	Ore held
OM	Ore on planet
P	Population
Y	Year
O	Oxygen
OS	Total ore sold
F	Fuel
N	Number of aliens

Listing

```
10    REM GANYMEDE
20    MI=0:M=2000:S=1:L=0:OBB=0
30    OM=0:P=50:Y=0:O=200
40    DEFFNR(R)=INT(RND(R)*R+1):OS=0
50    COLOR4,7,4:COLOR0,13,3
```

Clear All Variables; Print Instructions and Supplies

```
60    PRINT "▚■▲**▲G A N Y M E D E▲**"
70    PRINT :PRINT "■Y E A R▲▲▲▲▲▲▲▲▲▲▲"2000+Y:
      PRINT "■M O N E Y▲▲▲▲▲▲▲▲▲▲"M
80    PRINT "■P O P U L A T I O N▲▲▲"P:PRINT "■O X
      Y G E N▲▲▲▲▲▲▲▲"O
90    PRINT "■O R E▲H E L D▲▲▲▲▲"OB:PRINT "O R E
      ▲O N▲P L A N E T "OM
100   PRINT "■M I N E S▲▲▲▲▲▲▲▲▲▲"MI
110   PRINT "◥S H I P S▲▲▲▲▲▲▲▲▲▲"S:PRINT "S H I
      P S▲L O A D E D▲"L
120   PRINT :PRINT "■I N S T R U C T I O N S:"
130   PRINT "■1▲O X Y G E N ","◥2▲B U I L D ","◥3
      ▲L O A D ","■4▲M I N E S "
140   PRINT "■5▲R E C O V E R ","■6▲S E L L ":
      PRINT :PRINT "■T Y P E▲I N S T R U C T I O N "
150   GETA$:IF A$="W "THEN 190
160   IF A$<"1 "ORA$>"6 "THEN 150
170   PRINT "▚ ":ON VAL(A$)GOSUB 360,430,480,540,670,830:
      PRINT "■P R E S S▲A▲K E Y "
180   GETA$:IF A$=""THEN 180
```

Print Report for Game, Amount of Oxygen Left, Supplies Used

```
190   PRINT "▚◥▲▲▲R E P O R T▲F O R▲Y E A R ":Y
      =Y+1:PRINT
200   R=FNR(P/3):P=P+R:PRINT "■ "R"C H I L D R E N▲W E
      R E▲B O R N ":O=O-P
210   IF O<PTHEN PRINT "■ "P-O"P E O P L E▲D I E D ":
      PRINT "O F▲O X Y G E N▲S T A R V A T I O N ":P
      =0
220   IF MI>0ANDFNR(10)=10THEN PRINT "■M I N E "FNR(MI)"
      W A S▲D E S T R O Y E D ":MI=MI-1
230   IF MI>0ANDFNR(10)>5THEN 220
```

```
240   IF P<2THEN PRINT :PRINT "■L I F E ▲ O N ▲ B A S E
      ▲ ▲ ▲ ▲ ▲ ▲ ▲ ▲ ▲ ▲ ▲ E X T I N G U I S H E D ":
      GOTO 920
250   IF MI>0THEN R=FNR(MI*4)*FNR(MI):PRINT "■ "R"K G ' S
      ▲ O F ▲ O R E ▲ W E R E ":PRINT "M I N E D ":OM=OM
      +R
260   IF OS>3000THEN PRINT "◣ T H E ▲ G O V E R N M E N T
      ▲ H A S ▲ A L L ▲ T H E ▲ O R E ▲ I T ▲ W A N T S
      ":GOTO 920
270   R=FNR(P):PRINT "◣ "R"U N I T S ▲ O F ▲ O X Y G E N
      ":PRINT "▲ W E R E ▲ R E C Y C L E D ":O=O+R
280   IF P*1.3<=OORFNR(5)<3THEN 330
290   PRINT :PRINT "■ T H E ▲ P E O P L E ▲ R E V O L T E
      D "
300   IF M>200ANDP<75THEN 320
310   PRINT "◣ T H E Y ▲ O V E R - R A N ▲ T H E ▲ B A S
      E ▲ A N D ▲ ■K I L L E D ■ ▲ Y O U ":GOTO 920
320   PRINT :PRINT "■ Y O U ▲ S T O P P E D ▲ T H E M ":M
      =M-200:P=P-FNR(P/2):PRINT "■ T H E R E ▲ W E R E ▲
      C A S U A L T I E S "
330   PRINT :PRINT :PRINT "■ P R E S S ▲ A ▲ K E Y "
340   GETA$:IF A$=""THEN 340
350   GOTO 60
360   PRINT "■ ▲ ▲ ▲ ▲ ▲ ▲ ▲ ▲ ▲ ▲ O X Y G E N ":PRINT "■ Y O
      U ▲ H A V E "O"U N I T S "
370   R=FNR(15)+15:PRINT :PRINT "■ C O S T "R"F O R ▲ S H
      I P P I N G "
380   R1=FNR(2)+1:PRINT "A N D "R1"P E R ▲ U N I T ":
      PRINT :INPUT "■ B U Y ▲ H O W ▲ M U C H ";N
390   IF N=0THEN RETURN
400   IF N*R1+R>MTHEN PRINT "■ N O T ▲ E N O U G H ▲ M O
      N E Y ":GOTO 370
410   M=M-(N*R1+R):O=O+N
420   RETURN
430   PRINT "▲ ▲ ▲ ▲ ▲ ▲ ▲ ▲ ▲ ▲ ◣ S H I P S ":PRINT "■ Y O U
      ▲ H A V E "S"S H I P S "
440   R=FNR(15)+15:PRINT "■ C O S T "R"I N ▲ L A B O U R
      ▲ A N D ▲ M A T E R I A L S "
450   INPUT "■ B U I L D ▲ H O W ▲ M A N Y ";N:IF N*R>M
      THEN PRINT "■ N O T ▲ E N O U G H ▲ M O N E Y ":
      GOTO 450
460   M=M-R*N:S=S+N
470   RETURN
480   PRINT "▲ ▲ ▲ ▲ ▲ ▲ ▲ ▲ ▲ ▲ ◣ S H I P S ":PRINT "■ Y O U
      ▲ H A V E "S:PRINT L"A R E ▲ L O A D E D "
490   R=FNR(10)+25:PRINT :PRINT "◣ C O S T S "R"T O ▲ L O
      A D ▲ A ":PRINT "S H I P "
500   INPUT "L O A D ▲ H O W ▲ M A N Y ";N:IF N+L>S
      THEN PRINT "■ N O T ▲ E N O U G H ▲ S H I P S ":
      GOTO 500
```

```
510   IF R*N>MTHEN PRINT "N O T ▲ E N O U G H ▲ M O N E Y
       ":GOTO 500
520   M=M-R*N:L=L+N
530   RETURN
```

Send Ships to Set Up Mines; Check If Any Ships to Send

```
540   PRINT "■ Y O U ▲ H A V E "L"S H I P S ":PRINT "L O
      A D E D ▲ A N D ▲ R E A D Y "
550   INPUT "■ S E N D ▲ H O W ▲ M A N Y ";N:IF N>LORP/2
      <NTHEN PRINT "■ T O O ▲ M A N Y ":GOTO 550
560   IF N=0THEN RETURN
570   L=L-N
580   PRINT :PRINT "■ H O W ▲ M U C H ▲ F U E L ▲ F O R ▲
       ▲ ▲ ▲ ▲ M I S S I O N ":INPUT F
590   IF F>MTHEN PRINT "■ N O T ▲ E N O U G H ▲ M O N E Y
       ":GOTO 580
600   M=M-F
610   R=2/(FNR(4)+.5):IF R*10*N<=FTHEN 650
620   PRINT "■ N O T ▲ E N O U G H ▲ F U E L ":R=INT((R
      *10*N-F)/10):IF R=0THEN R=1
630   IF R>NTHEN R=N
640   S=S-R:PRINT "■ "R"S H I P S ▲ A R E ▲ S T R A N D E
       D ":N=N-R
650   PRINT :PRINT "■ "N"M I N E S ▲ W E R E ":PRINT "E S
       T A B L I S H E D ▲ O N ▲ ▲ ▲ ▲ ▲ ▲ ▲ ▲ ▲ ■ J U P I
      T E R "
660   MI=MI+N:RETURN
670   PRINT "■ Y O U ▲ H A V E "S"S H I P S "
680   INPUT "S E N D ▲ H O W ▲ M A N Y ";N:IF N>SORP/2<N
      THEN PRINT "■ T O O ▲ M A N Y ":GOTO 680
690   IF N=0THEN RETURN
700   IF N>S-LTHEN L=S-N
710   PRINT :PRINT "■ H O W ▲ M U C H ▲ F U E L ▲ F O R ▲
       ▲ ▲ ▲ ▲ M I S S I O N ":INPUT F
720   IF F>MTHEN PRINT "■ N O T ▲ E N O U G H ▲ M O N E Y
       ":GOTO 710
730   M=M-F:IF OM=0THEN R=0:GOTO 800
740   R=FNR(OM*2)/OM:IF R*10*N<=FTHEN 780
750   PRINT "■ N O T ▲ E N O U G H ▲ F U E L ":R=INT((R
      *10*N-F)/10):IF R=0THEN R=1
760   IF R>NTHEN R=N
770   S=S-R:PRINT "■ "R"S H I P S ▲ A R E ▲ S T R A N D E
       D ":N=N-R
780   R=INT(N*10*R+.5)
790   IF R>OMTHEN R=OM
800   PRINT "■ "R"K G ' S ▲ O F ▲ O R E ▲ W E R E ":
      PRINT "R E C O V E R E D "
810   OM=OM-R:OB=OB+R
```

```
820   RETURN
830   PRINT "▲ ▲ ▲ ■ S E L L ▲ ▲ T O ▲ ▲ ■ E A R T H ":
      PRINT :PRINT "Y O U ▲ H A V E "OB"K G ' S ":
      PRINT "T O ▲ S E L L "
840   F=FNR(5)+5:PRINT "■ T H E ▲ G O V E R N M E N T ▲ P
       A Y S "F:PRINT "P E R ▲ K G ":R=FNR(20)+25:R1=FNR(
      3)+3
850   PRINT "■ T R A N S P O R T A T I O N ▲ C O S T S ":
      PRINT R"F O R ▲ F U E L ":PRINT "■ A N D "R1"P E R
      ▲ K G ":PRINT "O F ▲ O R E "
860   PRINT "■ H O W ▲ M U C H ▲ D O ▲ Y O U ▲ W A N T ":
      INPUT "T O ▲ S E L L ";N
870   IF N>OBTHEN PRINT "■ Y O U ▲ D O N ' T ▲ H A V E ▲
      T H A T ▲ ▲ ▲ M U C H ":GOTO 860
880   IF N=0THEN RETURN
890   IF R1*N+R>MTHEN PRINT "■ N O T ▲ E N O U G H ▲ M O
      N E Y ":GOTO 860
900   OB=OB-N:M=M-(R1*N+R):PRINT "■ T H E ▲ G O V E R N M
       E N T ▲ O F ":PRINT "■ E A R T H ■ ▲ T H A N K S ▲
       Y O U "
910   M=M+F*N:OS=OS+N:RETURN
```

Print Message Thanking Player for Saving the Planet

```
920   FOR I=1 TO 5000:NEXT:PRINT "■ ■ T H E ▲ G O V E R N
       M E N T ▲ O F ▲ ▲ ▲ ▲ ▲ ■ E A R T H ■ ▲ T H A N K
      S ▲ Y O U "
930   PRINT "F O R ▲ Y O U R ▲ S E R V I C E ▲ O F "Y:
      PRINT "Y E A R S "
940   PRINT :PRINT "■ Y O U ▲ M A D E ▲ £ "M:PRINT :
      PRINT "■ A N D ▲ S O L D "OS"K G ' S ":PRINT "O F ▲
       O R E "
950   END
```

ChexSum Tables

10	= 0		330	= 1587		650	= 4369
20	= 2303		340	= 1214		660	= 939
30	= 1710		350	= 476		670	= 1640
40	= 2402		360	= 2942		680	= 4673
50	= 1121		370	= 3411		690	= 757
60	= 1401		380	= 4406		700	= 1506
70	= 3139		390	= 757		710	= 3244
80	= 2607		400	= 3503		720	= 2875
90	= 3125		410	= 1969		730	= 2332
100	= 1181		420	= 143		740	= 3016
110	= 2794		430	= 3058		750	= 4671
120	= 1706		440	= 4088		760	= 992
130	= 3481		450	= 5259		770	= 3530
140	= 4082		460	= 1528		780	= 1440
150	= 1311		470	= 143		790	= 1154
160	= 1533		480	= 3874		800	= 2947
170	= 4156		490	= 3873		810	= 1580
180	= 1212		500	= 4953		820	= 143
190	= 2781		510	= 3127		830	= 4728
200	= 4752		520	= 1502		840	= 6625
210	= 5301		530	= 143		850	= 6084
220	= 5494		540	= 3448		860	= 2925
230	= 1741		550	= 4880		870	= 3898
240	= 4583		560	= 757		880	= 757
250	= 6676		570	= 588		890	= 3502
260	= 5561		580	= 3116		900	= 6564
270	= 5198		590	= 2872		910	= 1891
280	= 2181		600	= 580		920	= 5508
290	= 2033		610	= 2970		930	= 2633
300	= 1497		620	= 4671		940	= 4353
310	= 4425		630	= 992		950	= 129
320	= 6801		640	= 3530		TOTAL	= 270053

Snakepit

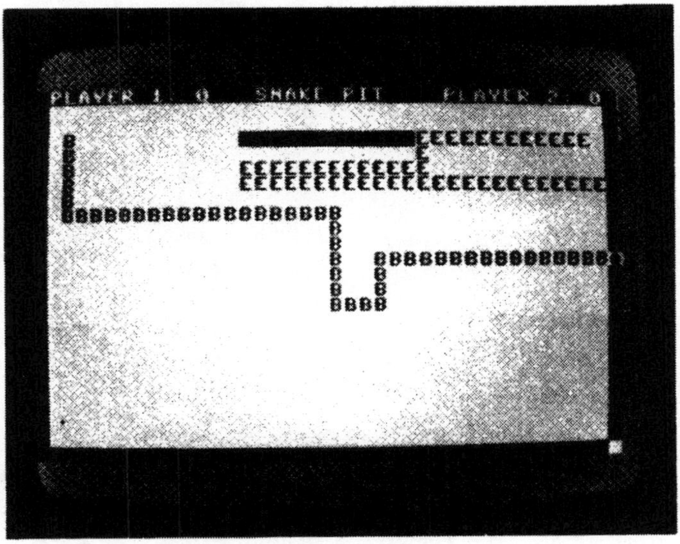

CLASSIFICATION: Evasion

You are one of two snakes placed in a pit, each trying to bite the other's tail off. The other snake can be either the computer or another opponent. Biting your own tail, turning back on yourself and running into the wall are all fatal to you. Try to block the other snake's path so that he runs into your tail. Seven bites of the tail determine the winner of each game. It is not necessary to hold keys down or hold the joystick in a fixed position, as the snake will continue travelling in the last direction it was pointed. For player 1 the keys to move up, left, right and down are W, A, S and Z. For player 2 they are I, J, K and M.

PROGRAMMING SUGGESTIONS

Give the opposing snake intelligence so that he can counteract your moves. Place obstacles on the board at random to make play more difficult.

PROGRAM
Variables

CO	Color offset address
UL	Left joystick
UR	Right joystick
X1	Left joystick X direction increment
Y1	Left snake Y direction increment
X2	Right snake X direction increment
Y2	Right snake Y direction increment
PI	Screen location of left snake
P2	Screen location of right snake
N	Number of players
F	Speed variable
S1	Left snake score
S2	Right snake score

Listing

```
10      REM   SNAKEPIT
20      VOL 8:GOTO 780
30      REM  GET DIRECTION
```

Scan Both Joystick Ports and the Keyboard; Call Move Snake

```
40      IF N=1THEN 60
50      IF JL<>0THEN 130
60      JL=JOY(1)
70      JL=15-(JLAND15)
80      IF JL=0THEN 130
90      IF JL=1THEN X1=0:Y1=-1:GOTO 290
100     IF JL=2THEN X1=0:Y1=1:GOTO 290
110     IF JL=8THEN X1=1:Y1=0:GOTO 290
120     IF JL=4THEN X1=-1:Y1=0:GOTO 290
130     JL=0:JR=JOY(2)
140     JR=15-(JRAND15)
150     IF JR=0THEN 200
160     IF JR=1THEN X2=0:Y2=-1:GOTO 290
170     IF JR=2THEN X2=0:Y2=1:GOTO 290
180     IF JR=8THEN X2=1:Y2=0:GOTO 290
190     IF JR=4THEN X2=-1:Y2=0:GOTO 290
200     GETA$:IF A$=""THEN 290
210     IF A$="I "THEN X2=0:Y2=-1:GOTO 290
220     IF A$="W "THEN X1=0:Y1=-1:GOTO 290
230     IF A$="M "THEN X2=0:Y2=1:GOTO 290
240     IF A$="Z "THEN X1=0:Y1=1:GOTO 290
250     IF A$="K "THEN X2=1:Y2=0:GOTO 290
260     IF A$="S "THEN X1=1:Y1=0:GOTO 290
270     IF A$="J "THEN X2=-1:Y2=0:GOTO 290
280     IF A$="A "THEN X1=-1:Y1=0:GOTO 290
```

Plot the Player on Screen and Check for Collision

```
290     REM PLOT PLAYER POSITION
300     P1=P1+X1+(Y1*40):P=P1:S=1:GOSUB 380
310     IF S=0THEN 990
320     IF N=1THEN GOSUB 610
330     P2=P2+X2+(Y2*40):P=P2:S=2:GOSUB 380
340     IF S=0THEN 990
350     POKE P1,81:POKE P1+CO,2
360     POKE P2,87:POKE P2+CO,5
370     FOR T=1 TO F*F+F*20:NEXT:GOTO 30
380     REM CHECK FOR HIT
390     IF PEEK(P)=32THEN RETURN
```

```
400   FOR I=5 TO 1 STEP -1:COLOR4,I,5:GOSUB 580
410   POKE P,81:FOR T=1 TO 60:NEXT
420   POKE P,81:NEXT
430   IF S=1THEN S2=S2+1:S=0
440   IF S=2THEN S1=S1+1:S=0
450   FOR T=1 TO 200:NEXT
460   IF S1<7ANDS2<7THEN RETURN
```

Print Out Who Won the Game and Prompt For Another

```
470   REM WINNERS ROUTINE
480   GOSUB 720:PRINT "■ ■ ■ ■ P L A Y E R ▲ 1 : ▲ ▲ ■ ■
      ■ ■ ■ ■ ■ ■ ■ ■ ■ ■ ■ ■ ■ ■ ■ ■ P L A Y E R ▲ 2 : ▲ ▲
      "
490   PRINT "■ ■ ■ "SPC(10)S1SPC(24)"■ "S2
500   IF S1<S2THEN N=2:PRINT "■ ■ ■ "
510   IF S2<S1THEN N=1:PRINT "■ ■ ■ "
520   PRINT "■ ■ ■ ■ ■ ■ ■ ■ ■ ■ ■ ■ ■ ■ ■ ■ ■ ■ ■ W I N N E
      R . . . . P L A Y E R ▲ ";
530   PRINT N
540   PRINT "■ ■ ■ ■ ■ ■ ■ ■ ■ ■ ■ ■ ■ ■ ■ ■ ■ ■ A N O T H E
      R ▲ G A M E ? ▲ ( Y / N ) "
550   GET A$:IF A$="Y "THEN RUN
560   IF A$<>"N "THEN 550
570   END
580   REM SOUND
590   FOR T=1 TO 10:SOUND 2,15,2:SOUND 1,30,4:NEXT
600   RETURN
610   REM COMPUTERS MOVE
620   IF PEEK(P2+X2+Y2*40)=32ANDRND(.)<.85THEN RETURN
630   XN=X2:YN=Y2:Y2=0
640   X2=1-(INT(RND(.)*3)):IF X2=0THEN 640
650   X=PEEK(P2+X2+Y2*40):IF X=32THEN IF X2=1THEN A$="K "
      :RETURN
660   IF X=32THEN IF X2=-1THEN A$="J ":RETURN
670   X2=0
680   Y2=1:X=PEEK(P2+X2+Y2*40):IF X=32THEN A$="M ":
      RETURN
690   Y2=-1:X=PEEK(P2+X2+Y2*40):IF X=32THEN A$="I ":
      RETURN
700   X2=XN:Y2=YN
710   RETURN
720   COLOR4,11,4:COLOR0,4,5
```

Draw Pit, Print Player Instructions and Enter Number of Players

```
730   PRINT "■ ■ ■ ▲ ▲ ▲ ▲ ▲ ▲ ▲ ▲ ▲ ▲ ▲ ▲ ▲ ▲ ▲ ▲ ▲ ▲ ▲ ▲ S N A K
      E ▲ P I T ▲ ▲ ▲ ▲ ▲ ▲ ▲ ▲ ▲ ▲ ▲ ▲ ▲ ▲ ▲ ▲ ▲ ▲ ▲ ▲ "
```

```
740   FOR I=1 TO 22:PRINT "■ ■ ▲ ▲ ":NEXT
750   PRINT "■ ■ ▲ ▲ ▲ ▲ ▲ ▲ ▲ ▲ ▲ ▲ ▲ ▲ ▲ ▲ ▲ ▲ ▲ ▲ ▲ ▲ ▲ ▲ ▲ ▲ ▲
      ▲ ▲ ▲ ▲ ▲ ▲ ▲ ▲ ▲ ▲ ▲ ▲ ▲ ▲ ▲ ▲ ▲ ▲ ▲ ▲ ▲ ▲ ▲ ■ ";"■ "
760   POKE 4031,160
770   RETURN
780   GOSUB 720
790   PRINT "■ ■ ■ ■ ■ P L A Y E R ▲ 1 ' S ▲ K E Y S ▲ ▲
      ▲ P L A Y E R ▲ 2 ' S ▲ K E Y S "
800   PRINT "■ ■ U P "SPC(9)"W "SPC(17)"I "
810   PRINT "■ ■ L E F T "SPC(7)"A "SPC(17)"J "
820   PRINT "■ ■ R I G H T "SPC(6)"S "SPC(17)"K "
830   PRINT "■ ■ D O W N "SPC(7)"Z "SPC(17)"M "
840   PRINT "■ ■ ■ J O Y S T I C K ( P O R T ▲ B ) ▲ ▲ ▲
      J O Y S T I C K ( P O R T ▲ A ) "
850   PRINT "■ ■ ■ E N T E R ▲ N U M B E R ▲ 1 ▲ O R ▲ 2
      ▲ F O R "
860   PRINT "■ ■ ■ ■ ■ ■ ■ ■ ■ ■ ■ N U M B E R ▲ O F ▲ P L A
      Y E R S . "
870   PRINT "■ ■ ■ T H E ▲ C O M P U T E R ▲ W I L L ▲ B
      E ▲ P L A Y E R ▲ 2 "
880   PRINT "■ ■ ■ ■ ■ ■ ■ ■ ■ ■ ■ W H E N ▲ O N L Y ▲ 1 ▲ P
      L A Y E R ▲ A V A I L A B L E . "
890   PRINT "■ ■ ■ N U M B E R ▲ O F ▲ P L A Y E R S : ▲
      ";
900   PRINT "■ ▲ ■ ";:FOR T=1 TO 80:NEXT:POKE 3072+999,16
      0
910   GETA$:IF A$="1 "ORA$="2 "THEN 930
920   PRINT "■ ▲ ■ ";:FOR T=1 TO 80:NEXT:GOTO 900
930   N=VAL(A$)
940   PRINT "■ ■ ■ ■ ■ ■ ■ ■ ■ ■ ■ ■ ■ ■ ■ ■ ■ ■ ■ ■ ■ ■ ■ ■
      ■ ■ ■ E N T E R ▲ S P E E D ▲ ( 1 : F A S T ▲ - ▲ 9
       : S L O W ) ▲ ";:GOTO 970
950   PRINT "■ ▲ ■ ";:FOR T=1 TO 80:NEXT
960   PRINT "■ ▲ ■ ";:FOR T=1 TO 80:NEXT
970   GETA$:IF A$<"1 "ORA$>"9 "THEN 950
980   F=VAL(A$):GOSUB 1140
990   GOSUB 720:PRINT "■ ■ ■ ■ P L A Y E R ▲ 1 : ▲ ▲ ■ ■
      ■ ■ ■ ■ ■ ■ ■ ■ ■ ■ ■ ■ ■ ■ ■ ■ ■ P L A Y E R ▲ 2 : ▲ ▲
       "
1000  PRINT "■ ■ ■ "SPC(10)S1SPC(24)"■ "S2
1010  REM SET RANDOM WALLS
1020  NW=INT(RND(.)*4):PRINT "■ ";
1030  IF NW=0THEN 1090
1040  FOR I=1 TO NW
1050  FOR J=1 TO RND((.)*6)+3
1060  PRINT :NEXT
1070  PRINT SPC((RND(.)*8)+8):FOR K=1 TO RND(.)*16+8:
      PRINT "■ ■ ▲ ";:NEXT
1080  NEXT
1090  REM SET INITIAL POSITIONS
```

```
1100  P1=3154:P2=3189:X1=0:X2=0:Y1=1:Y2=1:S=9
1110  IF N=2THEN 1120
1120  REM
1130  GOTO 150
1140  RETURN
```

ChexSum Tables

Line		Checksum
10	=	0
20	=	882
30	=	0
40	=	725
50	=	1051
60	=	686
70	=	1151
80	=	865
90	=	2348
100	=	2183
110	=	2190
120	=	2350
130	=	1151
140	=	1169
150	=	866
160	=	2355
170	=	2190
180	=	2197
190	=	2354
200	=	1213
210	=	2426
220	=	2435
230	=	2231
240	=	2247
250	=	2232
260	=	2241
270	=	2400
280	=	2393
290	=	0
300	=	2746
310	=	802
320	=	928
330	=	2753
340	=	802
350	=	1252
360	=	1251
370	=	2249
380	=	0
390	=	1117
400	=	2026
410	=	1431
420	=	530
430	=	1727
440	=	1729
450	=	374
460	=	1398
470	=	0
480	=	3236
490	=	1402
500	=	1493
510	=	1493
520	=	2208
530	=	231
540	=	2193
550	=	1263
560	=	1129
570	=	129
580	=	0
590	=	2164
600	=	143
610	=	0
620	=	3073
630	=	1521
640	=	2436
650	=	3915
660	=	2285
670	=	370
680	=	3666
690	=	3858
700	=	1061
710	=	143
720	=	1109
730	=	2724
740	=	1495
750	=	2530
760	=	584
770	=	143
780	=	299
790	=	3003
800	=	1460
810	=	1604
820	=	1719
830	=	1619
840	=	3196
850	=	2075
860	=	2004
870	=	2652
880	=	3023
890	=	1854
900	=	2568
910	=	1919
920	=	2307
930	=	654
940	=	4313
950	=	1534
960	=	1680
970	=	1924
980	=	1084
990	=	3236
1000	=	1402
1010	=	0
1020	=	1576
1030	=	932
1040	=	766
1050	=	1487
1060	=	342
1070	=	3752
1080	=	131
1090	=	0
1100	=	3408
1110	=	842
1120	=	0
1130	=	526
1140	=	143
TOTAL	=	179337

Break-In

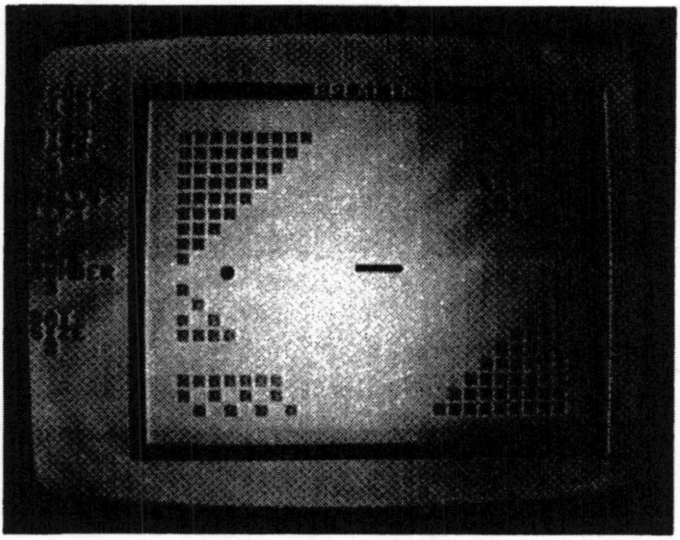

CLASSIFICATION: Co-ordination

You are inside a four-walled container with a series of brick walls, a moving ball and a bat. The ball is bouncing off the bricks and you must use your bat to stop it getting past you and hitting the wall. You are given nine balls for each game and you lose a ball each time one gets past your bat. The bat can be moved left and right using the I and P keys. There are three different brick wall configurations and two bat sizes. The smaller the bat, the more points scored.

PROGRAMMING SUGGESTIONS

Add more courts to the game so that the player has a greater choice of games. Make the ball change speed in midflight, i.e. accelerate or decelerate.

PROGRAM
Variables

SC	Start address of screen
CB	Color offset value
GM	Game number
BS	Bat size
GS	Game score
HS	High score
BV	Vertical position of bat
BH	Horizontal position of bat
BY	Vertical position of ball
BX	Horizontal position of ball
BA	Screen position of ball
DX	Horizontal movement value of ball
DY	Vertical movement value of ball
SW	Switch to allow screen refresh

Listing

```
10    REM  BREAKIN
```

Set Volume, Move Bat Left or Right; Check If Ball Hits Boundary

```
20    DN$="[HOME][24 DOWN][39 RIGHT]"
30    SC=3072:NB=9:GOTO 330
40    GOTO 20
50    VOL 8:SOUND 2,1,5:RETURN
60    REM  MOVE BAT
70    GETA$:IF A$=""THEN A=64
80    IF A$="I "THEN A=12
90    IF A$="P "THEN A=36
100   IF A=64THEN 170
110   PRINT LEFT$(DN$,BV)RIGHT$(DN$,BH);:FOR I=1 TO BS:
      PRINT "[UP] ";:NEXT
120   BH=BH+((A=12)-(A=36))*2
130   IF BH<8THEN BH=8
140   IF BH>38-BSTHEN BH=38-BS
150   PRINT LEFT$(DN$,BV)RIGHT$(DN$,BH);:FOR I=1 TO BS:
      PRINT "[RVS] [CLR] ";:NEXT:
160   REM CHECK BOUNDARY HIT
170   BX=BX+DX:BY=BY+DY:FF=21
180   IF BX<9THEN DX=-DX:GOSUB 50:GOTO 230
190   IF BX>36THEN DX=-DX:GOSUB 50:GOTO 230
200   IF BY<1THEN BY=1:DY=-DY:GOSUB 50:GOTO 230
210   IF BY>23THEN BY=23:DY=-DY:GOSUB 50
220   REM CHECK BAT/BRCK HIT & PRINT BALL
230   POKE BA,32:BA=SC+BY*40+BX
240   IF PEEK(BA)=120THEN BA=B1:DY=-DY:FF=133:GOSUB 50:
      GOTO 60
250   IF PEEK(BA)=207THEN DY=-DY:FF=35:GOSUB 50:GS=GS+1:
      PRINT "[HOME] [RVS] [DOWN] "GS
260   POKE BA,81
270   REM CHECK FOR MISSED BALL
280   IF GM=1ANDBY>22ANDDY=-1THEN NB=NB-1:PRINT "[HOME] [DOWN] [DOWN] [DOWN]
      [DOWN] [DOWN] [DOWN] [DOWN] [DOWN] [DOWN] [RVS] "NB
290   IF GM<>1ANDBY=12THEN NB=NB-1:PRINT "[HOME] [DOWN] [DOWN] [DOWN] [DOWN] [DOWN] [DOWN] [DOWN]
      [DOWN] [DOWN] [RVS] "NB
300   IF NB<1THEN 1090
310   IF INT(GS/100)-(GS/100)<>0THEN 60
320   ON GMGOSUB 830,900,990
```

Draw Title Screen; Select the Game Number and Bat Size

```
330   REM TITLE SCREEN
340   COLOR4,3,6:COLOR0,3,6:PRINT "♥QQQQ■▲▲▲▲▲
      ▲▲▲▲▲▲▲▲▲▲▲▲▲▲●"
350   FOR T=1 TO 100:NEXT
360   PRINT "♥QQQQQQ▣▲▲▲▲▲▲▲▲▲▲▲▲▲▲▲▲▲
      ▲▲●■●Я●"
370   FOR T=1 TO 100:NEXT
380   PRINT "♥QQQQQQQ▣▲▲▲▲▲▲▲▲▲▲▲▲▲▲▲▲
      ▲▲●▲■●▲Я●"
390   FOR T=1 TO 100:NEXT
400   PRINT "♥QQQQQQQQ∩▲▲▲▲▲▲▲▲▲▲▲▲▲▲
      ▲▲●▣●▲■●▲Я●⊏●"
410   FOR T=1 TO 100:NEXT
420   PRINT "♥QQQQQQQQQ∩▲▲▲▲▲▲▲▲▲▲▲▲▲
      ▲▲●▲▣●▲■●▲Я●▲⊏●"
430   FOR T=1 TO 100:NEXT
440   PRINT "♥QQQQQQQQQQ⊏▲▲▲▲▲▲▲▲▲▲▲▲
      ▲▲●∩●▲▣●▲■●▲Я●▲⊏●⊡●"
450   FOR T=1 TO 100:NEXT
460   PRINT "♥QQQQQQQQQQQ⊏▲▲▲▲▲▲▲▲▲▲
      ▲▲●▲∩●▲▣●▲■●▲Я●▲⊏●▲⊡●"
470   FOR T=1 TO 200:NEXT:FF=35:GOSUB 50
480   PRINT "♥QQQQQQQQQQQ⊏▲▲▲▲▲▲▲▲▲▲
      ▲▲B▲∩●▲▣●▲■●▲Я●▲⊏●▲⊡●"
490   FOR T=1 TO 200:NEXT:FF=21:GOSUB 50
500   PRINT "♥QQQQQQQQQQQ⊏▲▲▲▲▲▲▲▲▲▲
      ▲▲B▲∩R▲▣●▲■●▲Я●▲⊏●▲⊡●"
510   FOR T=1 TO 200:NEXT:FF=35:GOSUB 50
520   PRINT "♥QQQQQQQQQQQ⊏▲▲▲▲▲▲▲▲▲▲
      ▲▲B▲∩R▲▣E▲■●▲Я●▲⊏●▲⊡●"
530   FOR T=1 TO 200:NEXT:FF=21:GOSUB 50
540   PRINT "♥QQQQQQQQQQQ⊏▲▲▲▲▲▲▲▲▲▲
      ▲▲B▲∩R▲▣E▲■A▲Я●▲⊏●▲⊡●"
550   FOR T=1 TO 200:NEXT:FF=35:GOSUB 50
560   PRINT "♥QQQQQQQQQQQ⊏▲▲▲▲▲▲▲▲▲▲
      ▲▲B▲∩R▲▣E▲■A▲ЯK▲⊏●▲⊡●"
570   FOR T=1 TO 200:NEXT:FF=21:GOSUB 50
580   PRINT "♥QQQQQQQQQQQ⊏▲▲▲▲▲▲▲▲▲▲
      ▲▲B▲∩R▲▣E▲■A▲ЯK▲⊏I▲⊡●"
590   FOR T=1 TO 200:NEXT:FF=35:GOSUB 50
600   PRINT "♥QQQQQQQQQQQ⊏▲▲▲▲▲▲▲▲▲▲
      ▲▲B▲∩R▲▣E▲■A▲ЯK▲■I▲⊡N"
610   FOR T=1 TO 200:NEXT:FF=21:PRINT "QQ"
620   GOSUB 50
630   PRINT "■▲▲▲▲▲▲▲▲▲▲▣SELECT▲GAME▲
      NUMBER(1-3)":FOR T=1 TO 90:NEXT
```

```
640   PRINT "□ ▀ ▴ ▴ ▴ ▴ ▴ ▴ ▴ ▴ ▴ S E L E C T ▴ G A M E ▴
      N U M B E R ( 1 - 3 ) ";⬍FOR T=1 TO 90⬍NEXT
650   GETGM$⬍IF GM$<"1 "THEN PRINT ⬍PRINT "□ ";⬍GOTO 620
660   IF GM$>"3 "THEN PRINT ⬍PRINT "□ ";⬍GOTO 620
670   GM=VAL(GM$)⬍PRINT "▴ "GM⬍PRINT ⬍FF=35
680   GOSUB 50
690   PRINT "■ ▴ ▴ ▴ ▴ ▴ ▴ ▴ ▴ ▴ ▴ ▴ ▣ S E L E C T ▴ B A T ▴
      S I Z E ( 2 - 3 ) "⬍FOR T=1 TO 90⬍NEXT
700   PRINT "□ ▀ ▴ ▴ ▴ ▴ ▴ ▴ ▴ ▴ ▴ ▴ ▴ ▴ S E L E C T ▴ B A T ▴
      S I Z E ( 2 - 3 ) ";⬍FOR T=1 TO 90⬍NEXT
710   GETBS$⬍IF BS$<"2 "THEN PRINT ⬍PRINT "□ ";⬍GOTO 680
720   IF BS$>"3 "THEN PRINT ⬍PRINT "□ ";⬍GOTO 680
```

Draw Court, Print Score, High Score, Balls Left and Game Number

```
730   BS=VAL(BS$)⬍PRINT "▴ "BS
740   NB=9⬍GS=100*(4-BS)
750   FOR T=1 TO 500⬍NEXT
760   PRINT "◘ ■ ▴ ▴ ▴ ▴ ▴ ▴ ▴ ▴ ▴ ▣ ▴ ▴ ▴ ▴ ▴ ▴ ▴ ▴ ▴ ▴ ▴ ▴ ▴ ▴
      B R E A K I N ▴ ▴ ▴ ▴ ▴ ▴ ▴ ▴ ▴ ▴ ▴ ▴ ▴ ▴ ▴ "
770   FOR I=1 TO 23⬍PRINT "▴ ▴ ▴ ▴ ▴ ▴ ▴ ▴ ▴ ▣ ▴ ▀ ▴ ▴ ▴ ▴ ▴ ▴
      ▴ ▴ ▴ ▴ ▴ ▴ ▴ ▴ ▴ ▴ ▴ ▴ ▴ ▴ ▴ ▴ ▴ ▴ ▴ ▴ ▴ ▴ ▴ ▴ ▴ ▴ ▴ ▣
       ▴ "⬍NEXT
780   PRINT "■ ▴ ▴ ▴ ▴ ▴ ▴ ▴ ▴ ▴ ▣ ▴ ▴ ▴ ▴ ▴ ▴ ▴ ▴ ▴ ▴ ▴ ▴ ▴ ▴
      ▴ ▴ ▴ ▴ ▴ ▴ ▴ ▴ ▴ ▴ ▴ ▴ ▴ ▴ ▴ ▴ ▴ ▴ ▴ ▴ ▴ ▴ ▣ "
790   PRINT "▣ S C O R E "⬍PRINT GS⬍PRINT "▣ H I G H "⬍
      PRINT "S C O R E "⬍PRINT HS⬍PRINT "▣ B A L L S "
800   PRINT "L E F T "⬍PRINT NB⬍PRINT "▣ G A M E "⬍
      PRINT "N U M B E R "⬍PRINT GM
810   PRINT "▣ B A T "⬍PRINT "S I Z E "⬍PRINT BS
820   ON GMGOTO 830,900,990
```

Print Out the Courts for Games One, Two and Three

```
830   REM   GAME 1
840   PRINT "▣ ▣ ▣ ▣ "
850   FOR J=1 TO 4⬍PRINT "▣ ▣ ▣ ▣ ▣ ▣ ▣ ▣ ▣ ┏ ┏ ┏ ┏ ┏ ┏
       ┏ ┏ ┏ ┏ ┏ ┏ ┏ ┏ ┏ ┏ ┏ ┏ ┏ ┏ ┏ ┏ ┏ ┏ ┏ ┏ ┏ ┏ ┏ "⬍
      NEXT
860   IF GS>0THEN GS=GS+1
870   IF SW>0THEN 60
880   SW=1⬍BV=21⬍BH=17⬍BY=15⬍BX=18⬍BA=SC+BY*40+BX⬍DX=-1⬍D
      Y=-1
890   GOTO 110
900   REM GAME2
910   PRINT "▣ ▣ ▣ ▣ "
```

```
920  FOR J=1 TO 3:PRINT "■■■■■■■■■┌┌┌┌┌┌┌┌┌┌┌┌┌┌┌┌┌┌┌┌┌┌┌┌┌┌┌┌┌┌":
     NEXT
930  PRINT "■■■■■■■■■■■■"
940  FOR J=1 TO 3:PRINT "■■■■■■■■■┌┌┌┌┌┌┌┌┌┌┌┌┌┌┌┌┌┌┌┌┌┌┌┌┌┌┌┌┌┌":
     NEXT
950  IF GS>0THEN GS=GS+1
960  IF SW>0THEN 60
970  SW=1:BV=13:BH=20:BY=10:BX=21:BA=SC+BY*40+BX:DX=1:DY
     =-1
980  GOTO 110
990  REM GAME3
1000 PRINT "■■■"
1010 FOR I=0 TO 8:PRINT "■■■■■■■■■■";:FOR J=9
     -I TO 1 STEP -1:PRINT "■▀┌";:NEXT
1020 PRINT SPC(I*2+8);:FOR J=9-I TO 1 STEP -1:PRINT "┬"
     ;:NEXT:PRINT :NEXT:PRINT
1030 FOR I=0 TO 8:PRINT "■■■■■■■■■■";:FOR J=1
     TO I+1:PRINT "■▀┌";:NEXT
1040 PRINT SPC(((8-I)*2)+8);:FOR J=1 TO I+1:PRINT "┬";:
     NEXT:PRINT :NEXT:PRINT "■"
1050 IF GS>0THEN GS=GS+1
1060 IF SW>0THEN 60
1070 SW=1:BV=13:BH=16:BY=9:BX=24:BA=SC+BY*40+BX:DX=1:DY
     =-1
1080 GOTO 110
```

Check for Another Game

```
1090 REM END GAME
1100 PRINT "■■■■■■■■■■■■■■■■■■■■■■
     ■■    ANOTHER GAME(Y/N)"
1110 GETA$
1120 IF A$="N"THEN PRINT "⊡":END
1130 IF A$<>"Y"THEN 1110
1140 IF GS>HSTHEN HS=GS
1150 SW=0:GOTO 600
```

ChexSum Tables

10	=	0	400	=	3037	790	=	3959
20	=	3709	410	=	975	800	=	2957
30	=	1603	420	=	3147	810	=	1488
40	=	472	430	=	975	820	=	1282
50	=	1020	440	=	3941	830	=	0
60	=	0	450	=	975	840	=	317
70	=	1421	460	=	4073	850	=	8437
80	=	1139	470	=	1821	860	=	1448
90	=	1146	480	=	3945	870	=	821
100	=	834	490	=	1817	880	=	5699
110	=	3210	500	=	3816	890	=	526
120	=	2108	510	=	1821	900	=	0
130	=	1079	520	=	3676	910	=	317
140	=	1914	530	=	1817	920	=	8438
150	=	3604	540	=	3532	930	=	534
160	=	0	550	=	1821	940	=	8438
170	=	2291	560	=	3396	950	=	1448
180	=	2336	570	=	1817	960	=	821
190	=	2373	580	=	3252	970	=	5500
200	=	2844	590	=	1821	980	=	526
210	=	2332	600	=	3232	990	=	0
220	=	0	610	=	1853	1000	=	286
230	=	2008	620	=	247	1010	=	3802
240	=	3889	630	=	3625	1020	=	3941
250	=	4413	640	=	3827	1030	=	3397
260	=	444	650	=	2596	1040	=	4143
270	=	0	660	=	2123	1050	=	1448
280	=	4078	670	=	2072	1060	=	821
290	=	3307	680	=	247	1070	=	5463
300	=	913	690	=	3391	1080	=	526
310	=	2400	700	=	3593	1090	=	0
320	=	1056	710	=	2610	1100	=	2726
330	=	0	720	=	2128	1110	=	267
340	=	2812	730	=	1325	1120	=	1359
350	=	975	740	=	1644	1130	=	1199
360	=	2337	750	=	975	1140	=	1328
370	=	975	760	=	2593	1150	=	1015
380	=	2495	770	=	3324	TOTAL	=	248333
390	=	975	780	=	2264			

Minotaur

CLASSIFICATION: Educational

You are placed at the bottom centre of a matrix of numbers and symbols which you can move through by pressing keys as follows: W-up, X-down, A-left, D-right, Q-up left, E-up right, Z-down left and C-down right. It is easy to remember the keys because they form a diamond round the S key and each key points in the correct direction with reference to the S key. Your objective is to guess an integer (a whole number) in the range of Ø to 1ØØØ. You can get clues by moving over the X squares but in the least number of moves. Each number you move over is added to your score. If the number is too large, you are pursued by a minotaur which is placed in the centre of the screen at the start of each game, and which gradually creeps closer as you play. If he catches you, the game ends and you lose. When you think you have the number, move to the white block at the top of the matrix.

PROGRAMMING SUGGESTIONS

Make the board multilevel, and give the player and minotaur the ability to travel from level to level by landing on an appropriate spot.

PROGRAM

Variables

LD%	Level of difficulty
R%	Round
SN%	Secret number
D1%, D2%, D3%	Digits of a secret number (SN%)
PP%	Players' position
M%	Minotaur position
LS%	Last score
TS%	Total score
CU	Character under minotaur
NC%	Number of clues
T% ( )	Truth array for clues
MR%, MC	Minotaur row, colour
PR%, PC%	Player's row, colour

Listing

```
10     REM MINOTAUR
```

Set Screen Colours; Input the Difficulty Level; Print Board

```
20     PRINT "■ ";:COLOR4,9,4:COLOR0,7,5:PRINT TAB(10);"■
       M I N O T A U R ▲ M A S T E R - M I N D ":
30     PRINT :PRINT :PRINT
40     PRINT :PRINT "L E V E L ▲ O F ▲ D I F F I C U L T Y
        ? ( 1 - 9 ) ";
50     GETX$:IF X$=""THEN 50
60     IF VAL(X$)<1ORVAL(X$)>9THEN 50
70     LD%=VAL(X$):PRINT LD%
80     FOR T=1 TO 1000:NEXT
90     GOTO 250
100    FOR I=3273 TO 3833 STEP 40
110    FOR J=0 TO 37
120    K1=INT(RND(0)*13)
130    IF K1>9THEN 160
140    POKE I+J,K1+48
150    GOTO 220
160    IF K1<>10THEN 190
170    POKE I+J,24
180    GOTO 220
190    IF K1<>11THEN 210
200    POKE I+J,63:GOTO 220
210    POKE I+J,42
220    NEXT:NEXT
230    POKE 3292,160
240    RETURN
250    R%=1:SN%=INT(RND(0)*999+1)
260    D1%=INT(SN%/100):D2%=INT((SN%-D1%*100)/10):D3%=SN%
       -D1%*100-D2%*10
270    PRINT "■ ";:COLOR4,4,3:COLOR0,7,5:GOSUB 100
280    PP%=3852:M%=3572:IF PEEK(3852)>48THEN LS%=PEEK(3852
       )-48
290    IF PEEK(3852)=63ORPEEK(3852)=42ORPEEK(3852)=24
       THEN LS%=0:POKE 3852,48
300    TS%=TS%+LS%:CU=PEEK(3572):POKE 3572,13:POKE 3292,16
       0
```

Print Difficulty Level, Score and Total Score; Scan Keyboard

```
310    PRINT "■■R O U N D ▲ # ";R%;"■L E V E L ▲ O F ▲
       D I F F . ▲ ";LD%;"■ ";TAB(30);"■P L A Y E R ▲ 1 ■
        "
320    FOR I=1 TO 21:PRINT :NEXT:PRINT "■ ▲ T O T A L ▲ S
       C O R E ▲ ";TS%;TAB(21);"L A S T ▲ S C O R E ";LS%;
```

```
330   C=0:Q=1
340   GETX$:C=C+1
350   IF C=7THEN Q=1-Q:C=0
360   IF Q<>0THEN 390
370   IF PEEK(PP%)>63THEN POKE PP%,PEEK(PP%)-128:Q=1:
      GOTO 390
380   POKE PP%,PEEK(PP%)+128:Q=1
390   IF X$=""THEN 340
400   GOSUB 1940:IF PEEK(PP%)>64THEN POKE PP%,PEEK(PP%)
      -128
410   IF X$="W "THEN 510
420   IF X$="A "THEN 550
430   IF X$="D "THEN 590
440   IF X$="X "THEN 630
450   IF X$="E "THEN 670
460   IF X$="Q "THEN 710
470   IF X$="Z "THEN 750
480   IF X$="C "THEN 790
490   IF X$="T "THEN 830
500   GOTO 340
510   IF PEEK(PP%-40)=32THEN 340
520   LS%=PEEK(PP%)-48
530   POKE PP%,32:PP%=PP%-40
540   GOTO 850
550   IF PEEK(PP%-1)=32THEN 340
560   LS%=PEEK(PP%)-48
570   POKE PP%,32:PP%=PP%-1
580   GOTO 850
590   IF PEEK(PP%+1)=32THEN 340
600   LS%=PEEK(PP%)-48
610   POKE PP%,32:PP%=PP%+1
620   GOTO 850
630   IF PEEK(PP%+40)=32THEN 340
640   LS%=PEEK(PP%)-48
650   POKE PP%,32:PP%=PP%+40
660   GOTO 850
670   IF PEEK(PP%-39)=32THEN 340
680   LS%=PEEK(PP%)-48
690   POKE PP%,32:PP%=PP%-39
700   GOTO 850
710   IF PEEK(PP%-41)=32THEN 340
720   LS%=PEEK(PP%)-48
730   POKE PP%,32:PP%=PP%-41
740   GOTO 850
750   IF PEEK(PP%+39)=32THEN 340
760   LS%=PEEK(PP%)-48
770   POKE PP%,32:PP%=PP%+39
780   GOTO 850
790   IF PEEK(PP%+41)=32THEN 340
800   LS%=PEEK(PP%)-48
810   POKE PP%,32:PP%=PP%+41
```

```
820   GOTO 850
830   PR%=INT((PP%-3072)/40) :PC%=PP%-PR%*40-3072:
      GOSUB 1590:IF PP%<>M%THEN 830
840   GOTO 1770
850   PR%=INT((PP%-3072)/40) :PC%=PP%-PR%*40-3072
860   K1=PEEK(PP%):IF K1=63THEN GOSUB 950
870   IF PP%=M%THEN 1770
880   IF K1=24THEN GOSUB 970
890   IF K1=42THEN GOSUB 1440
900   IF K1=160THEN 1490
910   K1=PEEK(PP%)-48:IF LS%+K1>=10-LD%THEN GOSUB 1590
920   TS%=TS%+K1:GOSUB 1860
930   IF PP%=M%THEN 1770
940   GOTO 330
950   I=INT(RND(1)*10):POKE PP%,I+48
960   RETURN
970   POKE PP%,48
980   IF NC%>=9THEN GOTO 1430
990   K2=INT(RND(0)*9+1):IF T%(K2)=1THEN 990
1000  T%(K2)=1:NC%=NC%+1
```

At Random, Print a Clue at the Top of the Screen

```
1010  ON K2GOTO 1020,1050,1090,1130,1170,1210,1260,1290,1
      340
1020  GOSUB 1890:PRINT "S U M ▲ O F ▲ D I G I T S ▲ O F ▲
       S E C R E T ":PRINT TAB(9);"N U M B E R ▲ E Q U A
      L S ▲ ";
1030  PRINT D1%+D2%+D3%
1040  GOSUB 1910:RETURN
1050  GOSUB 1890:PRINT "S E C R E T ▲ N U M B E R ▲ I S ▲
       ";
1060  IF SN%/2=INT(SN%/2)THEN PRINT "E V E N ":GOTO 1080
1070  PRINT "O D D "
1080  PRINT :GOSUB 1910:RETURN
1090  K=INT(RND(1)*200)+SN%:J=K-200:IF J<0THEN J=0
1100  IF K>1000THEN K=1000
1110  GOSUB 1890:PRINT "N U M B E R ▲ I S ▲ B E T W E E N
       ";J:PRINT TAB(9);"A N D ";K
1120  GOSUB 1910:RETURN
1130  GOSUB 1890:PRINT "N U M B E R ▲ I S ▲ ";
1140  IF SN%/5=INT(SN%/5)THEN PRINT "D I V I S I B L E ":
      GOTO 1160
1150  PRINT "N O T ▲ D I V I S I B L E "
1160  PRINT TAB(9);"B Y ▲ 5 ":GOSUB 1910:RETURN
1170  L=D1%:IF D2%>LTHEN L=D2%
1180  IF D3%>LTHEN L=D3%
1190  GOSUB 1890:PRINT "L A R G E S T ▲ D I G I T ▲ I N ▲
```

```
      T H E ":PRINT TAB(9);"S E C R E T ▲ N U M B E R ▲
     I S ";L
1200 GOSUB 1910:RETURN
1210 GOSUB 1890:PRINT "F I R S T ▲ D I G I T ▲ I N ▲ T H
      E ▲ S E C R E T ":PRINT TAB(9);"N U M B E R ▲ I S
     ▲ ";
1220 IF D1%>5THEN PRINT "L A R G E R ▲ T H A N ▲ 5 ":
     GOTO 1250
1230 IF D1%<5THEN PRINT "L E S S ▲ T H A N ▲ 5 ":GOTO 12
     50
1240 PRINT "E Q U A L ▲ T O ▲ 5 "
1250 GOSUB 1910:RETURN
1260 GOSUB 1890:PRINT "S U M ▲ O F ▲ F I R S T ▲ A N D ▲
      T H I R D ":PRINT TAB(9);"D I G I T S ▲ I S ▲ ";
1270 PRINT D1%+D3%
1280 GOSUB 1910:RETURN
1290 GOSUB 1890:PRINT "O N E ▲ O F ▲ T H E ▲ D I G I T S
      ▲ I N ▲ T H E ":PRINT TAB(9);"S E C R E T ▲ N U M
     B E R ▲ I S ▲ ";
1300 K=INT(RND(1)*3):IF K=0ANDSN%>99THEN PRINT D1%:
     GOTO 1330
1310 IF K=1ANDSN%>9THEN PRINT D2%:GOTO 1330
1320 PRINT D3%
1330 GOSUB 1910:RETURN
1340 GOSUB 1890:PRINT "P R O D U C T ▲ O F ▲ T H E ▲ N O
      N - Z E R O ":PRINT TAB(9);"D I G I T S ▲ I S ";
1350 IF D1%=0ANDD2%=0THEN PRINT D3%:GOTO 1420
1360 IF D1%=0ANDD3%=0THEN PRINT D2%:GOTO 1420
1370 IF D1%=0THEN PRINT D2%*D3%:GOTO 1420
1380 IF D2%=0ANDD3%=0THEN PRINT D1%:GOTO 1420
1390 IF D2%=0THEN PRINT D1%*D3%:GOTO 1420
1400 IF D3%=0THEN PRINT D1%*D2%:GOTO 1420
1410 PRINT D1%*D2%*D3%
1420 GOSUB 1910:RETURN
1430 GOTO 1090
1440 POKE PP%,48
1450 IF TS%<11THEN RETURN
1460 I=INT(RND(0)*100):IF I>50THEN TS%=TS%-10:RETURN
1470 IF I<10THEN TS%=TS%+50:RETURN
1480 TS%=TS%+10:RETURN
```

Input the Secret Number; If Wrong, Then Give Player Clue

```
1490 GOSUB 1890:PRINT "G U E S S ▲ A T ▲ T H E ▲ S E C R
      E T ▲ N U M B E R ":PRINT TAB(9);
1500 INPUT "A N D ▲ H I T ▲ [K] R E T U R N ■ ";K$
1510 I=VAL(K$):IF I=SN%THEN 1770
1520 G1%=INT(I/100):G2%=INT((I-G1%*100)/10):G3%=I-G1%*10
     0-G2%*10
```

```
1530  PRINT "♥ ":PRINT :IF D1%=G1%THEN PRINT "F I R S T ▲
       D I G I T ▲ C O R R E C T ":PRINT
1540  IF D2%=G2%THEN PRINT "S E C O N D ▲ D I G I T ▲ C O
       R R E C T ":PRINT
1550  IF D3%=G3%THEN PRINT "T H I R D ▲ D I G I T ▲ C O R
       R E C T "
1560  IF D1%<>G1%ANDD2%<>G2%ANDD3%<>G3%THEN PRINT "N O ▲
      D I G I T S ▲ C O R R E C T "
1570  FOR T=1 TO 2000:NEXT
1580  R%=R%+1:GOTO 270
1590  MR%=INT((M%-1024)/40):MC%=M%-MR%*40-3072
1600  IF MC%<>PC%THEN 1630
1610  IF MR%>PR%THEN MR%=MR%-1:GOTO 1700
1620  MR%=MR%+1:GOTO 1700
1630  IF MR%<>PR%THEN 1660
1640  IF MC%>PC%THEN MC%=MC%-1:GOTO 1700
1650  MC%=MC%+1:GOTO 1700
1660  IF M%>PP%THEN 1690
1670  IF MC%<PC%THEN MC%=MC%+1:GOTO 1700
1680  MC%=MC%-1:GOTO 1700
1690  MR%=MR%-1
1700  K=3072+40*MR%+MC%:IF PEEK(K)=160THEN RETURN
1710  POKE M%,CU:IF CU=63THEN GOTO 1740
1720  IF CU>=48THEN GOTO 1740
1730  IF CU=24THEN GOTO 1740
1740  M%=K:CU=PEEK(M%)
1750  POKE M%,13
1760  RETURN
1770  PRINT "♥ ";:IF M%=PP%THEN 1810
```

Print the Score and Who Won, You or Minotaur; Print Magic Number

```
1780  FOR I=1 TO 18:PRINT "▲ ▲ ▲ C O N G R A T U L A T I
      O N S ! ▲ ▲ ▲ C O N G R A T U L A T I O N S ! ":
      NEXT:PRINT
1790  PRINT "Y O U ▲ H A V E ▲ D E F E A T E D ▲ T H E ▲
      M I N O T A U R ! ! ":PRINT "Y O U R ▲ S C O R E ▲
      I S ▲ ";TS%;
1800  PRINT "I N ▲ ";R%;"▲ R O U N D S ":GOTO 1830
1810  FOR I=1 TO 18:PRINT "■ ▲ ▲ ▲ M I N O T A U R ▲ W I
      N S ! ▲ ▲ ▲ ▲ M I N O T A U R ▲ W I N S ! ":NEXT:
      PRINT
1820  PRINT "T H E ▲ S E C R E T ▲ N U M B E R ▲ W A S ▲
      ";SN%
1830  PRINT :PRINT "H I T ▲ A N Y ▲ K E Y ▲ F O R ▲ A N O
       T H E R ▲ G A M E "
1840  GETX$:IF X$=""THEN 1840
1850  RUN
```

```
1860  PRINT CHR$(13);CHR$(145);"▲ T O T A L ▲ S C O R E ▲
       ▲ ▲ ▲ ▲ ▲ ▲ ▲ ▲ ▲ ";TAB(21);"L A S T ▲ S C O R E ▲ ▲
       ▲ ▲ ▲ ";
1870  PRINT CHR$(13);CHR$(145);"▲ T O T A L ▲ S C O R E ▲
       ";TS%;TAB(21);"L A S T ▲ S C O R E ";LS%;
1880  RETURN
1890  PRINT CHR$(13);:FOR I=1 TO 21:PRINT CHR$(145);:
      NEXT:PRINT "▣ ";
1900  PRINT TAB(9);:RETURN
1910  FOR I=1 TO 18:PRINT CHR$(17);:NEXT
1920  PRINT TAB(35);"◣ ";
1930  RETURN
1940  FOR I=3160 TO 3186:POKE I,32:NEXT
1950  FOR I=3200 TO 3226:POKE I,32:NEXT
1960  RETURN
1970  K1=INT(RND(0)*14):PRINT K1,:GOTO 1970
```

ChexSum Tables

10	=	0	310	=	4779	610	=	1451
20	=	4621	320	=	4912	620	=	534
30	=	585	330	=	680	630	=	1571
40	=	2389	340	=	903	640	=	1181
50	=	1196	350	=	1587	650	=	1505
60	=	1953	360	=	971	660	=	534
70	=	1204	370	=	3514	670	=	1570
80	=	1032	380	=	1638	680	=	1181
90	=	526	390	=	872	690	=	1513
100	=	1312	400	=	2944	700	=	534
110	=	709	410	=	969	710	=	1571
120	=	1207	420	=	957	720	=	1181
130	=	848	430	=	952	730	=	1507
140	=	943	440	=	978	740	=	534
150	=	527	450	=	959	750	=	1570
160	=	1089	460	=	971	760	=	1181
170	=	629	470	=	982	770	=	1512
180	=	527	480	=	955	780	=	534
190	=	1091	490	=	964	790	=	1571
200	=	1246	500	=	525	800	=	1181
210	=	629	510	=	1571	810	=	1506
220	=	320	520	=	1181	820	=	534
230	=	589	530	=	1506	830	=	5454
240	=	143	540	=	534	840	=	584
250	=	2063	550	=	1513	850	=	3533
260	=	5528	560	=	1181	860	=	1955
270	=	1987	570	=	1452	870	=	1060
280	=	3734	580	=	534	880	=	1043
290	=	4346	590	=	1513	890	=	1104
300	=	3293	600	=	1181	900	=	1022

910	=	3336
920	=	1338
930	=	1060
940	=	528
950	=	2055
960	=	143
970	=	515
980	=	1543
990	=	2619
1000	=	1484
1010	=	3081
1020	=	4787
1030	=	1009
1040	=	562
1050	=	2128
1060	=	2977
1070	=	441
1080	=	779
1090	=	3495
1100	=	1286
1110	=	3349
1120	=	562
1130	=	1513
1140	=	3423
1150	=	1236
1160	=	1472
1170	=	1700
1180	=	1168
1190	=	4879
1200	=	562
1210	=	4573
1220	=	2670
1230	=	2519
1240	=	941
1250	=	562
1260	=	4211
1270	=	656
1280	=	562
1290	=	5167
1300	=	3577
1310	=	2268
1320	=	311
1330	=	562
1340	=	4265
1350	=	2330
1360	=	2329
1370	=	2066
1380	=	2328
1390	=	2067
1400	=	2066
1410	=	1009
1420	=	562
1430	=	587
1440	=	515
1450	=	956
1460	=	3178
1470	=	1812
1480	=	1086
1490	=	3464
1500	=	1679
1510	=	1723
1520	=	5020
1530	=	3812
1540	=	3022
1550	=	2710
1560	=	4953
1570	=	1031
1580	=	1271
1590	=	3341
1600	=	1316
1610	=	2469
1620	=	1477
1630	=	1347
1640	=	2405
1650	=	1447
1660	=	1061
1670	=	2407
1680	=	1448
1690	=	810
1700	=	2898
1710	=	1928
1720	=	1571
1730	=	1370
1740	=	1195
1750	=	421
1760	=	143
1770	=	1569
1780	=	4920
1790	=	4976
1800	=	2036
1810	=	4653
1820	=	2254
1830	=	2713
1840	=	1321
1850	=	139
1860	=	4669
1870	=	4697
1880	=	143
1890	=	2969
1900	=	688
1910	=	1619
1920	=	828
1930	=	143
1940	=	1682
1950	=	1683
1960	=	143
1970	=	2328
TOTAL	=	346832

Star Trader

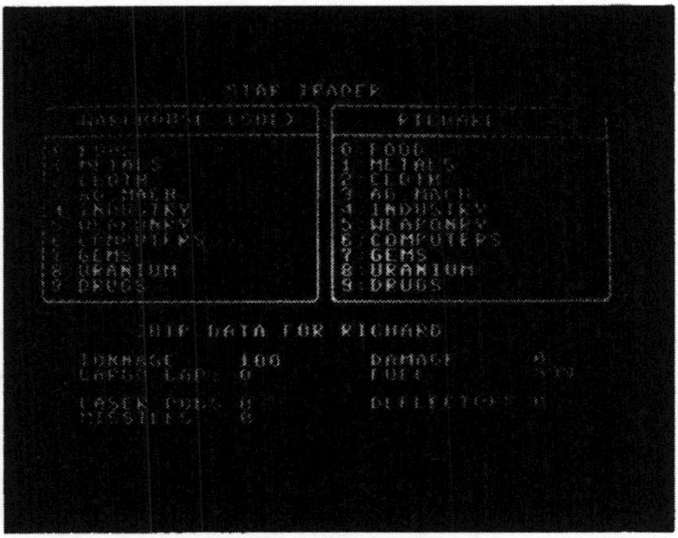

CLASSIFICATION: Strategy

You are the pilot of an interstellar merchant vessel. Using all of your charm and intelligence, you secure a loan from the Solar Interstellar Bank (Sol branch) to purchase a second-hand merchant ship. With the little cash left over, you decide to enter the hazardous world of interstellar speculation. Use your cash to purchase various items at cheap prices, then travel to worlds where the demand for these items is great and sell them at a profit. You must repay the bank your massive loan or risk repossession. Beware of pirates and space storms. Full instructions are contained within the game. May you make a gigabuck or two!

PROGRAMMING SUGGESTIONS

Limit the supply of goods available on each planet. Introduce random patrols searching for gems, drugs or uranium among the inner worlds. Add random events such as black holes, or robbers who attack you and try to steal your cash.

PROGRAM
Variables

S$	Ship name
GD	Goods in warehouse and ship
TP	Trade prices
T$	Trade items
CC	Cargo capacity
SS	Ship size
LP	Laser pods
MS	Missiles
DF	Deflectors
P%	Planetary data
PL$	Planetary names
CS	Cash
CR	Bank balance
DM	Damage to ship
DR	Current real damage
PF	Pirate fleet
SN	Number of pirates in fleet
SD	Star data
L	Current planetary system

Important Note

Star Trader is such a large program that it leaves no room for ChexSum to be merged with it.

You must therefore type in Star Trader in two sections, run ChexSum on each half in turn, then merge the two halves:

1 Enter lines 10 to 1440 of the first half of Star Trader which follow.

Listing

Initialise Game Variables

```
10    N$="▚ ■ ▲▲▲▲▲▲▲▲▲▲▲▲▲▲▲▲▲▲▲ S T A R ▲ T R A
      D E R "‡S$="B O L T ▲ B I N ▲ ▲ "‡VOL 8
20    PRINT "■ ";N$‡PRINT "▩ ▲▲▲▲▲▲▲▲▲▲▲▲▲▲▲ P
      L E A S E ▲ W A I T . . . "
30    RC$="▩ ▩ ▩ ▩ ▩ ▩ ▩ ▩ ▩ ▩ ▩ ▩ ▩ ▩ ▩ ▩ ▩ ▩ ▩ ▩ ▩ ▩ ▩ ▩ "
40    NL$="▲▲▲▲▲▲▲▲▲▲▲▲▲▲▲▲▲▲▲▲▲▲▲▲▲▲
      ▲▲▲▲▲▲▲▲▲▲▲▲▲▲▲▲▲▲▲▲▲▲▲ "
50    CY$="▩ ▩ ▩ ▩ ▩ ▩ ▩ ▩ ▩ ▩ ▩ ▩ ▩ ▩ ▩ ▩ "‡L$="≡ ≡ ≡ ≡ ≡ ≡
      ≡ ≡ ≡ ≡ ≡ ≡ ≡ ≡ ≡ ≡ ≡ ≡ ≡ ≡ ≡ ≡ ≡ "‡CD$="▩ ▩ ▩ ▩ ▩ ▩ ▩ ▩ ▩ ▩
      "
60    L1$="≡ ≡ ≡ ≡ ≡ ≡ ≡ ≡ ≡ ≡ ≡ ≡ ≡ ≡ + ≡ ≡ ≡ ≡ ≡ ≡ ≡ ≡ ≡ ≡ ≡ ≡ +
      ≡ ≡ ≡ ≡ ≡ ≡ ≡ ≡ ≡ ≡ ≡ ≡ ≡ ≡ ≡ ≡ ≡ ≡ ≡ ≡ ≡ ≡ ≡ ≡ "
70    LP=0‡MS=0‡DF=0‡DIMW%(9,1)‡DIMP(9,6)‡DIMPL$(9)‡SS=10
      0‡L=0
80    DIMPF(9,3)‡DIMGD(8,1)‡DIMTP(8)
90    DEFFNX(D)=INT(RND(0)*D*8-D*3)
100   DEFFNDS(D)=INT(SQR(ABS(P(D,0)-P(L,0))↑2+ABS(P(D,1)
      -P(L,1))↑2+ABS(P(D,2)-P(L,2))↑2))
110   RESTORE
120   DATASIRIUS,PROCYON,WESEN,ALTAIR,DENEB,DUBHE,VEGA,CA
      PELLA,CASTOR,POLLUX,ANTARES
130   DATAZOSMA,RIGEL,MEGREZ,MINTAKA,SAIPH,KOCHAB,PHAEDA
140   DATAETAMIN,ERIDANE,WOLF,HAMAL,ARIADNE
150   FOR I=1 TO 9‡IF RND(0)<.333THEN READPL$(I)‡READD$‡
      GOTO 180
160   IF RND(0)<.333THEN READD$‡READPL$(I)‡GOTO 180
170   READD$‡READPL$(I)
180   P(I,0)=FNX(I)‡P(I,1)=FNX(I)‡P(I,2)=FNX(I)
190   P(I,3)=91-10*I+INT(RND(0)*15)+INT(RND(0)*15)
200   P(I,4)=21-2*I-INT(RND(0)*3)‡P(I,5)=INT(2000/(P(I,3)
      *P(I,4))+1)
210   P(I,6)=FNDS(I)
220   NEXTI‡PL$(0)="S O L "‡P(0,3)=110+INT(RND(0)*20)‡P(0
      ,4)=20‡P(0,5)=1
230   DIMT$(9)‡T$(0)="▚ 0 ‡ F O O D ▲ ▲ ▲ ▲ "‡T$(1)="▚ 1
      ‡ M E T A L S ▲ ▲ "
240   T$(6)="▚ 6 ‡ G E M S ▲ ▲ ▲ ▲ "
250   T$(2)="▚ 2 ‡ W E A P O N S ▲ "‡T$(3)="▚ 3 ‡ C Y B O
      R G S ▲ "
260   T$(4)="▚ 4 ‡ U R A N I U M ▲ "‡T$(5)="▚ 5 ‡ D R U G
      S ▲ ▲ ▲ "
270   T$(7)="▚ 7 ‡ F U E L ▲ ▲ ▲ ▲ "‡T$(8)="▚ 8 ‡ R E P A
      I R S ▲ "
```

```
280  COLOR0,2:COLOR4,2
290  PRINT "▣▲▲▲▲▲▲▲WELCOME▲TO▲STAR▲TRADER!"
300  INPUT "▣▲▲▲▲▲▲▲ENTER▲NAME▲OF▲YOUR▲SHIP";S$:PRINT"▣"
310  GD(7,1)=10:CS=5000:CR=-5000:SD=5+INT(RND(0)*200)/100:GOSUB 2200:GOSUB 690:B=2*CS+500
```

Get Player's Command and Help Table

```
320  GETA$:IF A$=""THEN 320
330  IF A$="Q"THEN 530
340  IF A$="I"THEN GOSUB 690:GOTO 320
350  IF A$="M"THEN GOSUB 870:GOTO 320
360  IF A$="J"THEN GOSUB 990:GOTO 320
370  IF A$="B"ANDL=0ANDB>0THEN GOSUB 2400:GOTO 320
380  IF A$="D"ANDL=0ANDCS>0THEN GOSUB 2480:GOTO 320
390  IF A$="T"THEN GOSUB 1270:GOTO 320
400  IF A$="U"ANDL=0THEN GOSUB 570:GOTO 320
410  IF A$="L"ANDL=0THEN GOSUB 630:GOTO 320
420  IF ASC(A$)=13THEN 320
430  PRINT N$;"▣▣▣▣▲▲▲▲▲▲▲▲▲▲▲▲VALID▲COMMANDS▲ARE▲:":PRINT "▣▲'I'▲▲CARGO▲AND▲SHIP▲STATUS"
440  PRINT "▣▲'J'▲▲HYPER▲JUMP▲CHART":PRINT "▣▲'T'▲▲TRADE▲TABLE"
450  PRINT "▣▲'M'▲▲SYSTEM▲LIBRARY"
460  PRINT "▣▲'Q'▲▲TO▲QUIT▲GAME"
470  PRINT "▣▲'U'▲▲UNLOAD▲SHIP▲TO▲WAREHOUSE"
480  PRINT "▣▲'L'▲▲LOAD▲SHIP▲FROM▲WAREHOUSE"
490  PRINT "▣▲'B'▲▲BORROW▲CASH▲FROM▲BANK"
500  PRINT "▣▲'D'▲▲DEPOSIT▲CASH▲IN▲BANK"
510  GETA$:IF A$=""THEN 510
520  GOTO 330
530  PRINT "▣▣▣▲▲▲QUITTING:▲ARE▲YOU▲SURE▲?";
```

Quitting, Loading and Unloading, Inventory

```
540  GETA$:IF A$=""THEN 540
550  IF A$="Y"THEN 2860
560  GOSUB 690:GOTO 320
```

```
570  IN=-1:I$="":PRINT "■ ";CV$;NL$
580  PRINT CV$;"■▲U N L O A D I N G▲";
590  GOSUB 1620:IF IN>6THEN SOUND 1,200,5:GOTO 590
600  PRINT RIGHT$(T$(IN),8);:INPUT N:IF INT(N)>GD(IN,1)
     ORN<0THEN SOUND 1,200,5:GOTO 570
610  GD(IN,0)=GD(IN,0)+INT(N):GD(IN,1)=GD(IN,1)-INT(N)
620  PRINT CV$;NL$:GOSUB 2360:GOSUB 850:RETURN
630  IN=-1:I$="":PRINT CV$;NL$
640  PRINT CV$;"■▲L O A D I N G▲";
650  GOSUB 1620:IF IN>6THEN SOUND 1,200,5:GOTO 650
660  PRINT RIGHT$(T$(IN),8);:INPUT N:IF INT(N)>GD(IN,0)
     ORN<0THEN SOUND 1,200,5:GOTO 630
670  GD(IN,1)=GD(IN,1)+INT(N):GD(IN,0)=GD(IN,0)-INT(N)
680  PRINT CV$;NL$:GOSUB 2360:GOSUB 850:RETURN
690  PRINT N$:PRINT "■ ";L$;"■ ■ ";L$;"■ ";
700  PRINT "■▲▲W A R E H O U S E▲( S O L )▲■■▲
     ▲▲▲▲▲▲▲▲▲▲▲▲▲▲▲▲▲▲▲▲■ ";
710  PRINT "■ ■ ■ ■ ■ ■ ■ ■ ";RC$;S$
720  PRINT "■ ";L$;"■ ■ ";L$;"■ ";
730  FOR I=0 TO 6:PRINT T$(I);"▲▲▲▲▲▲▲▲▲■ ";T$(I)
     ;"▲▲▲▲▲▲▲▲▲■ ";:NEXT
740  PRINT "■ ■ ";L$;"■ ■ ";L$;"■ ":PRINT "■ ■ ■ "
750  GOSUB 2360:GOSUB 840:GOSUB 2460:GOSUB 850
760  PRINT CV$;"■ ■ ■ ■ ■ ■▲▲▲▲▲▲▲▲S H I P▲D A
     T A▲F O R▲";S$
770  PRINT "■ ■▲▲T O N N A G E▲▲▲■ ";:PRINT
     USING"# # # # # # # ";SS;
780  PRINT "■▲▲▲D A M A G E▲▲▲▲■ ";:PRINT
     USING"# # # # # ";DM
790  PRINT "■ ■ ■ ■ ■ ■ ■ ■ ■ ■ ■ ■ ■ ■ ■ ■ ■ ■ ■ ■
     ■ F U E L▲▲▲▲■ ";:PRINT USING"# # # # # . # ";
     GD(7,1)
800  PRINT :PRINT "■▲▲L A S E R▲P O D S▲▲■ ";:
     PRINT USING"# # # # # ";LP;
810  PRINT "■▲▲▲D E F L E C T O R S■ ";:PRINT
     USING"# # # # # ";DF
820  PRINT "■▲▲M I S S I L E S▲▲■ ";:PRINT USING"#
     # # # # # # ";MS;
830  RETURN
840  PRINT CV$;"■▲▲";PL$(L);"▲S T A R D A T E▲";:
     PRINT USING"# # # # # . # # ";SD;:RETURN
850  CC=SS:FOR I=0 TO 6:CC=CC-GD(I,1):NEXT:CC=CC-INT(GD(
     7,1))-10*(LP+DF)-MS
860  PRINT CV$;"■ ■ ■ ■ ■ ■ ■ ■ ■ ■ ■ ■C A R G O▲C A P
     . ■ ";:PRINT USING"# # # # # # # ";CC:RETURN
870  PRINT N$:PRINT :PRINT "S Y S T E M","P O P L .▲▲
     ▲▲T E C H .▲▲▲▲A G R I C U L T U R E":
     PRINT
```

Library Information

```
880   FOR I=0 TO 9:PRINT :IF L=ITHEN PRINT "* ";
890   PRINT PL$(I),P(I,3),P(I,4),P(I,5):NEXT
900   RETURN
910   PRINT N$:L1=L
920   PRINT "▣▮▲▲▲▲▲▲▲▲DESTINATION▲SYSTEM▲▣";PL$(L1)
930   FOR I=0 TO 4:PRINT "▣■";CHR$(I+48);"‡▣";:IF I=LTHEN PRINT "▣";
940   PRINT PL$(I);"▬▣";,P(I,6),;
950   PRINT "■";CHR$(I+53);"‡▣";:IF I+5=LTHEN PRINT "▣";
960   PRINT PL$(I+5);"▬▣";,P(I+5,6):NEXTI
970   PRINT "▣▣▣▲▲'0'..'9'▲TO▲SELECT▲DESTINATION":PRINT "▲▲▲▲▲▲▲THEN▲RETURN▲TO▲LAUNCH."
980   RETURN
990   IF CC<0ORGD(7,1)<=0THEN SOUND 1,200,5:RETURN
```

Hyperjump Table and Random Interstellar Events

```
1000  GOSUB 910
1010  GETA$:IF A$=""THEN 1010
1020  IF A$="Q"THEN 530
1030  IF L1=LANDASC(A$)=13THEN GOSUB 690:GOSUB 840:RETURN
1040  IF ASC(A$)<>13THEN 1110
1050  K=P(L1,6):L=L1:FOR Z=1 TO K:GOSUB 1140:SD=SD+.01:IF CR>0THEN CR=CR+CR/500
1060  IF CR<0THEN CR=CR+CR/150
1070  NEXTZ
1080  FOR I=0 TO 9:P(I,6)=FNDS(I):NEXT:GOSUB 2200:SOUND 1,1000,10
1090  IF RND(0)*CR*CR/1000000>50000/SDTHEN PRINT "▣■▲▲▲YOUR▲SHIP▲WAS▲REPOSESSED...":GOTO 2860
1100  B=2*CS+500:GOSUB 2540:GOSUB 690:RETURN
1110  IF ASC(A$)<48ORASC(A$)>57THEN 1010
1120  L1=VAL(A$):PRINT "▣▣▣▣▣▣▣▣▣";RC$;"▲▲▲▲▲▲▲▲▲▲▮▮▮▮▮▮▮▮▮▮";PL$(L1);
1130  GOTO 1010
1140  GD(7,1)=GD(7,1)-0.1
1150  IF GD(7,1)<0THEN PRINT "▣▣▲▲▲YOU▲RAN▲OUT▲OF▲FUEL▲IN▲MID-FLIGHT...":GOTO 2860
```

```
1160  IF RND(0)>.06THEN RETURN
1170  IF RND(0)>.3THEN 1220
1180  DM=DM+INT(RND(0)*5+1):SOUND 3,400,20
1190  PRINT CY$;"▣▣▣▣▣▣ ▴▴▴▴‖S P A C E ▴D E B
      R I S ! ! ▬ ":FOR J=1 TO 400:NEXTJ
1200  IF DM>=SSTHEN PRINT "▙▣▣▣▪ Y O U R ▴S H I P ▴
      W A S ▴D E S T R O Y E D ▴B Y ▴A ▴M E T E O R"
      :GOTO 2860
1210  RETURN
1220  IF RND(0)>.1THEN 1250
1230  GD(7,1)=GD(7,1)-INT(RND(0)*10)-1:SOUND 3,1000,20
1240  PRINT CY$;"▣▣▣▣▣▣▣▣ ▴▴▴▴‖M I S - J U M
      P ! ! ▬ ":FOR J=1 TO 400:NEXTJ:RETURN
1250  IF RND(0)>L↑2/120THEN RETURN
1260  GOSUB 1710:RETURN
```

Trading Goods and Trade Table

```
1270  PRINT N$:PRINT "▣▪ ▴▴▴▴▴▴▴▴▴▴▴▴▴▴T R A D E
       ▴P R I C E S ▴F O R ▴ ";PL$(L)
1280  PRINT "▞ ═ ═ ═ ═ ═ ═ ═ ═ ═ ═ ═ ┬ ═ ═ ═ ═ ═ ═ ═ ═ ═ ═ ═ ═
      ═ ┬ ═ ═ ═ ═ ═ ═ ═ ═ ═ ═ ═ ═ ═ ═ ═ ═ ▚ "
1290  PRINT "‖ ▴I T E M ▴▴▴▴▴‖ ▴▴▴▴P R I C E ▴
      ▴‖ ▴▴▴▴▴▴▴▴▴O W N E D ▴‖ ";
1300  PRINT "├ ";L1$;"┤ "
1310  FOR I=0 TO 6:PRINT LEFT$(T$(I),3);:IF IX=ITHEN
      PRINT "▧ ";
1320  PRINT RIGHT$(T$(I),8);"▀ ‖ ";:PRINT  USING"# # # #
      # # # . # # ";TP(I);
1330  PRINT "▴ ‖ ▴▴▴▴▴▴▴▴▴▴▴▴▴▴▴▴▴ ‖ ":NEXT
1340  PRINT "├ ";L1$;"┤ "
1350  PRINT T$(7);"‖ ";:PRINT USING"# # # # # # # . # # "
      ;TP(7);:PRINT "▴ ‖ ▴▴▴▴▴▴▴▴▴▴▴▴▴▴▴▴▴ ‖
      ";
1360  PRINT "├ ";L1$;"┤ "
1370  PRINT T$(8);"‖ ";:PRINT  USING"# # # # # # # . # #
      ";TP(8);:PRINT "▴ ‖ ▴▴▴▴▴▴▴▴▴▴▴▴▴▴▴▴▴ ‖
       ";
1380  PRINT "▚ ═ ═ ═ ═ ═ ═ ═ ═ ═ ═ ═ ┴ ═ ═ ═ ═ ═ ═ ═ ═ ═ ═ ═ ═
      ═ ┴ ═ ═ ═ ═ ═ ═ ═ ═ ═ ═ ═ ═ ═ ═ ═ ═ ▞ "
1390  PRINT "' B ' - B U Y ▴▴' S ' - S E L L ▴▴' Q '
      - Q U I T ▴▴' R ' - R E P A I R ":DN$="":GOSUB 16
      50
1400  IN=-1:I$="":GD(8,1)=0
1410  PRINT CY$;CD$;NL$
1420  GETA$:IF A$=""THEN 1420
1430  IF A$="Q "THEN GOSUB 690:RETURN
1440  IF A$<>"R "THEN 1480
```

ChexSum Tables

Line		Checksum
10	=	4035
20	=	2726
30	=	1068
40	=	2271
50	=	6608
60	=	8724
70	=	4329
80	=	1711
90	=	2395
100	=	6929
110	=	141
120	=	7007
130	=	4197
140	=	2885
150	=	3352
160	=	2623
170	=	809
180	=	3216
190	=	3436
200	=	4969
210	=	1033
220	=	4463
230	=	3695
240	=	1382
250	=	3317
260	=	3173
270	=	3178
280	=	834
290	=	2455
300	=	3124
310	=	6440
320	=	1216
330	=	946
340	=	1678
350	=	1678
360	=	1674
370	=	2779
380	=	2869
390	=	1750
400	=	2204
410	=	2194
420	=	1189
430	=	5673
440	=	3722
450	=	1733
460	=	1507
470	=	2564
480	=	2563
490	=	2285
500	=	2184
510	=	1212
520	=	528
530	=	2406
540	=	1212
550	=	1015
560	=	919
570	=	1958
580	=	1547
590	=	2379
600	=	4649
610	=	3794
620	=	1664
630	=	1760
640	=	1338
650	=	2384
660	=	4645
670	=	3794
680	=	1664
690	=	2221
700	=	3328
710	=	922
720	=	1673
730	=	3377
740	=	2311
750	=	1548
760	=	2503
770	=	2757
780	=	2507
790	=	3349
800	=	3023
810	=	2675
820	=	2783
830	=	143
840	=	3658
850	=	5941
860	=	3364
870	=	4202
880	=	1975
890	=	2077
900	=	143
910	=	723
920	=	2927
930	=	3492
940	=	1505
950	=	2925
960	=	2162
970	=	5823
980	=	143
990	=	2539
1000	=	303
1010	=	1276
1020	=	946
1030	=	2523
1040	=	1440
1050	=	5688
1060	=	1880
1070	=	221
1080	=	3244
1090	=	7374
1100	=	2022
1110	=	2124
1120	=	4628
1130	=	579
1140	=	1339
1150	=	5499
1160	=	1133
1170	=	1171
1180	=	2455
1190	=	3551
1200	=	5688
1210	=	143
1220	=	1168
1230	=	3139
1240	=	3513
1250	=	1636
1260	=	558
1270	=	3231
1280	=	8840
1290	=	3482
1300	=	970
1310	=	2902
1320	=	3126
1330	=	1562
1340	=	970
1350	=	4031
1360	=	970
1370	=	4037
1380	=	8830
1390	=	4214
1400	=	1743
1410	=	856
1420	=	1275
1430	=	1294
1440	=	1194

TOTAL= 385287

2 Save the first half of Star Trader by entering SAVE "STAR TRAD FIRST" for tape or SAVE "STAR TRAD FIRST", 8 for disk.

3 Load and run the Merge program by typing LOAD "MERGE" for tape or LOAD "MERGE",8 for disk, and then entering RUN.

4 From your games tape or disk, load the first half of Star Trader: enter LOAD "STAR TRAD FIRST" for tape or "LOAD STAR TRAD FIRST",8 for disk. Do not RUN the program at this time.

5 Enter SYS16331.

6 Load ChexSum by entering LOAD "CHEXSUM" for tape or LOAD "CHEXSUM", 8 for disk.

7 Enter SYS16355 to merge the first half of Star Trader with ChexSum.

8 Enter RUN 62000 to activate ChexSum.

9 The program will respond with the prompt:

LINE NUMBER: ?

Pressing the RETURN key at this point will cause ChexSum to start with the first line of Star Trader, first half. Entering a line number will start ChexSum at that line.

10 ChexSum next prompts with:

PRINTER (Y/N) ?

A 'Y' will send the ChexSum table to the printer or an 'N' will send it to the screen.

11 Check your grand total for the first half with that printed above. If they differ, a line has been typed incorrectly. Compare line numbers until you locate the bad lines and then edit them.

12 Repeat steps 8 to 10 until the games program is debugged. In step 8, enter the number of the first bad line to avoid ChexSum verifying the games program from the first line.

13 Erase ChexSum from the end of the first half by entering DELETE 62000-62196.

14 Save the first half as "STAR TRAD OK1".

15 Enter the second half of Star Trader, lines 1450 to 2880 (which follow), and save it: SAVE "STAR TRAD SEC" or SAVE "STAR TRAD SEC",8.

```
1450 PRINT CY$;CD$;"▫ ▴ ▴ R E P A I R S ▴ ";DM;:INPUT N:
     IF N>DMTHEN N=DM
1460 IF INT(N)*TP(8)>CSTHEN N=INT(CS/TP(8))
1470 DM=DM-INT(N):CS=CS-INT(N)*TP(8):GOSUB 1650:GOTO 141
     0
1480 IF A$<>"B "THEN 1560
1490 PRINT CY$;CD$;"▫ ▴ ▴ B U Y I N G ▴ ";
1500 IF IN<0THEN GOSUB 1620
1510 PRINT RIGHT$(I$,8);"( ";
1520 PRINT  USING"# # # # # # ";INT(CS/TP(IN));:PRINT ")
     ";
1530 PRINT "▴ ▴ ▴ ▴ ▴ ▴ ▴ ▴ ▴ ▴ ▴ ▴ ▪ ▪ ▪ ▪ ▪ ▪ ▪ ▪ ▪ ▪ ▪ ▪
     ";
1540 INPUT N:IF TP(IN)*INT(N)>CSTHEN N=INT(CS/TP(IN))
1550 CS=CS-TP(IN)*INT(N):GD(IN,1)=GD(IN,1)+N:GOSUB 1650:
     IN=-1:GOTO 1410
1560 IF A$<>"S "THEN SOUND 1,200,5:GOTO 1410
1570 PRINT CY$;CD$;"▫ ▴ ▴ S E L L I N G ▴ ";:IF IN>=0
     THEN PRINT "▫ ▫ ▫ ▫ ▫ ▫ ▫ ▫ ▫ ";:GOTO 1590
1580 GOSUB 1620:PRINT RIGHT$(I$,8);:IF IN>7THEN SOUND 1,
     200,5:IN=-1:GOTO 1410
1590 PRINT "▴ ▴ ▴ ▴ ▴ ▴ ▴ ▴ ▴ ▴ ▴ ▴ ▴ ▴ ▴ ▴ ▴ ▴ ▴ ▴ ▪ ▪ ▪ ▪
     ▪ ▪ ▪ ▪ ▪ ▪ ▪ ▪ ▪ ▪ ▪ ▪ ▪ ▪ ▪ ▪ ▪ ";
1600 INPUT N:IF INT(N)>GD(IN,1)THEN N=GD(IN,1)
1610 CS=CS+TP(IN)*INT(N):GD(IN,1)=GD(IN,1)-N:GOSUB 1650:
     IN=-1:GOTO 1410
1620 GETA$:IF A$=""THEN 1620
1630 IF ASC(A$)>=48ANDASC(A$)<=55THEN IN=ASC(A$)-48:I$
     =T$(IN):RETURN
1640 SOUND 1,200,5:GOTO 1620
1650 GOSUB 850:PRINT CY$;"▫ ▫ ▫ ▫ ▫ ▫ ▫ ▫ ▫ ▴ ▴ C A S H ▴
     ▴ ▴ ▴ ▴ ▴ ▴ ▴ ▴ ▴ ▴ ▴ ▴ ▪ ▪ ▪ ▪ ▪ ▪ ▪ ▪ ▪ ▪ ▪ ▪ ▪ ";
1660 PRINT USING "$ # # # # # # # # # # # . # # ";CS
1670 DN$="":FOR I=0 TO 6:PRINT "▫ ▫ ▫ ▫ ▫ ▫ ▫ ▫ ▫ ▫ ▫ ▫ ▫
     ▫ ▫ ▫ ▫ ▫ ▫ ▫ ";DN$;RC$;
1680 PRINT  USING"# # # # # # # ";GD(I,1):DN$=DN$+"▫ "
     :NEXT:DN$=DN$+"▫ ▫ ▫ ▫ ▫ ▫ ▫ "
1690 PRINT "▫ ▫ ▫ ▫ ▫ ▫ ▫ ▫ ▫ ▫ ▫ ▫ ▫ ▫ ";DN$;RC$;:
     PRINT USING"# # # # . # ";GD(7,1):
1700 PRINT "▫ ▫ ▫ ▫ ▫ ▫ ▫ ▫ ▫ ▫ ▫ ▫ ▫ ▫ ▫ ▫ ";DN$;RC$;
     :PRINT USING"# # # # # ";DM:RETURN
```

Ambushed By Pirates!

```
1710 PRINT "▫ ":COLOR1,8:COLOR0,2,4:DR=0:PS=480:SK=0:OS
     =0
1720 SN=0:BT=500:FOR I=1 TO INT(SS/100):SN=SN+INT(RND(0)
     *2):BT=BT+500+INT(RND(0)*600):NEXT
```

```
1730  PF(0,0)=SS+INT(RND(0)*SS/100+2)*100:IF SN>9THEN PF(
      0,0)=PF(0,0)+(SN-9)*100:SN=9
1740  PF(0,1)=INT(RND(0)*SS/100+2)+INT(RND(0)*L/2)
1750  FOR J=1 TO 9:PF(J,0)=INT(RND(0)*SS/10+SS/10):PF(J,1
      )=INT(RND(0)*SS/500+1)
1760  IF J>SNTHEN PF(J,0)=0
1770  NEXT
1780  FOR J=0 TO 9:PF(J,3)=30+INT(RND(0)*9):PF(J,2)=8+
      INT(RND(0)*6):NEXT:TG=0:OS=SN+1
1790  DR=DR-10*DF:IF DR<0THEN DR=0
1800  DM=DM+INT(DR):DR=DR-INT(DR)
1810  IF GD(7,1)<=0THEN PRINT "■■■■Y O U ▲R A N ▲O
      U T ▲O F ▲F U E L . . . ":DM=SS+1:FOR I=1 TO 1000
      :NEXT
1820  IF DM>=SSTHEN PRINT "■■■■■■■L O O T E D ▲B
      Y ▲P I R A T E S ! ":FOR I=0 TO 6:GD(I,1)=0:NEXT:C
      S=0:GOTO 2860
1830  PRINT N$:PRINT "■▲' E '▲E V A D E ▲' C '▲C L
      O S E ▲' 0 ' . . ' 9 '▲T A R G E T ":PRINT "▲'
      M '▲N U K E ▲▲' L '▲L A S E R "
```

Get Player's Combat Instructions
Draw Combat Display and Resolve Combat

```
1840  GOSUB 760:GOSUB 2050
1850  IF SN=-1THEN 1930
1860  PRINT CV$;RC$;CD$;"■■▲▲T A R G E T ▲▲▲▲▲▲
      ▲ ";:PRINT USING"# # ";TG;:GETA$:IF A$=""THEN 1860
1870  IF A$="L "ANDLP>0ANDPF(TG,0)>0THEN GOSUB 1970:
      GOTO 1790
1880  IF A$="M "ANDMS>0ANDPF(TG,0)>0THEN GOSUB 2000:
      GOTO 1790
1890  IF A$="E "ANDGD(7,1)>0THEN GOSUB 2040:GOTO 1790
1900  IF A$="C "THEN IF RND(0)<.7THEN EV=-3:GOTO 1790
1910  IF ASC(A$)>47ANDASC(A$)<58THEN TG=ASC(A$)-48:
      GOTO 1860
1920  GOTO 1860
1930  COLOR0,2:PRINT "■ ":IF OS<>SKTHEN RETURN
1940  PRINT "■■■■Y O U ▲D E F E A T E D ▲T H E ▲P
      I R A T E ▲F L E E T "
1950  CS=CS+BT:PRINT "■A N D ▲C O L L E C T E D ▲";:
      PRINT USING"# # # # # # # ";BT;:PRINT "▲I N ▲B
      O O T Y ! "
1960  FOR I=1 TO 2000:NEXT:PRINT "■ ":RETURN
1970  SOUND 3,1020,8:SOUND 1,970,8:PF(TG,0)=PF(TG,0)-(150
      *LP)/PF(TG,3)
1980  IF PF(TG,0)<=0THEN SOUND 3,900,20:SN=SN-1:SK=SK+1
1990  RETURN
```

```
2000  SOUND 3,600,20:MS=MS-1:IF RND(0)*100<PF(TG,3)
      THEN RETURN
2010  SOUND 3,800,30:PF(TG,0)=PF(TG,0)-INT(RND(0)*50)-
      INT(RND(0)*50)
2020  IF PF(TG,0)<=0THEN SOUND 3,950,20:SN=SN-1:SK=SK+1
2030  RETURN
2040  GD(7,1)=GD(7,1)-.1:EV=INT(RND(0)*3+1):RETURN
2050  POKE 3072+PS,42:POKE 2048+PS,127
2060  FOR J=9 TO 0 STEP -1:IF PF(J,0)<=0THEN 2180
2070  MV=INT(RND(0)*3):IF PF(J,3)+EV-MV>=1THEN PF(J,3)=PF
      (J,3)+EV-MV
2080  IF PF(J,3)>39THEN PF(J,0)=0:SN=SN-1:GOTO 2180
2090  IF INT(PS/40)>PF(J,2)ANDRND(0)<.3THEN PF(J,2)=PF(J,
      2)+1
2100  IF INT(PS/40)<PF(J,2)ANDRND(0)<.3THEN PF(J,2)=PF(J,
      2)-1
2110  IF J=0THEN POKE 3072+PF(0,2)*40+PF(0,3),65:POKE 204
      8+PF(0,2)*40+PF(0,3),127:GOTO 2140
2120  POKE 3072+PF(J,2)*40+PF(J,3)-40,J+48:POKE 2048+PF(J
      ,2)*40+PF(J,3)-40,113
2130  POKE 3072+PF(J,2)*40+PF(J,3),87:POKE 2048+PF(J,2)
      *40+PF(J,3),127
2140  IF RND(0)<PF(J,3)/40THEN 2180
2150  SOUND 3,1020-10*J,5:DX=(PF(J,1)*400)/(PF(J,3)↑2)
2160  DR=DR+DX:IF RND(0)<DX/(SS-DM+DX)ANDDF>0THEN
      SOUND 3,1020,10:SOUND 3,990,15:DF=DF-1
2170  IF RND(0)<DX/(SS-DM+DX)ANDLP>0THEN SOUND 3,1000,10:
      SOUND 3,900,10:LP=LP-1
2180  NEXTJ
2190  EV=0:RETURN
2200  TP(0)=20/SQR(P(L,5))
2210  TP(1)=2000/(5*P(L,4)+P(L,5)/5)
2220  TP(2)=40000/(10*P(L,4)+P(L,3))
2230  TP(3)=(12000+INT(RND(0)*2000))/SQR(10*P(L,4))
2240  TP(4)=100000/SQR(4*P(L,4))
2250  TP(5)=100000/SQR(P(L,5)/2)
```

Determine Trade Value of Goods

```
2260  TP(6)=15000*P(L,3)/(5*P(L,4))
2270  TP(7)=100/SQR(2*P(L,4))
2280  TP(8)=500-P(L,4)*22
2290  FOR I=0 TO 7:IF RND(0)<.4THEN TP(I)=TP(I)-RND(0)*(T
      P(I)/(7+L/2)):GOTO 2310
2300  TP(I)=TP(I)+RND(0)*TP(I)/(10+2*L)
2310  NEXT:IX=INT(RND(0)*7):IF INT(RND(0)*10)<>LORRND(0)
      <50/(SD*10)THEN IX=-1:RETURN
2320  NS=(RND(0)*P(L,3)+8)/4:G$="S H O R T A G E ":IF
      RND(0)<.5THEN G$="G L U T ":NS=4/NS
```

```
2330  PRINT "◘███◘T H E R E ▲ H A S ▲ B E E N ▲ A ▲
      ";G$;"▲ O F ▲ ";RIGHT$(T$(IX),8);". "
2340  PRINT "P R I C E S ▲ A R E ▲ █ ";:PRINT USING"# # .
       # # ";NS;:PRINT "▀ ▲ T I M E S ▲ N O R M A L ! ! !
       "
2350  FOR I=1 TO 2500:NEXT:TP(IX)=TP(IX)*NS:RETURN
2360  DN$=""
2370  PRINT "◘ ":FOR I=0 TO 6:PRINT "◙████████████
      ██████ ";DN$;:PRINT  USING"# # # # # # # # ";G
      D(I,0)
2380  PRINT "◙████████████████ ";RC$;DN$;:
      PRINT  USING"# # # # # # # # ";GD(I,1)
2390  DN$=DN$+"█ ":NEXT:RETURN
2400  PRINT CY$;NL$
2410  PRINT CY$;"◘ ▲ ▲ ▲ B O R R O W I N G ▲ ";
2420  INPUT N:IF INT(N)>BTHEN N=B
2430  CS=CS+INT(N):CR=CR-INT(N):B=B-INT(N):GOSUB 2460
2440  PRINT CY$;NL$
2450  RETURN
2460  PRINT CY$;"███ ▲ ▲ ▲ ▲ C A S H ▲ ▲ ▲ $ ▲ ";:
      PRINT  USING"# # # # # # # # # # # # # # . # # ";CS
2470  PRINT CY$;"████ ▲ ▲ ▲ ▲ C R E D I T ▲ $ ▲ ";:
      PRINT  USING"# # # # # # # # # # # # # # . # # ";CR
      :RETURN
2480  PRINT CY$;NL$
2490  PRINT CY$;"◘ ▲ ▲ ▲ D E P O S I T I N G ▲ ";
2500  INPUT N:IF INT(N)>CSTHEN N=CS
2510  CS=CS-INT(N):CR=CR+INT(N):B=B+INT(N):GOSUB 2460
2520  PRINT CY$;NL$
2530  RETURN
2540  IF RND(0)>P(L,4)/40THEN RETURN
2550  IF RND(0)>.2THEN 2620
2560  CT=P(L,4)*100+1000*RND(0)+RND(0)*(CS/1000)+CS/1000
2570  IF CT>CSTHEN RETURN
2580  PRINT "◘███▀Y O U ▲ H A V E ▲ B E E N ▲ O F F
      E R E D ▲ A ▲ B I G G E R ▲ S P A C E - "
2590  PRINT "█S H I P ▲ F R O M ▲ A ▲ C O M P A N Y ▲ O
      N ▲ ";PL$(L)
```

Special Offers When Arriving at a New Planet

```
2600  PRINT "█I T ▲ C O S T S ▲ ";:PRINT USING"# # # #
       # # # ";CT;:PRINT "▲ C R . ";
2610  PRINT "▲ W I T H ▲ A ▲ T R A D E - I N . ":GOSUB 28
      20:SS=SS+100:RETURN
2620  IF RND(0)>.25THEN 2680
2630  CT=160*(25-P(L,4))+RND(0)*(CS/1000)+CS/1000
2640  IF CT>CSTHEN RETURN
```

```
2650 PRINT "◣◙◙◙◘T H E R E ▲ I S ▲ A ▲ N E W ▲ L A
     S E R ▲ P O D ▲ F O R ▲ S A L E ▲ H E R E ."
2660 PRINT "◙I T ▲ C O S T S ▲ A ▲ M E R E ▲ ";÷
     PRINT USING"# # # # # # # # ";CT;÷PRINT "▲ C R ."
2670 GOSUB 2820÷LP=LP+1÷RETURN
2680 IF RND(0)>.15THEN 2740
2690 CT=200*(25-P(L,4))+RND(0)*(CS/800)+CS/800
2700 IF CT>CSTHEN RETURN
2710 PRINT "◣◙◙◙◘T H E R E ▲ I S ▲ A ▲ D E F L E C
     T O R ▲ S H I E L D ▲ A V A I L A B L E"
2720 PRINT "◙C O S T I N G ▲ J U S T ▲ ";÷PRINT USING"#
      # # # # # # # ";CT;÷PRINT "▲ C R ."
2730 GOSUB 2820÷DF=DF+1÷RETURN
2740 CT=70*(25-P(L,4))+RND(0)*(CS/1000)+CS/1000÷N=INT(
     RND(0)*P(L,4)/2+P(L,4)/3+1)
2750 IF CT*N>CSTHEN N=INT(CS/CT)
2760 IF N=0THEN RETURN
2770 PRINT "◣◙◙◙ ";N;"◘ ▲ N U C L E A R ▲ M I S S I L
      E S ▲ A R E ▲ O F F E R E D ."
2780 PRINT "◙T O T A L ▲ C O S T ▲ I S ";÷PRINT USING"#
      # # # # # # # ";CT*N;÷PRINT "▲ C R ."
2790 INPUT "◙H O W ▲ M A N Y ▲ D O ▲ Y O U ▲ W I S H ▲
     T O ▲ B U Y ";NM÷IF NM<0THEN NM=0
2800 IF NM>NTHEN NM=N
2810 MS=MS+NM÷CS=CS-NM*CT÷RETURN
2820 PRINT "◙A R E ▲ Y O U ▲ W I L L I N G ▲ T O ▲ M A
     K E ▲ T H E ▲ P U R C H A S E ▲ ?"
2830 GETA$÷IF A$<>"Y "ANDA$<>"N "THEN 2830
2840 IF A$="Y "THEN CS=CS-CT
2850 PRINT "◣ "÷RETURN
2860 PRINT "◘◙◙▲ ▲ ▲ ▲ ▲ ▲ ▲ ▲ ▲ C A S H ▲ P O S E S S
     E D ▲ ";CS÷PRINT "◙▲ ▲ ▲ ▲ ▲ ▲ ▲ ▲ ▲ B A N K ▲ B A L
      A N C E ▲ ";CR;
2870 PRINT "✕◙◙▲ ▲ ▲ ▲ ▲ ▲ ▲ ▲ ▲ G O O D S ▲ P O S E S
     S E D ◙"
2880 FOR I=0 TO 6÷PRINT "◘▲ ▲ ▲ ▲ ▲ ▲ ▲ ▲ ▲ ";T$(I);"÷ ◘
     ";GD(I,0)+GD(I,1)÷NEXT
```

ChexSum Tables

1450	=	3658
1460	=	2807
1470	=	3822
1480	=	1180
1490	=	1643
1500	=	1076
1510	=	916
1520	=	2438
1530	=	2484
1540	=	3302
1550	=	5255
1560	=	2248
1570	=	4274
1580	=	4000
1590	=	4136
1600	=	2517
1610	=	5255
1620	=	1277
1630	=	4538
1640	=	1272
1650	=	4444
1660	=	1404
1670	=	2863
1680	=	4046
1690	=	2764
1700	=	2685
1710	=	3461
1720	=	6817
1730	=	6856
1740	=	3505
1750	=	5764
1760	=	1410
1770	=	131
1780	=	6138
1790	=	2300
1800	=	2334
1810	=	5485
1820	=	6726
1830	=	5470
1840	=	739
1850	=	1112
1860	=	4851
1870	=	3416
1880	=	3414
1890	=	2665
1900	=	3018
1910	=	3736
1920	=	589
1930	=	2110
1940	=	3022
1950	=	4983
1960	=	1711
1970	=	4502
1980	=	3710
1990	=	143
2000	=	3560
2010	=	4207
2020	=	3715
2030	=	143
2040	=	3074
2050	=	1926
2060	=	2550
2070	=	5346
2080	=	3278
2090	=	3964
2100	=	3965
2110	=	6128
2120	=	5555
2130	=	4562
2140	=	1767
2150	=	3597
2160	=	6243
2170	=	5188
2180	=	205
2190	=	591
2200	=	1433
2210	=	2520
2220	=	2398
2230	=	3319
2240	=	1953
2250	=	1956
2260	=	2318
2270	=	1786
2280	=	1504
2290	=	5425
2300	=	2910
2310	=	5699
2320	=	6025
2330	=	3796
2340	=	4387
2350	=	2804
2360	=	445
2370	=	3773
2380	=	2783
2390	=	1247
2400	=	611
2410	=	1671
2420	=	1541
2430	=	3644
2440	=	611
2450	=	143
2460	=	3028
2470	=	3369
2480	=	611
2490	=	1762
2500	=	1717
2510	=	3644
2520	=	611
2530	=	143
2540	=	1647
2550	=	1173
2560	=	4246
2570	=	941
2580	=	3700
2590	=	2570
2600	=	3003
2610	=	3151
2620	=	1234
2630	=	3663
2640	=	941
2650	=	3790
2660	=	3507
2670	=	1382
2680	=	1234
2690	=	3558
2700	=	941
2710	=	3761
2720	=	3373
2730	=	1352
2740	=	7065
2750	=	2154
2760	=	757
2770	=	3406
2780	=	3654
2790	=	3988
2800	=	1144
2810	=	2362
2820	=	3452
2830	=	2405
2840	=	1640
2850	=	577
2860	=	4582
2870	=	2001
2880	=	3675
TOTAL	=	419602

16 Load Merge if you have reset or switched off your computer — see step 3.

17 From your tape or disk, load the second half of Star Trader: LOAD "STAR TRAD SEC" or LOAD "STAR TRAD SEC",8.

18 Perform steps 5 to 13 to run ChexSum on the second half of Star Trader.

19 Save the second half as "STAR TRAD OK2".

20 Load Merge if necessary — see step 3.

21 Load the first half by entering LOAD "STAR TRAD OK1" for tape or LOAD "STAR TRAD OK1",8 for disk.

22 Enter SYS16331.

23 Load the second half by entering LOAD "STAR TRAD OK2" for tape or LOAD "STAR TRAD OK2",8 for disk.

24 Enter SYS16355 to complete the merge.

25 The program will now run!

Appendix A
Using Joysticks

All the games in the book are designed to be played from the keyboard, usually using the following scheme:

KEY	ACTION
I	Left
P	Right
Q	Up
Z	Down
Space	Fire

The Commodore 16 has an inbuilt function JOY(N) which is used to read joystick input. The variable N is set to 1 to read joystick Ø and to 2 to read joystick 1. When the fire button is not depressed, the JOY(N) function returns values from Ø to 8 to indicate the deflection of the joystick; when the joystick is deflected and the fire button is depressed, values from 128 to 136 are returned (see diagram below and overleaf).

JOYSTICK VALUES, NOT FIRING

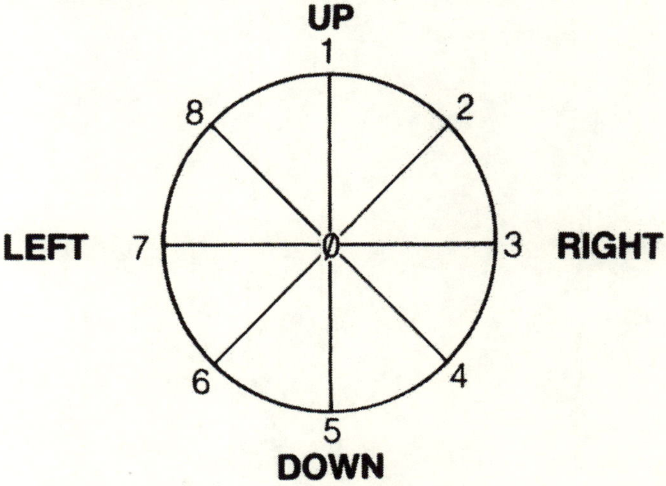

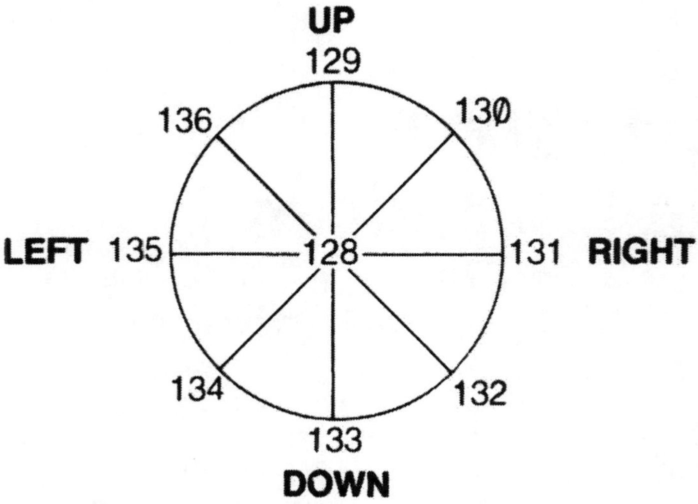

Thus, the statement

```
10 IF JOY(2) = 130 THEN (action)
```

would cause the appropriate action to take place when the joystick was moved to half-past two and the firing button depressed. Armed with this information, you should be able to alter the GET A$ statements in the programs so that they will operate with the joysticks.

Appendix B
Software Sprite Utility

WHAT IT IS AND HOW IT WORKS

This utility allows the user to move a block of characters in a 3 × 3 square around the screen. To use this program simply POKE the X and Y co-ordinates of the block into locations 16357, 16358 and then do a SYS16Ø5Ø. To move the block round the screen just change the X and Y co-ordinates and repeatedly call the SYS routine.

For this program to work correctly the screen must not scroll. Type in the program and save it to disk or tape, then run ChexSum on it.

When executed it will place a machine language program at 16Ø3Ø decimal and set the top of memory pointer to this location to prevent BASIC from overwriting it. Once executed, the program will sit there until you overwrite it, reset the top of BASIC pointers or switch off the computer. You can either tack it onto the ends of your programs and use it as a subroutine or load it in, run it and load in another program which calls it.

Sprite Utility

```
10    POKE 55,158:POKE 56,62:CLR
20    FOR I=16050 TO 16050+321:READA:POKE I,A:C=C+A:
      NEXT
30    IF C<>44960THEN  PRINT "C H E C K ▲ S U M ▲ E R R O
       R ▲ I N ▲ P R O G R A M ";C:STOP
40    STOP
50    DATA165,240,141,241,63,165,241,141,242,63
60    DATA173,232,63,201,0,208,7,173,231,63
70    DATA201,0,240,3,32,160,63,32,23,63
80    DATA32,92,63,173,230,63,141,232,63,173
90    DATA229,63,141,231,63,173,242,63,133,241
100   DATA173,241,63,133,240,96,169,0,133,240
```

```
110    DATA169,12,133,241,172,234,63,152,240,16
120    DATA24,165,240,105,40,133,240,169,0,101
130    DATA241,133,241,136,208,240,165,240,24,109
140    DATA233,63,133,240,169,0,101,241,133,241
150    DATA96,173,230,63,141,234,63,173,229,63
160    DATA141,233,63,32,234,62,160,0,140,235
170    DATA63,140,236,63,162,3,142,237,63,162
180    DATA3,142,238,63,174,235,63,172,236,63
190    DATA177,240,157,162,62,238,235,63,238,236
200    DATA63,206,238,63,208,234,173,236,63,105
210    DATA37,141,236,63,206,237,63,208,216,96
220    DATA173,229,63,141,233,63,173,230,63,141
230    DATA234,63,32,234,62,160,0,140,236,63
240    DATA169,127,141,240,63,162,3,142,237,63
250    DATA162,3,142,238,63,172,236,63,173,240
260    DATA63,145,240,238,236,63,238,240,63,206
270    DATA238,63,208,237,173,236,63,105,37,141
280    DATA236,63,206,237,63,208,219,96,173,232
290    DATA63,141,234,63,173,231,63,141,233,63
300    DATA32,234,62,160,0,140,235,63,140,236
310    DATA63,162,3,142,237,63,162,3,142,238
320    DATA63,174,235,63,189,162,62,172,236,63
330    DATA145,240,238,235,63,238,236,63,206,238
340    DATA63,208,234,173,236,63,105,37,141,236
350    DATA63,206,237,63,208,216,96,0,0,0
360    DATA0,0,0,0,0,0,0,0,0,0
370    DATA 0,130
```

ChexSum Tables

10	=	1207	130	=	2245	250	=	2090
20	=	3160	140	=	2128	260	=	2144
30	=	3991	150	=	2088	270	=	2140
40	=	145	160	=	2016	280	=	2157
50	=	2175	170	=	2010	290	=	2075
60	=	1992	180	=	2032	300	=	2014
70	=	1824	190	=	2211	310	=	1978
80	=	2025	200	=	2127	320	=	2093
90	=	2151	210	=	2079	330	=	2205
100	=	2096	220	=	2144	340	=	2157
110	=	2144	230	=	1959	350	=	1817
120	=	2086	240	=	2100	360	=	1120
						370	=	390
						TOTAL	=	74515

SPRITE DEMONSTRATOR

Type in the sprite utility and run it to place the utility in upper memory, then enter NEW to clear the BASIC loader. Now type in the following demonstration program:

```
10 PRINT CHR$(147);
20 FOR I=1 TO 20
30 POKE 16357, I   :REM SET X CO-ORDINATE
40 POKE 16358, I   :REM SET Y CO-ORDINATE
50 SYS 16050       :REM MOVE SPRITE
60 NEXT
70 GET KEY A$ : GOTO 20
```

When you run the program, the screen will clear and a block of characters will go from the top of the screen to the bottom. Hitting any key will move the block again. The characters in the block are from 127 ASCII to 135.

SHAPE DEMONSTRATION

It is possible to create differently shaped 'sprites' by redefining the characters in the 3 × 3 block. Enter this program:

```
 10 POKE 55,255: POKE 56, 47 :REM SET TOP OF
 15 B=12                     :REM MEMORY TO 12287
 20 POKE 65298, 192          :REM POINT AT NEW
 30 POKE 65299, 192+4*B      :REM CHARACTER DEFINITION
 40 P=1024*B
 50 SP=P+32*8                :REM DEFINE SPACE
 60 FOR I=SP TO SP+7:POKE I, 0 : NEXT
 70 IN=P+(127*8) :REM Define charsacters 127 - 135
 80 FOR I=IN TO IN+71=POKE I, 255 : NEXT
 90 POKE 16357, 5
100 POKE 16358, 5
110 SYS 16050
```

A solid 3 × 3 block will appear at co-ordinates 5, 5 on the screen.

In the program, lines 20 to 40 tell the computer to get its character set from memory starting at 12288. Each character is stored as eight bytes of memory and each bit in the byte represents one pixel (or dot) of the character. The first byte of the character represents the top pair of eight dots, while the second byte represents the next row of dots down and so on.

CHARACTER SHAPE VALUES

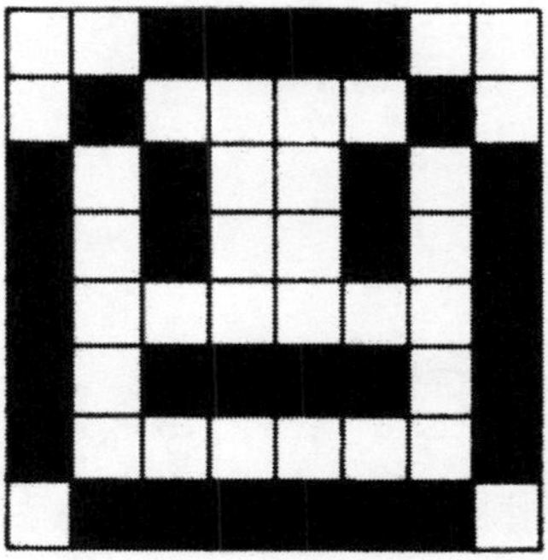

Binary		Hex	Decimal
Ø Ø 1 1	1 1 Ø Ø	3C	6Ø
Ø 1 Ø Ø	Ø Ø 1 Ø	42	66
1 Ø 1 Ø	Ø 1 Ø 1	A5	165
1 Ø 1 Ø	Ø 1 Ø 1	A5	165
1 Ø Ø Ø	Ø Ø Ø 1	81	129
1 Ø 1 1	1 1 Ø 1	BD	189
1 Ø Ø Ø	Ø Ø Ø 1	81	129
Ø 1 1 1	1 1 1 Ø	7E	126

To restore the normal character set, hold down the RUN/STOP key, then press reset. This will land you in the monitor! To escape, just press the X and then the RETURN key.

To find out the order of characters in memory, check the ASCII table in your reference manual. Use the formular SP=P+(A*8) to calculate the position of a character in memory, where A is the ASCII value of the character, and P is the start of character memory.

CAUTIONS

Please note these important facts:

1 The range of movement of the sprite is Ø to 37 for the X axis and Ø to 22 for the Y axis. The routine does no range testing, so it is up to you to make sure that the X and Y co-ordinates are in range.

2 The screen must not scroll.

3 Do not let your program place a sprite in location (Ø, Ø), which is reserved.

Appendix C
Merging Programs

The Merge program can be used to join other programs besides ChexSum and games programs, overcoming the lack of a MERGE command in Commodore BASIC. An important limitation to remember is that the smallest line number in the second program must be greater than the largest in the first program.

1 Load the Merge program by entering
LOAD "MERGE" for tape or
LOAD "MERGE", 8 for disk.

2 Enter RUN to cause Merge to place a machine language routine in high memory and to protect it by changing the top-of-memory pointer for BASIC.

3 Load the first program by entering
LOAD "first program" for tape or
LOAD "first program", 8 for disk.

4 Enter SYS16331.

5 Load the second program by entering
LOAD "second program" for tape or
LOAD "second program", 8 for disk.

6 Enter SYS16355 to complete the merge.

Appendix D
Printout Symbols

To aid clarity, the graphic symbols of the Commodore 16 computer have been represented in this book by special symbols designed to look like the pictographs which appear on the Commodore 16 keyboard.

COLOUR AND CONTROL CHARACTERS *

Symbol in book	Key
	CLR
	HOME
	CURSOR DOWN
	CURSOR UP
	CURSOR RIGHT
	CURSOR LEFT
	CTRL 1
	CTRL 2
	CTRL 3
	CTRL 4
	CTRL 5
	CTRL 6
	CTRL 7
	CTRL 8
	CTRL 9
	CTRL 0
	C= 1
	C= 2
	C= 3
	C= 4
	C= 5
	C= 6
	C= 7
	C= 8
	CTRL .
	CTRL .

* These characters are designed to emulate the characters which appear on the screen.

KEYBOARD CHARACTERS *

Symbol in book	Key	Symbol in book	Key
	C= E		C= ↑
	C= W	┬	C= R
	C= D	├	C= Q
	C= C		C= F
	C= B		C= V
	C= T		C= +
	C= U		C= Y
	C= O		C= I
	C= @		C= P
	C= G		C= –
	C= J		C= H
	C= L		C= K
	C= M		C= N
	C= S		C= £
	C= A		C= X
	C= *		C= Z
└	SHIFT L	┘	SHIFT @
┌	SHIFT O	┐	SHIFT P
	SHIFT I		SHIFT U
	SHIFT K		SHIFT J
○	SHIFT W	●	SHIFT Q
+	SHIFT +	✕	SHIFT V
╲	SHIFT M	╱	SHIFT N
♦	SHIFT Z	♥	SHIFT S
♣	SHIFT X	♠	SHIFT A
	SHIFT E		SHIFT D
	SHIFT *		SHIFT C
	SHIFT F		SHIFT R
	SHIFT T		SHIFT G
	SHIFT B		SHIFT –
	SHIFT H		SHIFT Y
	SHIFT £	←	SHIFT =
↑	SHIFT ZERO		

* These characters are designed to emulate the pictographs which appear on the front of the keys. The C= symbol is the special shift key located to the left of the left hand shift key.

Unfortunately different keyboard characters can produce identical symbols on the screen and printout. If a program doesn't work, these symbols may have been interchanged in a string:

	CTRL ,	CURSOR LEFT
	SHIFT *	SHIFT C
	SHIFT B	SHIFT –

You may also enjoy...

Made in the USA
Columbia, SC
24 March 2026

ce510df2-2c4a-45ef-b4fd-c2d26eb98f98R02